Notes on
the Role of Antisemitism
in Early Christianity

Monroe W. Strickberger

CONTENTS

PREFACE

My purpose in writing this monograph was to gather material on why and how antisemitism became incorporated into Gentile Christianity. It became clear to me that antisemitism was not a peripheral or tangential attachment to Gentile Christian development but served important purposes. Among these, as many scholars have noted, the need to gain status as an antique divinely revealed religion prompted Gentile Christianity to demonize Jews and replace them as heirs to the ancient Jewish Scriptures.

I realize this view, if taken seriously, will discomfort Christians who accept or ignore long-standing Christian anti-Jewish mythology. But since this mythology is not innocent of its terrible effects, I hope such Christians will seek a more truthful and more rational history of their religion and be willing to discard its mythological evils.

I pursued two related themes. 1) What explains the origin and persistence of Christian antisemitism? 2) In the wide gap that developed between Gentile Christianity and Judaism, what claims did Christians make against Jews, and what features of Christianity were rejected by Jews? Al-though this monograph may appear overly critical of Christian claims and doctrines, I believe it necessary for Christians to understand why Jews failed to adopt Christianity — a reason that was commonly given to justify antisemitism.

Organization of the monograph is based on a relatively short introductory review (pages 1–6) followed by a series of explanatory Notes, each indicated by a numbered superscript in the review. I felt that although the main theses can be briefly stated, somewhat fuller explanations supporting these arguments should include some of the historical backgrounds, events, literature, and attitudes that markedly affected Jews and Christians. Although a few major points may seem repetitive, it is difficult to treat some areas related to early Christian antisemitism without encountering the same agents.

For many fruitful discussions of content and organization, I am indebted to my wife, Ursula Rolfe, sons Paul and Neal, and Linda Oppen. I am grateful to the Graduate Theological Union Library, University of California, Berkeley, for access to their extensive collection of books and journals.

A version of this monograph can be found on the Internet at Christian antisemitism.com.

M. W. S.
April, 2019
Berkeley, California

Full references to sources cited in the Notes are in CITED REFERENCES. Biblical quotations are from the New Revised Standard Version, Oxford University Press. References to New Testament Gospels ascribed to the four evangelists ("Gospel of ......) are shortened to their names: St. Mark, St. Matthew, St. Luke, and St. John. Unless otherwise attributed, the abbreviations "ANF" and "NPNF" are used for translation sources; see CITED REFERENCES. Among more general surveys of the history of Jesus and early Christianity are books by Crossan (1991), Ehrman (1999), Fredriksen (1999), Horsley and Silberman, and the volumes edited by Esler (2000).

ON THE ROLE OF ANTISEMITISM
IN EARLY CHRISTIANITY

Among the many ways one can distinguish religions, I believe it reasonable that a primary feature of the assemblies St. Paul started was their non-Jewish ("Gentile") orientation. If we follow the chronology of St. Paul's letters, starting from about year 50 of the Common Era to perhaps late 60's C.E., Gentile Christianity, as distinct from that practiced by Jesus' original Jewish followers, arose within a generation after Jesus' death. Its recruits were urged by St. Paul to accept Jesus Christ as divinity and savior from sin; and to reject laws of the Jewish Torah, such as circumcision, dietary restrictions, Sabbath and Temple observances that particularly identified Jews. To St. Paul, one is "justified" by "faith" in Jesus Christ and not by "deeds" specified in Jewish Scriptures.[1]

Whether or not we call the changes in St. Paul's Gentile churches emblems of a new religion,[2] it seems clear from New Testament Gospels and other early Christian writings that Gentile Christianity became both a dominant and dominating form of Christianity by the beginning of the second century, supplanting the authority of Jesus' original Jewish followers. It is significant that aside from differences in beliefs among St. Paul's churches on whether Jesus Christ's body had been earthly or celestial, or whether end of the world is coming now or later — differences which must have seemed arcane to much of Roman society — Gentile Christianity, in its various forms, presented itself to the Roman world as separate from Jews by its non-Jewishness.[3]

Although Jews can draw some comfort that more Christian theologians now recognize the Jewishness of Jesus and his disciples,[4] a rarely discussed question that needs to be answered is: what led to Gentile Christianity's opposition to Jewishness despite the Jewishness of Jesus and his disciples? Specifically, what purposes did opposition to Jewishness serve in Gentile Christianity; especially in the virulent form it quickly adopted accusing the Jews of deicide? And why did it persist?

I think the sources and sustenance of Gentile Christianity's anti-Jewishness are not hard to find.

2

1. Anti-Jewishness helped evangelize Gentiles who viewed Jews and Jewish practices as "foreign," "unsociable," and "inhospitable" — regarding Jews as outside of Gentile society. [5]

2. Anti-Jewishness helped prevent the loss of Christian converts to Judaism and Jewish Christianity, by making "Jews" an object of derision. [6]

3. Anti-Jewishness helped disparage Jewish versions of the Jewish Bible that conflicted with Gentile Christian reinterpretations. These new interpretations claimed that Gentile Christianity was divinely envisaged in the Jewish Scriptures, yet Biblically commanded religious practices were no longer necessary. Such reinterpretation was also necessary to account for the historic absence of any persons named "Christian" before Gentile Christianity's initial appearance in the first century C.E. [7]

4. Anti-Jewishness enabled Christianity to pose as an unfairly persecuted group, whose salvific divinity, Jesus Christ, was martyred by Jews, an alleged immoral malevolent people— a "common enemy" — who then also oppressed his followers. [8]

5. Anti-Jewishness facilitated Christianity's relationship with Roman authorities and Roman converts by absolving Romans of crimes against Jews such as the murder of Jesus and the destruction of the Jerusalem Temple, which were blamed on the Jews themselves. [9]

6. Anti-Jewishness helped Christian leaders resolve internal conflicts by discrediting Christian dissidents for presumably following Jewish teachings. (See Note #17.)

Each of these advantages would have helped embed anti-Jewishness into Gentile Christianity's development, and some deserve to be further explored. Unfortunately, what seemed to have begun as differences with Jews on a religious level quickly advanced into demonizing Jews on a racial level — from anti–Jewishness to anti–"Jews." Issues raised against Jews included various myths used to explain why Christians were anti-Jewish.[10] Also, Jewish failure to adopt Christianity was ascribed to myths of sinfulness and intransigence, as though there could be no justifiable cause to reject this new self-proclaimed religion. However, if we discount such biased accusations, there were many valid reasons, both rational and religious, why Jews did not become Christian. [11]

In the New Testament, Gospel narratives [12] turned the few fragments known of Jesus the Jew into a mythic drama about Jesus Christ and his Jewish opponents. By the year 100 or so, the term "Jew" used 70 times in the New Testament Gospel of St. John, had already replaced "Scribes," "Pharisees," and other subgroup designations. Denouncing Jews as an ethno/racial entity — Jew-hatred now called *antisemitism* [13] — further widened the gulf between Judaism's synagogues and Gentile Christian churches and made Jew-hatred a common feature of Christian culture. [14]

Even earlier than St. John's Gospel, Gentile readers of the *Epistle of Barnabas* and the New Testament letter *Epistle to the Hebrews* mordantly concluded that the Jews had lost God's favor, now bestowed on Christians. Jesus the messianic Jew who preached a "Kingdom of God" for oppressed countrymen under Roman rule, [15] was transformed by literary means into the innocent victim of intolerant Jewish pietists. [16] The more loathsome and demonic any ties to Jews, the more difficult for potential converts to be attracted to Judaism, or for Christians to be proselytized by "Judaizers" into the "heresy" of Jewish Christianity, [17] or be attracted to any opposing view tainted with a "Jewish" label. However Gentile Jesus believers may have comported themselves religiously, and whether or not some Jews may have joined St. Paul's Gentile churches, any identity of Gentile Christianity with Jews quickly became "orthodox" Christian anathema.

Further discomfiting Christian leaders was Jewish disbelief in Christianity's basic theology of Jesus Christ as divinity (God or Son of God). Jewish denial placed Christianity's claim to Biblical legitimacy at issue, and early Christian leaders were engaged for centuries trying to align the meaning and context of passages in Jewish Scriptures with Christian needs. The Jewish Bible was therefore retained, not primarily for its rules and rituals, whose observance Gentile Christian leaders mostly condemned as anachronistic, but to claim divine support for the coming of Jesus Christ and convince Romans of Christian antiquity. [18]

The attempt to extract Christian legitimacy from the Jewish Bible led to apologetics and polemics claiming that "hard-hearted" Jews failed to fully understand and follow their own Bible because of Jewish sacrilege,

4

wickedness, and inferiority, as opposed to the sanctity, virtue, and superiority of its self-elected Christian successor. [19]

The inevitable consequences of Gentile Christianity's claims for Biblical legitimacy thus also led to Jew hatred:

- To present itself as a truly ancient religion Gentile Christianity reinterpreted Jewish Scriptures to show they prophesied Jesus Christ's appearance, life, and death. Now posing as the "True Israelites," Gentile Christians made clear they were supplanting antedated Jews.

- Jewish persistence in obeying Biblical religious laws was an abiding challenge to Christianity's presumption of Biblical antiquity and was blamed on the Jews for misunderstanding their own Bible.

A primary issue for Christian leadership was therefore how to confer religious authority on Gentile Christian beliefs and customs from Jewish Scriptures that proclaim contrary laws, doctrines, and practices. That is, how can the Jewish Bible be designated as a Christian document, and its writings reinterpreted, without denigrating Jews for not sharing such illusions? Antisemitism thus became inexorably tied to Christianity's self-identification as an antique "Gentile"-oriented religion, albeit with a Jewish-born savior. Had such Biblical claims not been made, as some Christians suggested, and a non-Jewish savior been found or created, Christianity, had it survived, would undoubtedly have had a different relationship with Jews. [20]

Unfortunately, despite absence of any Christian movement or "Church" during Israel's entire Biblical history, Christian Fathers held on to pretensions of being the "True Israel," and hostility to Jews never faltered. Jews were symbolized as malevolent "Christ killers," destined to wander the earth universally despised, exhibiting to all Christians the punishment for "deicide"— the murder of Jesus. Identifying "Jews" in this stereotyped racial/religious/cultural fashion thus provided a simple evil counterpart to "Christian godliness" that set up an impenetrable border between Jews and Christians. Demonizing these "rebellious" Jews, who fought wars against Roman rule in the first and second centuries of the Common Era, and blaming them for Jesus' death, also placed Christianity in a closer, concordant relationship with Romans who were thus absolved of crimes against Jesus and other rebellious Jews. [21]

In summary, antisemitism developed into a prominent and persistent feature of early Christian development, and the reasons for its introduction and expansion need to be examined and understood. Al-though serious measurement of social and religious factors leading to the success of Christianity remains difficult, [22] it seems clear that antisemitism, on both social and religious levels, helped Christianity to flourish, and was essential for its self-justification as a divinely revealed religion. The intensity and flagrance of anti-Jewish virulence by Christian saints and clerics through the first four centuries of Gentile Christian development appears otherwise unexplainable. [23]

Once Christianity reached its position of state power in the fourth and fifth centuries, and forcibly suppressed Judaistic influence, one might have expected antisemitic bigotry to diminish, since Christianity would no longer need to actively protect its authority and doctrines. In reality, antisemitism remained an obstinately entrenched Christian feature since Christian anathema could continually be focused on politically impotent Jews for their presumed enmity to Jesus. For example, "Passion Plays" portraying the Gospel story of Jesus with its fantasies of loathsome Jewish antagonists, provided a church-sponsored platform for antisemitic Christian education into present times. From "Judas" to "Jew" was not even a slip of the tongue. Early Christian theology, along with many of its later practitioners, thus established Jewish suffering as deserved retribution for supposedly opposing/betraying/convicting Jesus Christ the Savior by first century authorities. This invested Christian antisemitism with psychological/emotional justification that has lasted as long as Christianity itself — that one is punishing those who punished one's God.

From their beginning as Christianity's religious enemies, Jews could also be targeted for society's ills, as causative agents for famines, plagues, and other social calamities. Religious antipathy merged into racial/ethnic antipathy to provide a single vulnerable target — "Jews"— supposedly poisoning wells, sacrificing Christians in satanic rituals, and depriving honest Christians of their just rewards through monetary greed and secretive cabals. Antisemitic psychology thus turned Jews into convenient scapegoats on which to project Christians' own malevolent immoral feelings, resentments, and envious desires. [24] Demagogic clerics, politicians, and ideologues could then intensify these feelings, turning passive hatred into active violence. Two millennia of history show how markedly Christian concepts of

Jews affected Jewish lives.

Although persecution of Jews varied in time, place, and form, behind the persecutions lay the alleged "truth" of the Christian Gospels and their antisemitic stories, "canonized" as unchangeable divinely revealed texts. As the mainstays of Christian religious literature, the Gospels continue to be acclaimed by Christian clerics and theologians wherever Christianity is preached and practiced. It therefore seems clear that other than openly repudiating antisemitic themes in the Gospels and accompanying Christian literature, damaging effects of Christian antisemitism will remain. [25]

We should note that there are many Christian individuals and institutions that do acknowledge Christian antisemitism and seek to mediate its effects. [26] Nevertheless, we should also note that there is as yet no effort by Christian institutions or their leaders to renounce the New Testament's continually transmitted antisemitic messages, nor to seriously review the motivations that induced Christian antisemitism and kept it alive.

For Jews, there is a double aspect of how one can look at Gentile Christianity. On one hand, monotheistic, ethical, and social empathetic features of Judaism adopted by Christianity stand to its credit. On the other hand, Gentile Christianity's virulent anti-Jewishness and concomitant antisemitism was a sign of its leadership's failure to accept Jews as fellow human beings and treat them respectfully. Unfortunately, what is missing is tolerance, not only ethnic but religious. Theological differences between Christianity and Judaism, although heartfelt, cannot be tested. Since no religion or sect can prove it is the only communicant with God, it can hardly claim to be the only religious authority. As relates to all religions, the theology of how to configure and worship a god is a matter of variant beliefs and not evidential fact. Can we agree that human value rests on one's behavior and effect on others (one's humanity), not on one's theological beliefs?

1
ST. PAUL'S LETTERS AND
JEWISH CHRISTIANS

However one looks at St. Paul — as a renegade Jew or a Jew at heart — the message that Gentile readers obtained from his letters was not to be identified as a Jew in any sense that the Roman world recognized. That is, no circumcision, no dietary laws, no Sabbath, Jewish holidays, and Temple observances. *"You are observing special days, and months, and seasons, and years. I am afraid that my work for you may have been wasted"* (*Galatians* 4.10). Theological rationales St. Paul and other Christians used to justify these attitudes became significant in Gentile Christian doctrine, and some are briefly discussed in Notes #7, #10.5, #14, #17, #18, #19. The existential motive for St. Paul's message was clearly to attract Gentiles to belief in Jesus, as divine savior, without enduring those obstacles of Jewish Biblical practices followed by Jesus and his immediate disciples. St. Paul stigmatized Jewish practices as "rubbish" (*Philippians* 3.8; note that Greek usage of the term *skybalon* is not "rubbish" but includes "excrement," Kent, p. 145), making it quite easy for two millennia of readers to similarly stigmatize Jews and Judaism.

Nevertheless, we know that belief in Jesus was not unique to Gentile Christianity, since, at least for a time, one could be both a Jew and believer in Jesus as a Messiah (Note #15). On Jesus' death (ca. 30 C.E.), his Jewish followers founded an early "Jewish Christian" movement in Jerusalem led by a historical figure known as James the Just. *"As has been asserted more than once, the leaders of the Jesus movement thought as Jews, lived as Jews, and shared the aspirations of their fellow Jews. They remained subconsciously attached to the Law of Moses and when in Jerusalem, they went on participating in Temple ceremonies, and also used the forecourt of the sanctuary for preaching. They considered themselves, a small chosen unit within the large body of the Jewish people, the biblical 'remnant' entrusted with the correct understanding of Judaism, thanks to the instruction received from God's special envoy, Jesus. Baptism, a rite of repentance and purification, and the regular participation in a communal meal assured their group identity. They were also recognizable, at least during the first phase of the movement in Jerusalem, by a freely undertaken practice of religious communism"* (Vermes 2012, p. 81).

According to Tabor (pp. 39ff) and other scholars, the New Testament Letter of James bears concepts held by Jesus' Jewish disciples imploring Jesus followers not to abandon laws and commandments of the Jewish "Torah."

> 1.22: *"Be doers of the* [Torah's] *word, and not merely hearers who deceive themselves."*

> 2.14: *"What good is it, my brothers and sisters, if you say you have faith but do not have works? Can faith save you?"*

> 2.17: *"Faith by itself, if it has no works, is dead ... I by my works will show you my faith."*

These sayings help show how distinct the separation between Jesus' Jewish followers who settled in Jerusalem, and St. Paul, who promulgated concepts completely opposite. It indicates that the supposed "Jerusalem Conference" between the two groups, signifying St. James' agreement of St. Paul's mission to abandon Jewish practices, is probably fictional, created by St. Paul and St. Luke (ascribed author of Acts of the Apostles) to forge an unbroken link between Jesus' Jewish disciples and St. Paul's Gentile Christians. (Note #10, page 90). Other remaining documents that may have been influenced by Jewish Jesus-believers are in an early record, *The Didache* or *The Teaching of the Twelve Apostles* (Vermes 2012, pp. 136–148; Milavec) and in a "Pseudo-Clementine" literature known from fifth century Latin translations (Burns 2016, pp. 149–156).

The letters of St. Paul show that within a generation after Jesus' death, differences in adherence to Jewish practices led to serious disputes between Jewish Christians and their Gentile Christian colleagues. In Rome's early Christian church, for example, members obeying Biblical laws were actively derided, and were characterized by St. Paul as Christians "weak/sickly in faith" (Note #10.*4*); and Jewish Christians who insisted that Gentile church members also adhere to Jewish practices were denounced as "Judaizers" (Note #17).

In Jerusalem and other cities, Jewish Christians, who organized assemblies of their own, such as that of James the Just, remained isolated from "orthodox" Gentile Christian churches, disappearing from view by the fourth or fifth centuries. Names given to these extinct Jewish-Christian groups included "Nazoreans," "Ebionites," "Elchasaites," and so forth. Each group, depending on its description by a Christian historian, professed distinctive Jewish-Christian beliefs and practices (Luomanen, see also Horrell 2000). Nonetheless, whatever their denomination, Jewish Christians were, in due course, officially labeled "heretics" by Gentile Christian Fathers (Eusebius, ca. 330, *Ecclesiastical History* 3.27).

It would seem that the Gentile Christian church did not oppose Jewish Christian belief that Jesus was a Messiah but objected to Jewish Christian religious practices in which a "Christian" can also be a "Jew." Acts of the Apostles (21.21) may have obliquely credited St. Paul with beginning this process by being accused in a visit to Jerusalem: "*They* [Jews] *have been told that you teach all the* [Jesus-believing?] *Jews living among the Gentiles to forsake Moses, and that you tell them not to circumcise their children or observe the customs.*" In St. Jerome's words (ca. 400, *Epistles* 112.13): "*Since they want to be both Jews and Christians, they are neither Jews nor Christians.*" Or, as stated by St. Ignatius of Antioch (ca. 100), "*It is absurd to profess Christ Jesus, and to Judaize*" (*Letter to the Magnesians* X, ANF vol. 1, p.62). "*If anyone preach the Jewish law unto you, listen not to him*" (Ibid. *Letter to the Philadelphians* VI, p. 82). In St. John's Gospel (8.31–59), believers in Jesus who hold on to Jewish themes and practices are lumped together with non-believers as responsible for Jesus' persecution and death. One can ask why

Gentile Jesus-believers who chose not to follow Jewish practices must be unconditionally opposed to Jewish practices by Jews or Gentiles who also believed in Jesus — an unremitting antagonism that extended to Jewishness of any sort. To the Gentile Christian Fathers, Gentile Christians were not only to be non-Jewish but anti-Jewish.

Even earlier than Eusebius, Christians who followed Jewish practices were declared "heretics" by St. Irenaeus (ca. 180), who was among the first to establish Christian "orthodoxy" from prevailing varieties of Christian belief. To St. Irenaeus, Jews and their practices had no more standing than the Biblical Esau in the book of Genesis, from whom God's favor and his father's (Isaac's) blessing was usurped by his brother Jacob (now identified as Christian!) (ANF vol. 1, p. 493; Freeman, p. 157; see also Note #19).

Thus, although the Jewish followers of Jesus are commonly placed under the modern rubric *"Jewish Christians,"* the name would really be an oxymoron for that time, since Gentile Christianity excluded being a simultaneous practicing Jew and Christian, and it was the Gentile Church that defined "Christianity." Moreover, Christianity's differences from Jews of any kind, Jesus followers or not, proceeded on many levels: not only in discarding Jewish practices, but in its adoption of distinctively different customs and precepts. These include the communal ceremony of symbolically eating Jesus' flesh and drinking his blood (Note #11.*f*), and the elaborate theology ("Christology") of proclaiming Jesus' membership in a "Holy Trinity" in which he shares creation of the universe with God (Note #11.*b*).

As indicated above, practicing Jews who believed in Jesus as a "Jewish" Messiah were identified by Christian historians as other than "Christian."

2

WHAT AND WHEN WAS "PARTING OF THE WAYS"? (Also Note #14)

Some scholars claim that as long as Jewish Christians remained on the scene, there was no real "Parting of the Ways" between Jews and Christians (Becker and Reed; Jackson-McCabe). We should nonetheless keep in mind that however many kinds of Jesus-believing groups existed in the first several centuries (Ehrman 2003), ranging from partly or entirely Gentile to entirely Jewish, it was Gentile Christianity in its singular Pauline non-Jewish/anti-Jewish form that became ensconced from 50 C.E. onward as the popular and dominating form of "Christianity." St Paul's strictures against Jewish Christian "Judaizers," branded as oddities and "heretics" by Christian Fathers (Note #17), separated them from St. Paul's mainstream Gentile Christian movement from the first century onward.

In terms of belief and practice, St. Paul stands at the center of Gentile Christianity's separation from Jews and Judaism (also Notes #7, #14). *"In him* [St. Paul] *and his heritage the emergence of Christianity as a religion of gentiles as distinct from that Judaism which was still rather diverse ("Judaisms") becomes apparent. Paul was a major impetus to this manifestation of two distinct world religions"* (Pervo 2010, p. 235). Among the distinctive elements St. Paul used to separate his Gentile converts from Jews are the following:

- St. Paul repudiated the sanctity of the Scriptural covenant between Abraham and his progeny and the Jewish God Yahweh. *"Every male among you shall be circumcised"* (Genesis 17.10); *"You must diligently keep the commandments of Yahweh your God, and his decrees, and his statutes"* (Deuteronomy 6.17). Instead, he created a unique "Gentile Christian covenant" that "cursed" the basic Biblical commandments conferring Jewish identity. *"Christ redeemed us from the curse of the* [Jewish] *law ... in order that in Christ Jesus the blessing of Abraham might come to*

12

the Gentiles" (*Galatians* 3.13–14). In the *Letter to the Hebrews* (8.6-7, 8.13), a first century document once attributed to St. Paul: "*Jesus has now obtained a more excellent ministry, and to that degree he is the mediator of a better covenant, which has been enacted through better promises. For if that first covenant had been faultless, there would have been no need to look for a second one. ... [H]e has made the first one obsolete. And what is obsolete and growing old will soon disappear.*"

- St. Paul declared his unique vision of a new Gentile Christianity that had divine origin revealed only to him. "*The Gospel that was proclaimed to me is not of human origin, for I did not receive it from a human source, nor was I taught it, but I received it through a revelation of Jesus Christ*" (Galatians 1.11–12; see also Note #14, p. 169).

- In this imagined "Gospel" ("good news"), St. Paul changed the image of Jesus, from a Jewish Messiah observing Jewish Scriptural law, to a transethnic divine figure venerative for non-observant Gentiles: "*Christ Jesus, who ... was in the form of God*" (*Philippians* 2.5–6). "*[T]he grace given me by God to be a minister of Christ Jesus to the Gentiles in the priestly service of the gospel of God, so that the offering of the Gentiles may be acceptable, sanctified by the Holy Spirit*" (*Romans* 15.14–16). St. Paul's letters thus initiated a new theology based on Jesus Christ. "*Every assertion about God is simultaneously an assertion about 'Christ,' and vice versa. For this reason and in this sense Paul's theology is, at the same time, Christology*" (Matera, p. 217).

- To invest his views with ancient Scriptural authority, St. Paul instituted the practice of reinterpreting and misinterpreting the Jewish Scriptures (Note #7), changing the meaning of ancient Jewish history into accounts and revelations that sanctified newly created Gentile Christianity.

- St. Paul insisted that Jews who did not agree with his reinterpretations and his Gospel were obstinately perverse because "the god of this world has blinded the minds of the unbelievers, to keep them from seeing the light of the Gospel of Christ, who is the image of God" (*2 Corinthians* 4.4). To St. Paul and the theologians that followed, the dilemma of how non-Jews can claim antique ancestry in Jewish Scriptures was resolved by insisting that the Scriptures were not truly meant for Jews to whom they were incomprehensible, but for Gentiles. Gentile Christian need for antiquity showed little concern that the plain meanings and intentions of Jewish Scriptural writers did not at all comply with those of Christian theologians appearing many centuries later.

- St. Paul established a cornerstone sacrament of Gentile Christianity by changing a Jewish purification rite (the "mikvah") into a mystical baptism signifying death and rebirth. *"Do you not know that all of us who have been baptized into Christ Jesus were baptized into his death? Therefore we have been buried with him by baptism into death, so that, just as Christ was raised from the dead by the glory of the Father, so we too might walk in newness of life"* (*Romans* 6.3–4).

- St. Paul changed the celebration of a communal Jewish meal from blessing God's gift of bread and wine into a mystical "Eucharist" ceremony of eating Jesus' flesh and blood. *"For I received from the Lord what I also handed on to you, that the Lord Jesus on the night when he was betrayed took a loaf of bread ... broke it and said, 'This is my body that is for you. Do this in remembrance of me.' In the same way he took the cup also, after supper, saying,*

'This cup is the new covenant in my blood. Do this, as often as you drink it, in remembrance of me'" (*1 Corinthians* 11.23–25). The Eucharist and Baptism were *"the central liturgical practices of early Christians"* (Lynch, p. 117).

- St. Paul established the doctrine replacing "fleshly" literal-minded Jews in God's favor with "spiritual" Gentile Christians ("supersessionism"). *"Our competence is from God, who has made us competent to be ministers of a new covenant, not of* [Jewish Scriptural] *letter but of spirit, for the letter kills, but the Spirit gives life"* (*2 Corinthians* 3.5–6). Gentile Christians thus took on the status of "True Israelites" (Note #19), becoming *"God's people, now redefined around Jesus the Messiah"* (Moo, p. 403).

- St. Paul introduced the concept of two distinct Abrahamic lineages: one through Abraham's "faith," inherited by un-circumcised Christian *"children of the promise"*; and the other through Abraham's "flesh," inherited by circumcised Jewish *"children of the flesh."* The former, Gentile Christians, are Abraham's *"true descendants, true Israelites, the children of God,"* whereas the latter, Torah-observant Jews, do not *"truly belong to Israel"* (*Romans* 9.6–8). Ignored was the fact that the Jewish Scriptures, *Israel's* religious documents, are concerned only with the history and welfare of Father Abraham's biblical descendants, circumcised Jews. It is essential to note that before St. Paul invented the mainstays of Gentile Christianity, there is no evidence that any congregation or church of uncircumcised "faithful" Gentile Christians — Abraham's imagined *"children of the promise"* — existed during the fifteen-hundred-year interval between Abraham and St. Paul. (See also Notes #7, p. 60; #14, p. 165; #18, p. 212.)

- St. Paul preached that rituals prescribed for "fleshly" Jews were worthless: that one is "justified by Christian faith" and not by the "deeds" prescribed by Scriptural laws — a source of delinquent "sin." *"Gentiles who did not strive for righteousness have attained it, that is, righteousness through faith; but Israel* [Jews] *who did strive for the righteousness based on the law, did not succeed in following the law. Why not? Because they did not strive for it on the basis of faith, but as if it were based on works"* (*Romans* 9.30–32). *"For his* [Jesus Christ's] *sake I have suffered the loss of all* [Jewish] *things, and I regard them as rubbish, in order that I may gain Christ and be found in him, not having a righteousness of my own that comes from the* [Jewish] *law, but one that comes through faith in Christ, the righteousness of God based on faith"* (*Philippians* 3.8–9).

- By using "faith" and "spirit" rather than "works," St. Paul thus provided the rationale allowing Gentile recruits to reject Jewish Scriptural rules ("works") and thus separate themselves from observant Jews, whether Jesus-believing or not. To the question of whether "faith" really replaces "works," a modern Christian theologian replies: *" 'Works of the law,' like any other human 'work,' always fall short of what God expects of his creatures, leaving incorporation into Christ by faith as the only means of achieving righteousness"* (Moo, p. 27). However, since Yahweh's righteousness correlates with behavioral deeds/"works" (Genesis 18.19 *"Keep the way of the Lord by doing righteousness and justice"*), the question arises why and how does the presumed righteousness of "faith in Christ" exclude or exceed the Scriptural righteousness of "works"? Ignored in all such claims of "faith" over "works" was an implicit motivation: by replacing Covenantal Scriptural "works" with "faith" in Jesus Christ, proselytized Gentiles achieve Scriptural sanctity without interfering with Gentile life styles.

- In rejecting Jewishness, St. Paul contrasted his "sinful" Jewish-Christian opponents ("Judaizers," Note #17) to his "sanctified" Gentile Christians in most vituperative ways: *"Beware of the* [Jewish] *dogs, beware of the evil workers, beware of those who mutilate the flesh! For it is we* [Christians] *who are the true circumcision, who worship in the spirit of God and boast in Christ Jesus and have no confidence in the flesh"* (*Philippians* 3.2–3).

- In castigating his Gentile converts for assuming an alleged bad habit of *"observing special days and months and seasons and years"* (*Galatians* 4.10), St. Paul obviously referred to the Jewish festivals, disparaging them as "slavery" to *"weak and beggarly elemental spirits"* (Ibid. 4.9). This opposition to "Jewishness" of any kind thus precedes later reproofs by Christian Fathers that one cannot be simultaneously Jewish and Christian (Note #1).

- In focusing on Jesus Christ as a divine savior (*"we are expecting a Savior, the Lord Jesus Christ"* *Philippians* 3.20), St. Paul changed emphasis from Jesus' messianic call for social action (Note #15) to ecclesiastical piety and forgiveness of sin. *Colossians* 1.13: *"He has rescued us from the power of darkness and transferred us into the kingdom of his beloved Son, in whom we have redemption, the forgiveness of sins."* While anticipating heavenly reward, Christian faithful were to patiently accept one's station in life — whether oppressed, slave, or master (*Colossians* 3.18–22). *"Whatever your task, put yourselves into it, as done for the Lord and not for your masters, since you know that from the Lord you will receive the inheritance as your reward"* *Colossians* 3.23–24. In substituting saving Christian souls for improving Christian lives, St. Paul thus justified what became a common ecclesiastical defense of social stratification — a far cry from the social struggle for which Jesus was executed. St. Paul gives *"nonpolitical applications to [Scriptural] passages that originally had primarily sociopolitical implications. ... [H]e displayed no interest in using his ministry for broader humanitarian concerns"* Ellis (p. 154). *"None of* [St. Paul's] *writings would lead one to understand that good news for the poor was a central feature in the message of Jesus.* [St. Paul's] *focus is rather on the reconciling effects of the cross for humanity alienated by sin"* Loader (p. 31). *"Messianism, we must reiterate, is not the salvation of souls, but the redemption of bodies, the redemption of history"* Ruether (1979, p. 246).

- St. Paul's attacks on Jewish "works of the law" also had a strong racist tone, helping to mark distinction between his Gentile converts and ethnically/racially different "Jews." Dunn (2008, p. 109) makes clear that St. Paul's opposition to Covenantal Jewish Scriptures specifically meant opposition to those Jewish features (circumcision, dietary restrictions, Sabbath observances, etc.) functioning as *"identity markers, they served to identify their practitioners as Jewish in the eyes of the wider public, they were the peculiar rites which marked out the Jews as that peculiar people."*

Although St. James and others of the Jerusalem Jewish Christians recognized St. Paul as a fellow apostle, there is not the slightest historical evidence they authorized any of St. Paul's anti-Jewish themes. It was not belief in Jesus as Messiah that separated St. Paul's Gentile Christians from observant Jews, Jesus-believing or not, but rather St. Paul's insistence on preventing Jewish ethnicity and rituals from affecting Gentile recruitment. *"There was no sign of any fissure in the united body of Jesus' followers until* [St. Paul's] *principle that non-Jews could become full members of the Jesus movement without passing through Judaism. Paul's successful missionary activity among gentiles is the primary source of the parting of the ways*" (Vermes 2013, p.23). "*The split (as we see it in the New Testament sources) was brought on by what was primarily the ethnic division between Gentile (Pauline) Christianity and Jewish/Palestinian (Petrine? Jacobite?) Christianity*" (Porter and Pearson, p. 115).

Among those who followed St. Paul's example, *The Epistle of Barnabas* (ca. 100) devotes full chapters denouncing Jewish rituals and practices such as Temple sacrifices (II), Jewish fasts (III), circumcision (VIII), dietary restrictions (X), Sabbath observances (XV); exclaiming that it is not Jews who are the heirs of Abraham's covenant with God but Jesus Christ believers who are in "*a state of uncircumcision* [Gentiles]" (XIII, ANF vol. 1, p. 146). Further *Barnabas* anti-Jewish denunciations are included in two chapters entitled: "*Antichrist is at hand: Let us therefore avoid Jewish errors*" (IV, Ibid., p. 138); "*The New Covenant, founded on the sufferings of Christ, tends to our salvation, but to the Jews destruction*" (V, Ibid., p.139). Horbury comments, (p. 12): "*Christian sense of accepted separation from the Jewish community seems first detectable in writings from about the end of the first century onward, notable the Epistle of Barnabas.*"

Thus, although Jewish Christians may seem like intermediaries joining Jewishness with newly emerging Gentile Christianity, their presence was regarded by Gentile Christian leaders as an unwelcome incursion. Virulent resistance to adopting Jewish practices in St. Paul's churches far overwhelmed sharing common beliefs in Jesus as Messiah.

Since there was little if anything recognizably Jewish remaining in St. Paul's Christianity, the Jesus concept he bequeathed to Gentile Christianity was not the transition of Jesus from a Jewish Messiah to a divine Jewish Prophet, such as Elijah — a concept that some Jewish Jesus-believers may have already initiated. Instead, he changed Jesus from a Jewish Messiah into a universal "Christian" spiritual divinity, only peripherally related to Jews by birth. Since

Christianity was not presented to Gentiles in the form of either Jewish beliefs or rituals, the prime advantage of preserving Jesus' Jewish natal connection was to enable St. Paul and his successors to endow this new Christian divinity with age-old historic credentials through bold and fanciful reinterpretations of the Jewish Scriptures, and to develop a theology ("Christology") centered on Jesus' divine sacrifice. For St. Paul's Christianity, "Parting of the Ways" thus became tied to its fundamental Gentile needs: (1) to present Jesus as a divine savior transcending the Jewish cultural ethos, (Note 11.*b*); (2) to supplant Jews with Gentiles as the true "Israelite" possessors of the antique Jewish Scriptures (Notes #7, #19), (3) to decry Jewish Scriptural law that interferes with Gentile traditional practices (Note #18).

As noted above (*Galatians* 1.11–12), the authority that St. Paul gave to these innovations was a self-proclaimed apostleship he received from an imagined vision of Jesus, unshared and unwitnessed by any of Jesus' disciples. It seems reasonable to ask: What "divine" criteria allowed Gentile Christian leaders to claim that St. Paul's imaginary views against Jewishness were more authoritative than those of Jews and Jewish Christians who derived their outlooks and practices from the Jewish Scriptures?

Although it is continually debated (Carleton Paget, pp. 3–24), there is little doubt that however nebulous or firm the early boundaries between Christians and Jews, it did not take long for Romans to recognize these two groups as separated both religiously and ethnically. St. Paul's "ecclesia" ("churches") did not engage in Jewish male circumcision, Jewish Sabbath observances, Jewish dietary restrictions, Jewish holiday celebrations, Jewish pilgrimages to the Judean homeland, nor Jewish Temple worship. Leaders of St. Paul's churches did not identify themselves as "Jews" but as "Christians" (Note #5) and made clear that Jews were mostly hostile elements ranging from "Christ killers" to "demons" (Notes #6, #8, #10, #17, #19). Thus, despite clothing itself with antiquity by postulating exclusive possession of the Jewish Scriptures (Note #7), Gentile

Christianity rejected Scripturally based rituals and practices to nullify any identification with Jews in either history or practice.

The earliest unequivocal mention of Christians in Roman literature is by Tacitus writing about the great fire in Rome (64 C.E.). Years before any of the New Testament Gospels appeared, division between Christians and Jews at that time was already sufficient for Emperor Nero to persecute Christians without any reference to Jews or their Jewish origin. *"Picking out Christians as his victims was probably no random choice for the emperor in that respect. Especially those Christians who were not Jewish and could not claim the right to the Jewish privilege of monotheism could immediately be seen ... as people who had turned their backs on Roman society by distancing themselves from the Roman gods. Their behavior could disturb the pax deorum* ["Peace of the Gods"], *jeopardizing the well-being of the Roman state and its citizens"* (Heemstra, pp. 92–93; see also M. H. Williams, pp. 158–159).

Similarly, in his letter to Emperor Trajan on investigating Christians for presumed disloyalty (ca. 112 C.E.), Pliny the Younger uses the term "Christian" without any mention or connection to "Jews" (Ferguson, pp. 556–558). According to Carleton Paget (p. 254), late first century and early second century Christian writings (*1 Clement*, and *Hermas*), "[B]*etray no signs of any interactions with a wider Jewish community; Judaism is no longer an issue for these writers."* As noted by Judge (p. 366): *"A socially clear-cut separation from an early stage must be assumed if we are to explain the fact that Romans seem to have been unaware of the links between Jews and Christians."*

Also, in spite of Roman persecution, Christian leaders stressed their ethnic backgrounds and social habits as more like Romans but definitely unlike Jews. *Epistle to Diognetus* (ca. 130): *"For the Christians are distinguished from other men neither by country, nor language, nor the customs which they observe. For they neither inhabit cities of their own, nor employ a peculiar form of speech, nor lead a life which is marked by any singularity"* (V, ANF vol. 1, p. 26).   Tertullian (ca. 198): *"We are from among you* [Romans/Greeks]: *Christians are made, not born* [like Jews]" (*Apology* 18, see Lieu 2004, p. 298).   *"We neither accord with the Jews in their peculiarities in regard to food, nor in their sacral days, nor even in their well-known bodily sign* [circumcision], *nor in the possession of a common name"* (Ibid. *Apology* XXI, ANF vol. 3, p. 34). We *"are living among you, eating the same food, wearing the same attire, having the same habits, under the same necessities of existence. ... We sail with you, fight* [as soldiers] *with you, and till the ground with you"* (Ibid. *Apology* XLII, ANF vol. 3, p. 49).

"By the middle of the second century, Christians had separated from Judaism, but had also lost many of the cultural markers that defined them in Roman eyes as members of a distinct society. There was no distinctively Christian dress, no food or purity rules, no one quarter of the Roman city where Christians alone lived....it is impossible to distinguish Christian from non-Christian culture in funerary art, symbols, inscriptions, and even buildings" (Denzey, p. 503). Such accommodation to Roman society helped diminish persecution and, as described in Note #22, enhanced their Roman identification, allowing extensive periods when the Church could grow "at peace." Eventually, the Church even permitted Christians to become magistrates in Roman civil colonies as long as they *"keep away from Church and worship during their year in office"* (Markschies, p. 123).

With few exceptions, the second century and beyond provided Gentile Christianity with significant intervals of amity and expansion. For example, despite suppressing Jewish rebellions in Cyrene and Alexandria, as well as the large Bar Kochba Palestinian rebellion (132–135 C.E.; see Note #15, p. 189), Emperor Hadrian (117–138 C.E.) launched a process of tolerance towards divergent religious groups providing they maintained loyalty to Rome.

Considering the rapidity in which Jewish Christians became isolated from St. Paul's Gentile Churches (Note #1), there is little to support the view that they or their "Jewishness" played a significant role in Gentile Christianity's transition from its first century beginnings to its fourth century Nicene creed (325 C.E.). According to Neusner (2001, p. 18): "*Christianity was born on the first Easter with the resurrection of Jesus Christ, as the Church saw matters. That event was unique, absolute, unprecedented. Christianity did not have to present itself as a reformation of Judaism, because it had nothing to do with any other formation within Israel.*" That Jewish Christians saw Jesus as an inspired messianic Jew who maintained his Jewishness, (Notes #4, #15), not only aroused the ire of Christian Church Fathers during this period but were also subject to St. Paul's vituperative strictures against "Judaizers" (Note #17).

However, no matter the many invectives Gentile Christianity threw against Jews and Judaizers, inherent contradictions in claiming Jewish Scriptural antiquity while rejecting Biblical religious practices remained difficult to justify authoritatively. St. Paul repeatedly claimed but never clarified why "faith in Jesus Christ" circumvents observance of expressly decreed Biblical commandments. Statements, such as that in *Galatians* 5.4 are unexplained: "*You who want to be justified by the* [Jewish] *law have cut yourself from Christ; you have fallen from grace.*" Also inexplicable is St. Paul's insistence that circumcision and observance of Sabbath and Jewish holidays would be no different from enslavement to idolatry. "*How can you want to be enslaved to them* [idols] *again?*" (*Galatians* 4.9).

Similarly, St. Augustine's claim that "*all the things in the Old Testament which you think are not observed by Christians because Christ destroyed the law are in fact not observed because Christ fulfilled the law*" (ca. 400, *Reply to Faustus* XIX.11, NPNF Series 1, vol. 4, p. 243), left the matter of "Christ's fulfillment" at issue. That is, why would fulfillment of the "Law" by Jesus (Note #4) preclude fulfillment of the Law by others? St. Augustine's somewhat lame explanation that Jesus' "fulfillment of the law" was not seriously meant but done only to appease the Jews (Ibid. NPNF p. 239) seems contradictory to all we know from the Gospels on law-observant historical Jesus and Jesus' law-observant disciples who sent out law-observant "Judaizers." Essentially, as mentioned earlier, Christian condemnation of Jews and Jewish Christians for observing Biblical commandments had no divine authorization other than St. Paul's Gentile Christianity's need to reject Biblical practices which conflict with Gentile life styles.

The first of the New Testament Gospels, that of St. Mark, created a prime narrative justification for St. Paul's anti–"Judaizing" ideology by extending it back to the time of Jesus the Jew. In St. Mark, Jesus gains little unqualified regard from his allegedly self-centered Jewish disciples (later to become St. James' "Jewish Christians") who are perplexed by Jesus' announcement of his death and resurrection, and blind to his claim to be the divine "Son of Man" (Chapters 8–10). The disciples appear *"remarkably obtuse, even fearful, stupid, cowardly, and treacherous"* (Telford, p. 238). Separating Jesus from his Jewish background and relationships (even his family rejects him), St. Mark's Gospel essentially recreates St. Paul's Jesus. That is, not a Jewish Messiah attempting to liberate his people from oppression (Note #15), but a divine god-like figure vainly trying to convince Jews of his role as a savior from sin, a role that only becomes properly espoused by Gentiles.

Disconnecting Jesus from the Jews was further extended in St. John's Gospel in which Jesus is a God or semi-God, whose earthly opposition, in almost every respect, are "Jews" (Note #12). To the following famous quote by E. Käsemann (Telford, p. 180), we need add only one bracketed word: *"John changes the Galilean teacher into the* [persecuted] *God who goes about on earth."* From Jesus onward, New Testament "Jewishness" is set up as an ungodly affront to Christianity, and the accusation of being tainted with any sign of

"Jewishness" became sufficient for Christian clerics to excommunicate other Christians as "heretics" (Note #17).

It is also clear that although "Parting of the Ways" — whether assigned to an early or later century — may have intensified Gentile Christian anti-Jewishness, such animosity did not await "Parting of the Ways." St. Paul's persistent polemics against "Judaizers" and their Jewish practices show that the gap between his Gentile Christian churches and the synagogues of Jews (and even of Jewish Christians) was already significant within his lifetime. *"As the* [first] *century proceeded, the boundary becomes ever clearer and ever more stable"* (S. J. D. Cohen 2013, pp. 232–233).

St. Paul's oft-quoted *"There is no longer Jew or Greek, slave or free, male or female; for all of you are one in Christ Jesus'* (*Galatians* 3.28), is not a claim for equality on earth for all people, nor does it erase boundaries between Gentile Christians and other groups, but applies only to those desiring entrance into St. Paul's future spiritual "Heavenly Kingdom" by: 1) embracing faith in the divinely sanctified "Christ Jesus'; 2) being baptized into St. Paul's Gentile Christian community; 3) curtailing Jewish religious practices (the "Law"). Even then, St. Paul insists that economic, social, and gender differences be sustained. *"In whatever condition you were called, brothers and sisters, there remain with God. For the present form of this world is passing away"* (*1 Corinthians* 7.24–31).

Unlike Jesus and the Jewish prophets (Note #15), St. Paul never protests injustice in wealth and power. Nor does he challenge the great extent of unremitting poverty and slavery in the Roman empire. In the fourteen letters ascribed to St. Paul, his three appeals for *"giving alms"* and *"remembering the poor"* (*Romans* 15.26, *2 Corinthians* 9.9, *Galatians* 2.10) are matters of personal discretion, not a plea for social change. For St. Paul, *"equality exists 'in the sight of God' and has no relation whatever to temporal affairs. The distinction between slave and master in this world is no more seen as needing to be changed as that between male and female*" (Ste. Croix 2006, p. 349).

Whatever the religious differences among his recruits, St. Paul makes clear that "Jewishness" is a flawed attribute. As noted by Nirenberg (p. 56), "*To the extent that Jews refuse to surrender their ancestors* [e.g., Abraham], *their lineage, and their scripture, they could become emblematic of the particular, of stubborn adherence to the conditions of the flesh, enemies of the spirit, and of God.*" Since anti-Jewishness played such a significant role in early Gentile Christianity, how could it not have affected "Parting of the Ways" between Gentile Christianity and Judaism? How easy then for Christian Fathers to move on from anti-Jewishness to anti-Jew?

3
JEWS, CHRISTIANS, AND ROMAN LEGITIMACY

In response to political and military support from Jewish rulers, Julius Caesar, followed by Emperor Augustus, conferred upon Jews exceptional civic and religious rights. Jews were exempt from sacrifice to Roman civic gods and Emperor worship prescribed for all Roman subjects, as well as from other civic practices forbidden by Jewish monotheistic beliefs and the Jewish Scriptures. These concessions were not easily given, and often resented, since such sacrifice and worship provided a symbolic yet politically important means to unify the vast Empire and venerate a powerful ruler whose good graces provided protection and benefits for the populace. Even so, there is no sign that such license granted Jews political independence since the Jewish elite were fully expected to help maintain Roman rule and safeguard Roman interests.

In coping with religious diversity, Romans were generally tolerant. Although Romans showed no special fondness for Jews because of Jewish religious customs and Jewish rebellions, they generally respected the Jewish religion as a *religio licita* (legitimate religion) because of its antiquity. As long as an individual complied with the rules of the Roman state, did not interfere with social conventions, and earned citizenship, "*a Roman could be Jewish and a Jew could be Roman*" (Goodman 2007a, p. 155).

Matters were very different with the Christians, who had ex hypothesi abandoned their ancestral religions. ... The Christians asserted openly either the pagan gods did not exist at all or that they were malevolent demons. ... As a result, because a large part of Greek religion and the whole of the Roman state religion was very much a community affair, the mass of pagans were naturally apprehensive that the gods would vent their wrath at this dishonor not upon the Christians alone but upon the whole community; and when disasters did occur, they were only too likely to fasten the blame on to the Christians" (Ste. Croix 2006, pp. 135–136).

Having abandoned Judaism, Gentile Christianity was thus regarded as an illegitimate *superstitio*. A common Pagan complaint was that defection from prevailing tradition shows that Christians represent neither a true nation, people, or tradition, nor do they have *"authority for their doctrine"* (Conzelmann, p. 100). *"The followers of Christ were usually rebuked for a twofold betrayal: not only had they abandoned the beliefs of their fathers* [polytheistic paganism] *and joined a 'barbaric' religion, but they had changed the faith of the Jews and thereby committed a second kind of infidelity"* (Moreschini and Norelli, p. 422). *"If a religion was new, it could scarcely be true"* (Ehrman 2012b, p. 132). Gentile Christians who refused to engage in Emperor worship were hence considered alien elements disloyal to Rome, violating the *pax deorum* ("peace of the Gods").

"The time-honored method of deciding whether a given person was a Christian was the 'sacrifice test' ...the individual concerned was asked to sacrifice, offer incense, or make a libation to the gods or the emperor.... The government, as a rule, took actions against Christians only in response to popular clamor or individual delation [accusation]*"* (Ste. Croix 2006, p. 41).

Persecution, when it occurred, was not for believing in Jesus Christ, or for refusing to curse Jesus Christ, but for rejecting the required sacrifice to the civic gods of the Roman Empire, an exemption given only to Jews. This exemption separated Jews from Christians early on, since St. Paul's Christians were not included, nor did they include themselves, in the Jewish exemption.

In answering Pliny the Younger's letter on persecuting Christians (Note #2, p. 20), the Emperor Trajan's (98–117 C.E.) instruction is relevant (Judge, p. 361): *"Incomprehensible as the activities of Christians were, they could be tolerated providing (as Romans) they did not abandon their national duty of sacrifice to the Roman gods. The Romans had always understood and accepted that this was impossible for Jews, for whom exemption was secured.*" However, to Trajan: "*there is no hint that anyone ever tried to suggest* [to Christians] *such a solution* [exemption]."

In further separation from Jews, Christians acquitted themselves from a tax (*Fiscus Judaicus*) imposed on Jews for their 66–72 C.E. rebellion. When the tax became more liberal and voluntary in 96 C.E., applying only to those who claimed a Jewish religious exemption from Emperor worship, Christians still sought exception to the tax although "*it would have spared them two centuries of misunderstanding and haphazard persecution*" (Judge, p. 367).

Nevertheless, despite Pagan complaints, Christianity gradually gained popularity and acceptance (Note #22), spreading even among the upper classes "*because it could assure them that the new religion would not present a threat to their friendship and family networks, institutions so critical to maintaining aristocratic status. Such guarantees of status were a significant factor facilitating conversion*" (Salzman, p. 15). From St. Paul onward, New Testament accounts made accommodating to Roman society and authority a significant part of Christian practice. Thus, in St. Luke's Gospel, the redemption Jesus enacts "*is not deliverance from the Roman Empire*" but "*deliverance from the kingdom of Satan*" — only on Jesus' awaited second coming (the "Parousia") will Rome be replaced (Kim, Chapters 8, 9; see also Notes #21, #22).

Eusebius (ca. 330), "Father of Church History," echoes common Christian notions that, in spite of occasional Roman hostility, the Empire was respectful of Christians, and Christians dutiful to the Empire, whereas Jews are Christianity's persistent enemies because of their refusal to accept Jesus Christ as their Messiah (*Ecclesiastical History* 3.5). To the Gentile Christian Church, Roman victories over Jews and destruction of Jerusalem's Temple did not come from Jewish conflict with Roman tyranny, but was rather a sign of God's revenge for Jewish intransigence in not accepting "Jesus Christ." (See St. Justin Martyr, ca. 150, *Dialogue with Trypho, a Jew* CVIII, ANF vol. 1, p. 253; Origen, ca. 240 C.E., *Contra Celsum* 4.22; Eusebius, *Ecclesiastical History*, ca. 330 C.E., 3.5–8; and also Note #8, p. 68ff.) It is ironic that Christians could claim God's judgment as the cause for Jewish misfortunes while ignoring God's judgment for misfortunes that befell Christians, such as wars, plagues, and famines. By some obverse logic, Roman persecution and Christian martyrdom was conceived as the sign of God's redemption (M. S. Taylor, pp. 120–121).

Also notable is that during the Roman persecutions of Christians, the difference between Christians and Jews was of marked significance to the Roman public and authorities. Christian leaders' resentment against Jews was then fed by Judaism's legality offering sanctuary to Christianity persecuted as a non-legal superstition. *"The Jews in Smyrna even offered sanctuary in the synagogues to Christians obliged to sacrifice* [to Roman gods] *under the edict of Decius AD 150"* (Judge. p. 367). A study of St. Aphrahat (ca. 330) showed that the Saint's attacks on Jews came on the heels of a Persian persecution when Christians *"may have been flocking to the synagogue to receive charity and perhaps to Aphrahat's chagrin, something more"* (A. H. Becker, p. 305).

4

JESUS THE JEW

The little we know of Jesus is unfortunately limited to New Testament Gospels primarily written for theological purposes: *"The good news of Jesus Christ, the Son of God"* (St. Mark 1.1). Among the main historical elements we can discern about the short one to two-year period that the Gospels cover:

- Jesus was born and raised in the Galilean province of Israel. Along with Syria, Israel had been dominated by Roman rule since the 63 B.C.E. Pompey conquest. Replacing a century of independence (165–63 B.C.E.), the Romans governed Israel as a dominion or client state with collusion of native aristocratic and priestly families.

- Socially and economically, Jesus' Israel was primarily an agrarian society whose peasantry lived under a regimen of Roman, royal, and priestly taxes, and usurious loans (Note #15).

- Jesus' audiences were Jews from Israel's Galilean and Judean countryside. *"In so far as we can trust the specific information given us by the Gospels there is no evidence that Jesus ever entered the urban area of any Greek city"* (Ste. Croix 2006, pp. 330–331).

- Jesus' reformist preachings were influenced by a Jewish social reformer, John the Baptist (ca. 4–29 C.E.), whose core message was *"Repent, the Kingdom of God is at hand."* This theme reflected Jewish dependence on God Yahweh's supremacy and goodwill — *"Yahweh is our king; he will save us"* (Isaiah (33.22). More than just a prophet, John the Baptist also headed a movement censuring the existing aristocratic order, leading to his execution by Herod's son, Herod Antipas — the Roman-approved overlord of Jesus' Galilean homeland.

- To both John the Baptist and Jesus, the "Kingdom of God" was imminent here on earth. "[T]*he time is fulfilled, and the Kingdom of God has become near, repent*" (St Mark 1.15, St. Matthew 4.17). "*There are some standing here who will not taste death until they see that the Kingdom of God has come with power*" (St Mark 9.1, St. Matthew 16.28, St. Luke 9.27). Both also showed concern that it provides justice for the oppressed. "*Will God not grant justice to his chosen ones who cry to him day and night*" (St. Luke 9.27).

- Both Jesus and John the Baptist believed they shared God's "authority" (St. Mark 11.29–32), while the ruling class saw both as subversives.

- After John the Baptist was killed, Jesus preached in the Galilean countryside for a one or two-year period during the reign of Roman emperor Tiberius (14–37 C.E.).

- Jesus kept membership in his movement informal, with no special baptism or initiation requirements.

- To Jesus, nothing in one's past or present, whether of personal needs or family, should hold one back from imminent action in fighting for the "Kingdom of God." "*No one who puts a hand to the plow and looks back is fit for the kingdom of God*" (St. Luke 9.62). "*Whoever comes to me and does not hate father and mother, wife and children, brothers and sisters, yes and even life itself, cannot be my disciple*" (Ibid., 14.26).

- Jesus observed the laws and rituals prescribed in the Jewish Scriptures: such as circumcision, dietary laws, observance of Jewish Holidays, and pilgrimage to the Jerusalem Temple (Note #16).

- Jesus visited Jerusalem for Passover celebrations during the Roman rule of the Procurator Pontius Pilate (26–36 C.E.).

- Jesus was involved in a disturbance in the Jerusalem Temple.
- Jesus was accused of a capital offence ("sedition"), and crucified in Jerusalem with other Jews by order of Pontius Pilate.
- After Jesus' death, all that remained of his original movement in Roman Palestine was a small network of Jewish followers, headed by St. James ("James the Just"), which moved from Galilee to Jerusalem.

Throughout Jesus' history, his Jewish orientation is notable, and New Testament sayings that can reliably be ascribed to Jesus show that his message was specifically to Jews, not Gentiles. *"These twelve [disciples] Jesus sent out with the following instructions: 'Go nowhere among the Gentiles, and enter no town of the Samaritans, but go rather to the lost sheep of the house of Israel. As you go, explain the good news* [of the Kingdom of God]'" (St. Matthew 10.5–6). Jesus' use of "twelve" is a symbolic reference to the twelve tribes of Israel; that is, to Israel itself, in which Jesus' disciples, like the prophets before them, are to help achieve justice and freedom from oppression (Horsley 2012, p. 121).

His exclusive mission to fellow Jews and low regard for Gentiles is also recorded in other sayings (St. Matthew 5.47, 6.7, 6.32, 18.17), and most harshly in an encounter with a Gentile woman asking for help for her daughter. Jesus replies *"I was sent only to the lost sheep of the house of Israel ... It is not fair to take the* [Jewish] *children's food and throw it to the dogs* [Gentiles]" (St. Matthew 15.24–26, St. Mark 7.27). Although the woman pleads, and Jesus relents, this show of anti-Gentile bias is striking, and many Gospel sayings attempt to counter its hostility.

According to unprejudiced scholars, sayings attributing a "universal" evangelizing message to Jesus were added by later Christian writers to accord with a Gentile audience. *"No authentic command to bring the good news to all nations of the world can be traced to Jesus'* (Vermes 2012, p. 67). Other concepts held by Jesus' disciples, such that Jesus was completely human and not divine, and commandments by Jesus to retain their Jewish identity, were, according to Ehrman (2011a), later modified by New Testament writers to coincide with new "orthodoxies."

Jesus' renowned statement *"the sabbath was made for man, not man for the sabbath"* (St. Mark 2.27), does not contest Jewish belief but is actually of Pharisaic origin, as is his engagement in Sabbath healing (E. P. Sanders 1985, pp. 264–267). Gospel accounts in which Jesus supposedly disclaimed observance of the Sabbath and defied Jewish dietary restrictions contradict the traditional practices and beliefs of the Jewish Christian movement led by his own disciples. Such non-Jewish notions were most likely introduced to comply with St. Paul's new "Gospel of Christ" that Jewish Scriptural commandments be ignored to accommodate to Gentile life styles (Notes #2, #14), and oppose Jewish Christian "Judaizers" (Note #17). In an extensive chapter called "Jesus Kept Kosher," Boyarin (2012, p. 103) shows that Jesus *"saw himself not as abrogating the Torah but as defending it. There was controversy with some other Jewish leaders as to how best to observe the Law, but none ... about 'whether' to observe it."*

Towards his countrymen, Jesus' fundamental social ethic stems directly from Jewish Scriptures. *"You shall not take vengeance or bear a grudge against any of your people, but you shall love your neighbor as yourself"* (Leviticus 19.18). *"Act with justice and righteousness, and deliver from the hand of the oppressor anyone who has been robbed. And do no violence to the alien, the orphan, and the widow, or shed innocent blood"* (Jeremiah 22.3). Thiessen and Merz (p. 394): *"Jesus' ethic is a Jewish ethic... the centre of its content lies in the Torah... Jesus presents it as a Jewish rabbi."* In the words of Rabbi Hillel, early in the first century C.E., *"What is hateful to you do not do to your fellow man. That is the whole Torah."*

34

"The true distinguishing mark of Jesus' piety lies in his emphasis on the inner significance of commandments" (Vermes 2010, p. 8). *"The general Gospel picture of Jesus is that of a Jew who conforms to the principal religious practices of his nation in contrast to St. Paul's open antipathy towards all form of 'Judaizing'"* (Ibid. p. 23). *"There is no instance in the Gospels in which Jesus sets out to criticize the Torah itself; all the controversial statements turn on conflicting laws or on the precise understanding of a precept"* (Ibid. p. 25; also Note #16, p. 196). E. P. Sanders (2002, p. 41) claims: *"There is some good evidence that Jesus accepted purification and sacrifice (as well as other ancient views, such as that God especially dwelt in the Temple), and there is not good evidence against it."* In contrast to St. Paul's abandoning Jewish dietary laws (*Romans* 14), St. Peter's refusal to eat non-kosher meat (Acts of the Apostles 10.14) shows that Jesus' disciples followed Jesus' observance of Jewish dietary laws. According to Vermes (2012, p. 52), the phrase *"he declared all foods clean"* (Mark 7.19) is an editorial "addendum" by a "redactor" for Gentile Christian consumption. (Redactors: *"editors who revised* [Gospel] *traditions in the light of new historical situations and new theological viewpoints"*; Kelsey, p. 144.)

Significantly, the language used by Jesus, his disciples, and his Jewish audiences was Aramaic, Israel's common Semitic language of the time, rather than Greek of the Christian New Testament, a different language directed to different people. For example, we know that the first account of the Jewish-Roman 66–72 C.E. War by Josephus, the Jewish historian, was in Aramaic for Jews in the Eastern Mediterranean, and only later did Josephus write in Greek for a *"broader reading public"* (Barclay 1996, p. 346). We also know of a large Aramaic literature that translated and paraphrased the Jewish Scriptures, enabling Jewish villagers to study and worship their Bible in local dialect (Chilton et al., pp. 37–42).

Also noteworthy, the "Gospel" of the Jewish Christian Nazorean sect, although lost, was probably in Aramaic, written in

Hebrew script and not New Testament Greek (Petersen 1992, also Ehrman and Pleŝe, p. 199). Despite considerable confusion about the content and numbers of lost Jewish Gospels (Ehrman and Pleŝe, pp. 197–200), it is significant that the Nazoreans, who marked their descent from Jesus' original Galilean followers, continued to use Aramaic rather than the Greek of the "Hellenists" (see below).

"As for Jesus, how much Greek he knew will never be clear, but he most likely would not have needed it to be a carpenter, to teach the Galilean crowds, to travel around the lake, or to venture into the villages associated with Tyre, Caesarea, Philippi, and the Decapolis cities....It is unlikely that literacy would have been widespread among such a group [Jesus' followers] *and unclear why the rare literary member would have chosen to compose such a text* [Jesus' sayings] *in Greek rather than Aramaic"* (Chancey, pp. 163–164). "[I]*t is obviously in the Aramaic-speaking rural communities dependent on them, and not in the Hellenized urban centres themselves that* [Jesus'] *interests lie"* (Scholer, p. 9).

According to Casey (2010, p. 158), Aramaic *"was the only language used in the Galilean countryside."* Feldman (1992, pp. 20–21): *"Indeed, it is clear that the predominant language of the* [Palestinian] *Jews from the time of the Babylonian captivity in 586 B.C.E. until after the Arab conquest of Palestine in 640 C.E. was not Greek, but Aramaic"* Of all mentioned communities in which Jesus preached, none were major Galilean cities such as Tiberias, Scythopolis, and Sepphoris (E. P. Sanders 1992, p. 64), which may have had some Greek-speaking populations.

By contrast to the Aramaic of Jesus and his disciples, the New Testament Gospels, each claiming to recount details of Jesus' life, actions, and sayings, were written in Greek by writers and editors ("redactors") who were not his countrymen or disciples, nor shared the immediate concerns of his audiences. Thus, the disparity between Jesus' oral Aramaic speeches and the later literary Gospels' Greek accounts and interpretations (Note #12), follows a disparity between different languages aimed at distinctly different cultural audiences. On one hand were Aramaic-speaking Galilean Jewish peasants counterpoised to St. Paul's cosmopolitan urban Greek speakers from outside the Jewish homeland, who were Gentiles with few, if any, Jews (see also Note #14).

Horsley (2005, p. 12) makes the point that *"Galilean and Judean villagers spoke a dialect of Aramaic, so they would hardly have understood Hebrew if it were read to them. The Gospel of Luke is projecting* [later] *Greek urban practices onto the synagogue in Nazareth in its portrayal of Jesus opening a scroll of Isaiah and reading from it."* However, even if Hebrew language education were prevalent, as some scholars suggest, there is little if any evidence that Jewish villagers would have conversed in Greek, nor would they have read or quoted the Greek version of the Jewish Scriptures (called the "Septuagint LXX"). Thus, in referring to other scholarly work, R. N. Longenecker (1999, page 47) poses the question: *"Why, if Jesus spoke and taught in Aramaic, is it that not only are his words recorded in Greek but his biblical quotations are based on the* [Greek] *LXX, and not on a Hebrew or Aramaic version?"* It is apparent that Jesus' Aramaic speeches were rewritten, and perforce edited, in a language foreign to him and his listeners.

The author of Acts of the Apostles divides early Christians after Jesus' death into two groups: "Hebrews," native Judeans/Galileans which would have included Jesus' original disciples, speaking primarily Aramaic; and "Hellenists," Greek-speaking Jesus-followers who came from outside Israel. *"Thus it is now thought that it was this community of Christian Hellenists who accelerated the transferal of the Jesus tradition from Aramaic into Greek, who helped bring Christian theology fully into the realm of Greek thought freed from Aramaic pre-acculturation, who were instrumental in moving Christianity from its Palestinian setting into the urban culture of the larger Empire, who first saw the implications of Jesus' resurrection for a Law-free Gospel for the Gentiles (and for Jews), and who were the bridge between Jesus and Paul. These Christian Hellenists were the founders of Christian mission outside Palestine, and a theological tradition capable of articulating a gospel for the Greco-Roman world"* (T. W. Martin, p. 136). Although it is still unknown whether these Hellenists were Jews or non-Jews (Kee 2013b, p. 80), it is quite unlikely that any such Greek-speaking Hellenists were among Jesus' Galilean disciples and followers.

Since Jesus is believed to have been killed about the year 30 C.E., the Gospels are distanced from Jesus the Jew by their time as well as by their language. According to modern scholars, the earliest of the four "canonized" Gospels (St. Mark's) was written about 70 C.E., forty or more years following Jesus' death, and the last Gospel (St. John's) was written no earlier than the close of the first century C.E. or beginning of the second. It was not until the end of the second century; more than 150 years after Jesus' death, that final edited versions of the Gospels were generally accepted as the primary Christian Scriptures about the life of Jesus, although many differences between them, textual and narrative, endured (Note #12). Thus, M. Grant (p. 106) claims that neither oral or written sources can provide reliable information on Jesus' actual sayings: *"[A]n oral tradition, if it is concerned with material relating to religious and miraculous beliefs stands no chance of surviving unchanged for more than thirty years. As to written sources, it seems only too likely that those who listened to Jesus had no idea of writing down his words or actions at the time, for transmission to posterity."*

According to detailed studies by more than 70 New Testament scholars, less than one out of five sayings attributed to Jesus in the Gospels were actually said (Funk et al. 1993), and very few of the actions attributed to Jesus actually occurred (Funk et al. 1998). *"Not Mark, and even less so any other gospel, can give us reliable information about the course of Jesus' ministry or tell us anything about Jesus' motivations, his experiences, or his self-consciousness"* (Koester 2007, p. 271).

Unfortunately, although St. Paul's letters (ca. 50–68 C.E.) are the earliest known Christian writings, he records nothing of Jesus' life or death, except his crucifixion and presumed resurrection. Other than imagined visions, St. Paul never saw or heard Jesus, nor does he show any interest in Jesus' life as a radical and reformer, activities which gave Jesus fame and followers. *"When we come to the 'bio-graphical' elements in Jesus' life, the resemblance between Gospels and Pauline Epistles totally disappear. The Epistles had shown an astonishing, total, ignorance of every single fact of Jesus' life before the Last Supper"* (M. Grant, p. 213). As discussed in many places throughout this monograph, St. Paul's concern was to fit Jesus into basic themes of a new Gentile Christian faith. He focused on a myth-ical non-historical Jesus, Jesus Christ: *"I decide to know nothing among you except Jesus Christ, and him crucified"* (*1 Corinthians* 2.2):

- that Jesus Christ was a divine or semi-divine figure sent to save Gentiles from sin;
- that although Jesus Christ was born and lived as a Jew, his message as Savior was not to follow the Jewish law;
- that one is saved by forming a mystical bond with Jesus Christ through "faith."

St. Paul's statement *"we have the mind of Christ"* (*1 Corinthi-ans* 2.16), was made to justify the mystical claim that one can pro-pound beliefs, values, and thoughts of an imagined universal divine "savior" in whom one must have "faith." To enhance this necessity of faith, St. Paul transfers Adam's "original" sin of disobedience in the Garden of Eden to all descendants, for whom *"the wages of sin is death, but the free gift of God [for faithful Christians] is eternal life in Christ our Lord"* (*Romans* 6.23). *"As all die in Adam, so all will be made alive in Christ"* (*1 Corinthians* 15.22). However, to St. Paul, Christ's redemption is not conferred evenly on all "sins" and all "sinners." That is, one is not redeemed by faith in Christ for sins committed in trying to follow Jewish Scriptural "Law" (*Galatians*

5.4: "*You who want to be justified by the law have cut yourself off from Christ*") — but, strangely, faith in Jesus Christ redeems one from ancestral Adam's sins (for which one is not really culpable).

Because St. Paul's letters added so little historical information, gaining details about Jesus' life must rely on New Testament Gospels appearing decades later. Unfortunately, as in St. Paul, it is a Jesus of "faith" that prevails in Gospel accounts, while historical aspects of Jesus lie hidden in stories designed to provide and minister to religious beliefs of the Gospel communities. "*To read a Gospel is to be led out of Galilee, out of Jerusalem, into the Church community of a later day*" (Rousseau, p. 50). "*The Gospels derive from a process of accretion in which an original image of Jesus was overlaid with all kinds of later material which expresses the faith of the early Church but does not go back to Jesus*' (Watson, p. 160).

Also, the dramatic theatrical style of the Gospels was designed to help favor Christianity's attractiveness and not to present an unbiased portrayal of events. "[T]*he popularity of the [Gospel] genre among early Christians as a way of spreading the word about Jesus' life and teaching may be ascribed in part to the novelty of this sort of writing*" (Goodman 2007a, pp, 179–180). The new "Gentilized" Jesus was torn from his provincial "Kingdom of God" movement and placed by New Testament writers on a lofty Greco-Roman stage as a divine Jesus Christ, Son of God, and savior of mankind, product of an occultic birth, life, death, and resurrection (see Notes #11.*d*, and #22, pp. 243*ff*).

However, other than endorsing a "Kingdom of God," Jesus' authentic message bore no further theological notions. He neither proclaimed nor indicated that he was a non-human divinity and member of a Holy Trinity — concepts that became basic Gentile Christian "Christological" doctrines. (See also Note #11.*b*.) "[T]*he church transformed the metaphorical content of kingdom of God. It removed the implications for social and political change the term had for Jesus, just as it transformed Jesus into a more spiritual savior"* (Kaylor p. 75).

St. Paul's letters and Gospel stories of Jesus' opposition to Jewish practices, enabled Gentile Christian leaders to create a religion in which the "Jewishness" of Jesus was muted to little more than a natal connection. By contrast: *"Jesus certainly did not intend to found a new religion. He did not repudiate Scripture — far from it. And he did not call in question the law of Moses, though on occasion he emphasized some Scriptural principles at the expense of others"* (Stanton, p. 296). *"Insofar as Jesus' position, unswerving on monotheism ... was wholly unthreatening in respect of circumcision, Sabbath and food laws, he was at one with each and every other member of his people. That he attracted attention on how a law should be interpreted and applied, which he did, is not the same as attracting criticism for setting a law aside, which he did not. Much the same can be said of his position vis-a-vis the Temple"* (Catchpole, p. 301).

Considering that Jesus' disciples continued observance of the Temple after his death, it is quite clear that Jesus' action which led to his crucifixion must have been to reform its priestly governance (perhaps in accord with an Essene doctrine) and not to destroy the Temple — a political not religious act (Note #21). Notwithstanding his condemnation of apparent exploitative practices, Jesus saw the Temple as a sacred place for worship (St. Mark 1.44, St. Matthew 23.19). Jesus' statement, *"Do you see these great buildings? Not one stone will be left here upon another; all will be thrown down"* (St. Mark 13.2, St. Matthew 24.2, St. Luke 21.6) appears as a fabricated prophecy of the Roman 70 C.E. destruction 40 or so years after Jesus' death. It was obviously designed to turn Jesus' anger at priestly corruption against the Temple itself, the prime Jewish religious structure extant at the time.

In Oakman's terms (2008, p. 4), far from contesting Jewish religious practices, we can discern that *"the peasant aims of Jesus was profoundly political — encompassed symbolically under an image about God's power — and entirely social as might be expected of a peasant sage and reformer*." Jesus' social and political activity in first century Israel, efforts for which he died — "the Jesus of History" — is therefore quite different from the "Christology" and religious innovations St. Paul and the Gospels conferred on Jesus in the Gentile Christian Church — "the Jesus of Faith."

Thiessen (1999, pp. 33–34): "*Jesus had a Jewish identity. He revitalized the sign language of Judaism. He revived it in light of its central content — belief in the one and only God.... His conflicts with his contemporaries were conflicts within Judaism and not with Judaism. He did not represent an exodus from Judaism but a renewal movement within it. Here he belonged in a series of renewal movements within Judaism since the period of the Maccabees — in an unbroken series of attempts to revitalize the Jewish religion. Since almost always this happened directly or indirectly as a response to the challenge from the great powers that dominated Judaism, none of these renewal movements — including the Jesus movement — can be understood without this political framework.*"

In sum, one can say: Gentile Christianity's Jesus Christ was not the Jesus of the Jews to whom he preached. Jesus was Jewish, St. Paul's Gentile Christianity was not (Notes #2, #14).

For further studies of Jesus the Jew, see, for example: Casey 1991, pp. 72–74; Gray; Swidler, pp. 42–74; Vermes 1993.

5

RECRUITING GENTILES AND EFFECT OF THE NAME "CHRISTIAN"

Although ethno/racist prejudices were common in Greek/Roman societies, there was no systematic persecution of any specific group (Isaac). Nevertheless, the Gentile Christian message rejecting association with Jews and Jewish laws would have found a willing audience among Greeks and Romans who shared disdain for Jewish practices such as male circumcision, refusal to eat pork, and refraining from labor on the Sabbath. According to Barclay (1996), such Gentile hostility was also abetted by Jewish opposition to "idolatry" (p. 274), and by Jewish "exclusivity" (p. 272), expressed in fears *"that the Jewish community was of influence and importance—perhaps growing importance—within the life of the city"* [p. 276], coupled with *"their social cohesion—a feature which malevolent observers would interpret as clannishness or misanthropy"* (p. 287). Barclay lists other *"faults"* and *"contrary"* practices ascribed to Jews by Roman writers such as Tacitus (ca. 110 C.E.) including their increase in numbers caused by Jewish "lust," and their *"refrain from intercourse with foreign women"* (p. 411). Goodman (1987, p.61) notes that the absence of Jewish infanticide and abortion also generated Tacitus' *"amused contempt."*

Since there was no connection to "Jew" in the Greek appellation "Christian," its first century adoption by Antioch Christians (Acts of the Apostles 11.26) and St. Paul (Ibid. 26.28–29) would have removed Christians from the status of being solely a Jewish sect. By the year 100 C.E., St Ignatius already defined Gentile Christianity as uniquely distinctive: *"It is absurd to speak of Jesus Christ with the tongue, and to cherish in the mind a Judaism which has now come to an end. For where there is Christianity there cannot be Judaism"* (Letter to the Magnesians X, ANF vol. 1, p. 63).

"The name 'Christianoi' (Acts 11.26...) is an unmistakable indication that the Church has detached itself from the synagogue.

With this step it had freed itself from the obligation to observe Jewish purity laws and the circumcision commandment but had also placed itself outside Judaism and affiliation with the people of salvation [Jewish Jesus-followers — 'Nazoreans']" (J. Becker (p. 147). "[W]*hat was distinctive about such communities that might explain why they in particular were marked out by the authorities as a recognizable, and therefore namable, group was precisely that they comprised former 'pagans' rather than Jews*" (Townsend, p. 219).

Use of the name "Christian" thus marked both a religious and ethnic separation in "Parting of the Ways" between early Gentile Christian and Jewish communities, whether or not the latter were Jesus-believing. That is, religious, cultural, and ethnic features which distinguished Gentile communities from Jews also distinguished St. Paul's Gentile Christian churches ("ecclesia") from synagogues of any Jewish sect. "*In social reality Paul's churches were distinct from synagogues, and their predominantly Gentile members unattached to the Jewish community*" (Barclay 1996, p. 386, also Esler 2015). By the second century, Christian writers "*self-consciously use the term 'Christian' for insiders, portraying this membership in terms of descent and kinship as well as transformation*" (Kimber Buell, p. 183).

6

CHRISTIAN ANTI-JEWISH RHETORIC

St. John Chrysostom (ca. 386), Bishop of Antioch and Constantinople, revered as a "Holy Hierarch of the Orthodox Church," had some nine hundred sermons preserved by church authorities, among which are probably the most inflammatory denigrating attacks ever made on Jews. In *Against the Jews, Oration* 1, he proclaims: "*Do you see that the demons dwell in their* [Jewish] *souls…they insult the Master of the prophets himself…they are the common corruption and disease of the whole world…what manner of transgression haven't they eclipsed by their bloodthirstiness? They sacrificed their own sons and daughters to demons…they became more savage than any wild beasts. What else do you want me to tell you — their acts of plunder, greed, their betrayal of the poor, their theft and cheating?*" (Mayer and Allen, pp. 161–162).

Parkes (p. 163): "*In* [Chrysostom's] *discourses there is no sneer too mean, no gibe too bitter for him to fling at the Jewish people. No text is too remote to be able to be twisted to their confusion, no argument is too casuistical, no blasphemy too startling for him to employ.*" St. Jerome (ca. 400), Latin translator of Bibles, enthroned as "Doctor of the Church," declares: "*The ceremonies of the Jews are pernicious and deadly, and whoever observes them whether Jew or Gentile, has fallen into the pit of the devil. For Christ is the end of the Torah*" (Epistle 75, Michael, p. 21). "*For up to the present day they persecute our Lord Jesus Christ in the Synagogues of Satan*" (Epistle 84, NPNF Series 2, vol. 6, p. 176)

As Parkes and others have shown, one reason for these anti-Jewish attacks was Christian attendance at Jewish festivals and rituals. St. John Chrysostom (*Against the Jews Oration* 1): "*Another very serious disease bids me to speak in order to cure it … What's this disease? The festivals of the wretched and unsociable Jews are about to approach, thick and fast: the Trumpets, the Tabernacles, the Fasts. Of the many in our ranks who go to watch the festivals, who say they think as we do, some will both join in the festivities and take part in the Fasts. This bad habit I want to drive out of the Church right now"* (Mayer and Allen, p. 150).

Christian Fathers, beginning with St. Paul (*2 Corinthians* 3.5–6, see Note #7), long argued that Jewish practices and traditions offer no religious benefit, since Christianity replaced Judaism in God's favor. A similar attitude of supplanting Judaism is expressed by writers of the *Didascalia Apostolorum* (ca. 300 C.E.), condemning female Jewish converts to Christianity who continue practicing Jewish water immersion (the "mikvah") to regain religious purity after menstruation.

Despite such guarded reactions, there is no substantial evidence that Christian participation in Jewish rituals ("heteropraxis") changed Gentile Christianity, making it more Jewish. Attending a ritual of a different religion does not change the religion being attended nor change the rituals of the attendee's religion. Even when some renegades/apostates completely circumvent them, barriers between religions remain. What appears at stake were fears that claims for having replaced Judaism fell on some deaf Christian ears, stimulating Christian leaders, beginning with St. Paul, to respond to any intrusion of Jewish customs vituperatively and illogically.

Such unaccommodating defensive attitudes helped make the border between Gentile Christianity and Judaism fixed and immutable. The Sabbath was changed to Sunday, fast days from Mondays and Thursdays to Wednesdays and Fridays, Passover to Easter, and so forth. In sum, it was the anti-Jewish precepts, doctrines, and contentions, from the time of St. Paul onwards, that held sway through the centuries, reaching an early political apogee when Emperor Constantine legitimatized Christianity (313 C.E.) and Emperor Theodosius (379–395 C.E.) established it as the only sanctioned state religion.

It is significant that the controversy between Christian Churches about whether the Easter date should or should not accord with Jewish Passover was settled by Emperor Constantine. His pertinent letter displays the virulent antisemitism induced by his Christian mentors. *"In the first place it was decreed unworthy to observe that most sacred festival in accordance with the practice of the Jews; having sullied their own hands with a heinous crime, such blood-stained men are as one might expect mentally blind. ... Let there be nothing in common between you and the detestable mob of the Jews! ...Let us with one accord take up this course, right honorable brothers, and so tear ourselves away from that disgusting complicity. ... What could those people calculate correctly, when after that murder of the Lord, after that parricide, they have taken leave of their senses, and are moved, not by any rational principle, but by uncontrolled impulse"* (Cameron and Hall, p. 128).

Note that even after gaining state power, Christian animus to heteropraxy continued, as we have seen in St. John Chrysostom's and St. Jerome's fulminations. Stringent governmental laws against Jews and their synagogues (Note #23) then augmented Gentile Christianity's long-sustained non-Jewish/anti-Jewish identity.

7
CHRISTIAN REINTERPRETATION OF THE JEWISH BIBLE

Of the three parts of the Jewish Bible/Hebrew Scriptures, the Five Books of Moses, from Genesis to Deuteronomy, called the "Torah," is considered the "Written Law." It stipulated Jewish monotheistic beliefs and served as the "Covenant" (agreement) prescribing rules and behavior (e.g., the Ten Commandments) for an abiding protective and worshipful relationship between Jews and their God ("Yahweh"). The other two parts of the Jewish Bible are the "Prophets" (from *Joshua* to *Malachi*) and the "Writings" (from *Psalms* to *Chronicles*).

Throughout much of Biblical history, prophets served as Israel's religious and moral conscience, through writings embodying both religion and politics. That is, not only how to behave in worshipping Yahweh, but the behavior expected from rulers and institutions governing the people who worship Yahweh. Prophets became Israel's champions of accountability to a higher power (Yahweh), adamant opponents of pagan idolatry, and prime advocates for justice and caring social relationships. *""I have been Yahweh your God ever since the land of Egypt; you know no God but me, and beside me there is no savior"* (Hosea 13.4). "[The idolater] *makes it* [wood] *into a god, his idol, bows down to it and worships it, he prays to it and says, 'Save me, for you are my god!'"* (Isaiah 44.17). *"These things that are made of wood and overlaid with gold and silver are like stones from the mountain, and those who serve them will be put to shame. Why then must anyone think that they are gods, or call them gods?"* (Letter of Jeremiah 39–40).

"Is not this the fast that I [Yahweh] *choose: to loose the bonds of injustice, to undo the thongs of the yoke, to let the oppressed go free. and to break every yoke? Is it not to share your bread with the hungry, and bring the homeless poor into your house; when you see the naked to cover them, and not to hide yourself* [turn your back]

from your own kin?" (Isaiah. 58.6–7). *Scoundrels are found among my people; they take over the goods of others. Like fowlers they set a trap; they catch human beings. ... their houses are full of treachery ... they have grown fat and sleek. They know no limits in deeds of wickedness; they do not judge with justice the cause of the orphan ... and they do not defend the rights of the needy"* (Jeremiah 5.26–28). *"What does Yahweh require of you but to do justice, and to love kindness, and to walk humbly with your God"* (Micah 6.8).

In time, Scriptural Law and prophetic aspirations gained firm ethical structure so that *"basic moral principles were laid down. God is just, and justice is his prime demand — not justice as a vague abstraction, but as applied in the daily affairs of men, to strangers as well as to the home-born"* (Blank (p. 180). *"For the Lord your God is God of gods and Lord of lords, who is not partial and takes no bribe, who executes justice for the orphan and the widow and who loves strangers, providing them with food and clothing. You shall also love the stranger, for you were strangers in the land of Egypt"* (Deuteronomy 10.17–19).

The Scriptural theme, *"Remember you were slaves in the land of Egypt"* was continually repeated, exhorting Jews to be moral exemplars; enabling them to abide on Yahweh's "Holy Hill" of ethical behavior. *"Those who walk blamelessly, and do what is right, and speak the truth from their heart, who do not slander with their tongue, and do no evil to their friends, nor take up a reproach against their neighbors; in whose eyes the wicked are despised, but who honor those who fear Yahweh; who stand by their oath even to their hurt; who do not lend money at interest, and do not take a bribe against the innocent"* (Psalm 15).

At the height of all Biblical cultic commands is perhaps the ritualistic tie to Yahweh in Genesis 17.10: *"This is my covenant, which you* [Abraham] *shall keep, between me and you, and your offspring after you: every male among you shall be circumcised."* Deuteronomy (30.6, 9–14) broadens the circumcision covenant not only as outwardly visual but emotionally internal: *"The Lord [Yahweh], your God, will circumcise your heart and the hearts of your descendants ... For the Lord will again take delight in prospering you, just as he delighted in prospering your ancestors, when you obey the Lord by observing his commandments and decrees that are written in this book of the law ... [T]his commandment ... is not in heaven, that you should say, 'Who will go up to heaven for us, and get it for us so that we may hear it and observe it?' Neither is it beyond the sea, that you should say 'Who will cross to the other side of the sea for us so that we may hear it and observe it?' No. the word is very near to you; it is in your mouth and in your heart for you to observe."*

The circumcision covenant is endless: *"Remember [God's] covenant forever, the word that he commanded, for a thousand generations, the covenant he made with Abraham, his sworn promise to Isaac, which he confirmed to Jacob as a statute, to Israel as an everlasting covenant"* (1 Chronicles 16.15–16). ("Covenant" and "circumcision" are both celebrated by Jews using the same Hebrew term, "Bris.")

In more than one hundred verses (Exodus 20–24), the Jewish Scriptures set out a code of law, justice, and ritual that begins with the Ten Commandments and ends with *"you shall not boil a kid in its mother's milk."* Overlooked by St. Paul and Christian critics of Jewish "Law" were the communal spirit and sentiments that served as important elements in fulfilling its rituals and commandments. *"[B]urnt offerings, public sacrifices, music and song, thanksgiving sacrifices and the eating joyful meals together — allows people of the Second Temple era to realize what their God intended for them in their Jerusalem temple: praise, thanksgiving, and petition, offered to God in a ritual complex that can help them realize their identity as the people of God"* (Endres, p. 187). Hezekiah's prayer (2 Chronicles 30.19) emphasized spiritual devotion over meticulous observance: *"The good Lord pardon all who set their hearts to seek*

God, the Lord of their ancestors, even though not in accordance with the sanctuary's rule of cleanness." (See also Japhet, p. 252.)

For Jews, the Torah was not merely instructive but, through historical accounts, formed and strengthened Jewish identity. "[I]*ts legends of cultural perseverance sustained a national culture grounded in religion but far exceeding its domain. Jewish identity in antiquity was not simply about cultic reverence. It was about kinship and tradition, about loyalty to a proud and historic people destined to withstand their political subjugation in order to reclaim the past glories documented in their sacred scriptures. ... Simply put, there would have been no Jewish religion had there not been a cohesive polity to support it. One therefore cannot account for one without accounting for the other"* (Burns 2016, pp. 80–81). This close tie between Jewish ethnicity, Jewish religion, and Jewish culture prevailed even though Israel/Judea came repeatedly under foreign rule: by Assyrians (722 B.C.E), Babylonians (586 B.C.E.), Persians (538 B.C.E.), Greeks, (322 B.C.E.), and Romans (63 B.C.E.).

Although considered irrevocable, there were obvious needs to modify some religious rituals after the Romans destroyed the Jerusalem Temple and displaced its priestly class (70 C.E.); events not unlike those in the Babylonian exile centuries before. Adapting Biblical commands to existing conditions was accomplished by lay religious teachers ("Rabbis") in conferences and debates, out of which came relevant codes of conduct, codified in the Jewish Mishnah and the Jewish Talmud. Despite controversies and varied Scriptural interpretations, they all adhered to identifiable Jewish principles and rituals. Among these were monotheism and moral social behavior; the observance of circumcision, the Sabbath, and dietary laws; celebration of holidays that commemorated historical events such as the exodus from slavery; and shared Hebraic literature that sanctified these beliefs and practices. *"The Mosaic covenant stood at the center of Israelite tradition. It was, in effect, the constitution of Israelite society"* (Horsley 2012, p. 122).

Unfortunately for Jews, the interpretive allegorical methods Rabbis used to adapt Jewish Scriptures to Jewish needs gave license to St. Paul and his successors to adapt Jewish scriptures to quite opposite Christian needs. That is, Christian "exegesis" (Scriptural interpretation) turned the main themes of the Jewish Scriptures against the Jews themselves, introducing new "spiritual" criteria that repudiate explicit Scriptural meanings and intent.

For example, the Scriptural commandment that Jews must *"live by the Law"* without asking *"who will ascend into heaven"* and *"beyond the sea"* (Deuteronomy 30.12–13, page 49 above), St. Paul changed into a spiritual warning to exercise "faith" by not asking who will *"bring Christ down"* or *"bring Christ up"* (*Romans* 10.6–7). The Deuteronomy sentence, *"the word* [Law] *is very near to you; it is in your mouth and in your heart for you to observe,"* was changed by St. Paul into *"the word of faith that we proclaim; because if you confess in your lips that Jesus is Lord and believe in your heart that God raised him from the dead, you will be saved"* (*Romans* 10.8–9).

Similarly, St. Paul deemed the circumcision covenant in Genesis and other Scriptural books worthless because it was a literal interpretation of the "Law" based on supposed *"praise from others,"* rather than a spiritual interpretation derived *"from God"* (*Romans* 2.25–29). In his letter to the Galatians, God's covenant with Jews was turned into a spiritual "promise" made not to *"his offsprings"* (plural, the Jews) but to *"his offspring"* (singular, the Savior): *"that is to one person, who is Christ"* (3.18), *"if you belong to Christ, then you are Abraham's offspring"* (3.29). *"Our competence is from God, who made us competent to be ministers of a new covenant, not of letter* [the Torah] *but of spirit; for the letter kills, but the Spirit gives life"* (*2 Corinthians* 3.5–6).

As shown in Note #2, these novel meanings and interpretations produced a "New Covenant," unshared by Jesus of the Gospels or any of his disciples, that was ascribed by St. Paul to an exclusive personal vision given to him by a phantom Jesus. In his unique dream, Jesus instructed St. Paul to engage his followers in a new ceremony — a Christian sacrament called the Eucharist, which St. Paul dated to Jesus' Last Supper (that he never attended!) — to eat bread and drink wine to simulate sharing Jesus' body's flesh and blood. *"The Lord Jesus on the night when he was betrayed took a loaf of bread, ... and said, 'This is my body that is for you. Do this in remembrance of me.' In the same way he took the cup also ... saying, 'This cup is the new covenant in my blood. Do this, as often as you drink it, in remembrance of me'"* (*1 Corinthians* 11.23–25; also Note #11.*f*, p. 121). According to Koester (2007 p. 250), St. Paul's "New Covenant" forged the *"unity of the many Christian communities"* in which *"the primary bond was the Eucharist as the ritual of the new Christian nation."* This was then embodied in the "New Testament" for which the Jewish/Hebrew Bible, named as "Old Testament," was merely the presumed forerunner.

Nevertheless, since the Old Testament was the primary source for St. Paul's Gentile Christianity's claim to antiquity, it could not simply be ignored. History provided no other ancient text in which to construe interpretations that a Jesus Christ existed before the first century C.E. Searching for Jewish Scriptural sources to support Christianity's antique claims thus became a common theological enterprise, and, by facile interpretation, Jesus Christ was placed in Old Testament history as far back as the Book of Genesis. In the New Testament, hundreds of passages therefore quote, parallel, or allude to Jewish Scriptural sources in attempts to justify such Christian claims (C. A. Evans, pp. 190–219).

St Paul, for example, uses approximately 130 Biblical quotations (Scheffler 2011b, p. 274) to support his views, many grossly misinterpreted or misquoted as shown above (see also R. N. Longenecker 1999, pp. 96–116). *"Paul changes the wording of more than half of his* [Biblical] *citations for stylistic and rhetorical reasons. At times, Paul's treatment of a passage seems cavalier. For example,*

*in Deut. 30.10–14, cited in Rom. 10.6–8, Paul replaced all refer-ences to "doing" with references to Jesus' death and resurrection.
... Paul derives meaning foreign to the traditional understanding of this passage and imports his innovative understanding into the text itself"* (Norton, p. 137). In other examples, St. Paul also blatantly shifted Biblical references made to God, from Israel's "Yahweh" to "Jesus' (Lüdemann 2002b, p. 96).

"One can conclude that in his use of the Old Testament (whether by direct quotation, reference or allusion) Paul most of the time reads the old Testament out of context" (Scheffler 2011b, p. 276). In St. Paul's audiences, according to Stanley (p. 154): *"Those with extensive knowledge of Scripture would have found Paul's quo-tations troubling, to say the least, and some might even have con-cluded that contextual reading of Paul's quotations offered more support for the views of Paul's opponents than for Paul."* That St. Paul's creations and misquotations escaped his audience's examina-tion shows they *"were written for a very different type of audience* [mainly, if not entirely, Gentiles], *one that was largely illiterate and possessed only a limited acquaintance with the text of Scriptures"* (Ibid. p. 145).

Also, despite prolific use of the Jewish Scriptures, St. Paul seems to purposely ignore quotations that would broaden the scope of his readers beyond the "Christ event." For example, although St. Paul repeatedly condemns Jews for using "deeds" to atone for sins rather than "faith" and "spirit" (e.g., *Romans* 3.20), he completely overlooks the prophetic theme that true Jewish sacrifice to God is a contrite repentant heart rather than burnt sacrificial offerings (*Psalm* 51, see also Note #9, p. 74). As listed by Scheffler (2011b, p. 277), among St. Paul's other purposeful omissions are:

- critical wisdom of Job and Qohelet;
- positive evaluation of sexuality as expressed in Genesis and Song of Songs;

54

- political struggle of prophets such as Jeremiah, Ezekiel, Amos and Micah;
- positive appreciation of nature in the Psalms (e.g. 8, 9, 104 and 139);
- engagement for the socially marginalized in Deuteronomy, the prophets and the Psalms.

St. Paul's Scriptural handpicking and misinterpretation served for centuries as models in which almost any Christian notion could be ascribed to a "divine" message hidden in a Jewish Scriptural passage: interpretations far removed from their intended Jewish meanings. For example, although the life and trials of Gentile Christianity's "Jesus Christ" is nowhere mentioned in any Jewish Biblical document, St. Paul exclaims, "*Christ died for our sins in accordance with the Scriptures, and that he was buried, and that he was raised on the third day in accordance with the Scriptures*" (*1 Corinthians* 15.3–4). Quotations from Jewish Scriptures could even be invented, as in St. John's Gospel (7:38): "*As the Scripture has said 'Out of the believer's heart shall flow rivers of living waters.'*"

Thus, with most imaginative detail, St. Justin Martyr (ca. 150 C.E., *1 Apology* XXXI) declares: "*In these books, then, of the prophets we found Jesus our Christ foretold as coming, born of a virgin, growing up to man's estate, and healing every disease and every sickness, and raising the dead, and being hated, and unrecognized, and crucified, and dying and rising again, and ascending into heaven, and being, and being called, the Son of God. We find it also predicted that certain persons should be sent by Him into every nation to publish these things, and that rather among the Gentiles (than among the Jews) men should believe on Him. And He was predicted before He appeared, first 5,000 years before, and again 3,000, then 2,000, then 1,000, and yet again 800; for in the succession of generations prophets after prophets arose*" (ANF vol. 1, p. 173).

St. Melito of Sardis (ca. 170) imposes even further fantasies on Biblical narratives: "*This is He* [Jesus Christ] *who was pilot to*

Noah; He who was guide to Abraham; He who was bound with Isaac; He who was in exile with Jacob; He who was sold with Joseph; He who was captain of the host with Moses" (*On Faith*, ANF vol. 8, p. 757).

Moreschini's and Norelli's (p. 138) comment: "*What we see here is an important episode in the 'expropriation' of the Scriptures and religious tradition of Judaism that was carried on by Christians, especially in the second century, as they claimed for Christianity the authentic understanding of the Bible and continuity with the 'true Israel.' In this perspective, polemical violence against the Jews came naturally in the effort to prove that the Jews had no right to appeal to the* [Scriptural] *revelation that the Christians had inherited from them, but of which the Christians now claim to be the sole possessors. We see this process in* [St.] *Justin in the area of biblical interpretation; in* [St.] *Melito it is applied to the very core of Jewish identity as represented by the celebration of Passover.*" (See Note #8, p. 68.)

Gentile Christian exegesis exercised no limit, and St. Augustine (ca. 400 C.E.) extends Gentile Christian interpretive dominance from the book of Genesis to all succeeding Jewish Scriptures: "*To enumerate all the passages in the Hebrew prophets referring to our Lord and Savior Jesus Christ, would exceed the limits of a volume ... The whole contents of these Scriptures are either directly or indirectly about Christ*" (*Reply to Faustus* XII.7, NPNF Series 1, vol. 4, p. 185). This echoes a saying St. Luke (24.44) ascribes to Jesus' resurrected image: "*Everything written about me in the Law of Moses, the prophets, and the psalms must be fulfilled.*"

Young (1997, pp. 23–24) points out that according to Christian Fathers such as Origen (ca. 240 C.E.): "*The words and teachings of Christ are not simply those recorded from his days on earth. For Moses and the prophets were filled with his spirit. ... it was the Spirit's skopos* [doctrines] *to enlighten the prophets and apostles so they became partakers in all the doctrines of the Spirit's counsel.*

These doctrines prove to be those concerning God, his only be-gotten Son, and the cause of his descent to the level of human flesh. ...[W]here the earthly [Scriptural] *narrative did not fit, bits were woven in to represent the more mystical meaning. The coherence of scripture, we might say in summary, lies at its heart, in its soul and spirit, not its physical reality.*" (See also Note #12, p. 138.)

When Jews objected to exotic Christian reinterpretations by pointing to more lucidly clear Scriptural statements, Christian apologists claimed they had been purposely rewritten to thwart Christians. St. Justin Martyr (*Dialogue with Trypho, a Jew* LXXI): "*...I wish you to observe that they* [Jews] *have altogether taken away many Scriptures from the translation effected by those seventy elders who were with Ptolemy* [the 'Septuagint' Greek translation of the Jewish Bible], *and by which this very man who was crucified* [Jesus] *is proved to have been set forth expressly as God, and man, and as being crucified, and as dying. ...You contradict the statement 'Behold, the virgin Shall conceive,' and say it ought to be read, 'Behold, the young woman shall conceive*'" (ANF vol. 1, p. 234). (Note that the Biblical Hebrew word "almah" in Isaiah 7.14 was translated in the Greek Septuagint Bible as "parthenos," and was used by Christians to mean "virgin." In Hebrew, however, "almah" means no more than "young woman," or even "married young woman," and the Hebrew term for a virgin is not "almah" but "bethulah" (Genesis 24.16, 1 Kings 1.2))

Similarly, in attempting to justify Biblical prophecy of Jesus' crucifixion, St. Justin Martyr (*Dialogue with Trypho, a Jew* LXXIII) accuses Jews of deleting "from the wood" in *Psalm* 96.10, which reads "*Declare among the nations, 'the Lord is King'* [or '*the Lord reigns*']," claiming it should read "*the Lord reigns from the wood* [Jesus' cross]" (ANF vol. 1, pp. 234, 235). St. Justin Martyr also replaces the Jewish God Yahweh with Jesus Christ in Yahweh's famous call to Moses from the burning bush (Exodus 3). "*This same*

One [Jesus Christ] *who is called an Angel and **is** God, appeared and communed with Moses"* (ANF vol. 1, p. 227).

Like St. Paul's Scriptural liberties, such forced departures from the Old Testament could only have passed muster when presented to Biblically uninformed Gentile audiences. *"It is clear that Justin's assertions in fact have little to do with serious textual enquiry on his part and that theological polemic over possession of the truth prevents his being an impartial or even informed witness to developments among Greek biblical texts"* (Rajak, p. 127).

By the sixth century C.E., flagrantly created Christian prophecies, drawn from imagined renditions of Jewish Scriptures, became legalized in Christian Emperor Justinian's pronouncement that literal interpretations by Jews of their Scriptures are to be prohibited. *"It was right and proper that the Hebrews, when listening to the Holy Books, should not stick to the bare letters but look for the prophecies contained in them, through which they announce the Great God and the Saviour of the human race, Jesus Christ"* (Smelik, p. 145).

Even in modern times, trying to justify Christian non-literal readings of the Jewish Scriptures, remains a significant part of Christian theology (Moyise, pp. 111–117). According to Lohse (p. 24), the "deeper meaning" of the Jewish Scriptures *"can be discerned only when the Old Testament is read from the point of view of its fulfillment in Jesus Christ."* Similarly, despite St. Paul's purposeful Scriptural misreadings and theological inventions, Dunn (2013, p. 36) characterizes St. Paul's mission to establish Gentile churches as *"scripturally valid and theologically sound."*

To Christian theologians, meaning of a Jewish Biblical text is not determined by the original writer but by the Christian interpreter ("exegetist") and his Christian audience. For a Christian reader to think otherwise — that the meaning of a text is based on the author's intention — *"leads to determinate readings that are incapable of acknowledging the mystery of God"* (Spinks, p. 65). Emphasizing Scriptural history instead of Christian interpretative theology prompts Christian protest against Jews and disbelievers rejecting *"Christian [Fathers'] claims regarding Jesus Christ as the key to all the Scriptures"* (Treier, p. 47).

To religious Christian doctrinaires and theologians, "History" is thus a persistent threat to "Faith," no matter that "Faith" can blatantly distort and subvert history. In the words of a modern Christian theologian (Seitz, p. 105), *"It is important to reiterate that Christian theological reflection on the Old Testament has a life proper to itself"* and should not succumb to *"historical-critical inquiry."* Similarly, Moberly focuses *"on reading the Hebrew Bible as Christian Scripture"* (p.3), and theological exegesis must *"not be restricted to original meaning and be able to move beyond it"* (p. 161). Thus, to Childs (1997, p. 61), original contexts of the Jewish prophets are to be ignored, and interpreting Isaiah as *"a witness to Jesus Christ...is not only possible, but actually mandatory for any serious theological reflection."* Lienhard (p.7): *"[T]he first problem of the historical method; of itself, it can only discern discrete facts from the past. As such, it cannot provide the foundation for faith."*

New Testament authors and editors were thus arbitrarily endowed with a "divine spirit" that obviated any need for sustaining original orientations and objectives of Jewish Scriptures. *"Thus while their interpretative procedure was flawed, the* [Christian] *meaning they wrote down was inspired"* (Beale, p. 2). One rationale offered for reinterpreting Jewish Scriptures ("OT") in favor of the New Testament ("NT") is that *"history is an interrelated unity, and God has designed the earlier parts [OT] to correspond and point to the latter parts [NT], especially to events that have happened in the age of eschatological fulfillment in Christ ... Consequently, the concept of prophetic fulfillment should not be limited to fulfillment of direct verbal prophesies from the OT but broadened to include also an indication of the 'redemptive historical relationship of the new, climactic revelation of God in Christ"* (Ibid. p. 98). Kelsey (p. 149): *"It declares the resurrection of Jesus of Nazareth, an event central to the religious sense of the New Testament, to be beyond the competence of the methods one needs to use the historical sense of the texts.*" Since it is doubtful that any one Christian theologian or theological group is more privy than others to God's presumed Scriptural designs (Note #11.*b*, p. 111), it is apparent that Christian theologians and "*New Testament authors modify the Hebrew Bible quotations to create support for their particular views*" (Chilton et al., p. 24). According to Stendahl (p. 210) this leads to an appropriate question: "*What does it profit an exegete to understand the words and miss the intention?*"

A primary distortion of Biblical history was to argue that "true" Christians include ancient Abraham (circumcised Father of the Jews!) and even Biblical Adam (Notes #2, #14, #18, #19). As noted earlier, Abraham's circumcision had no sacrosanct meaning to St. Paul since "*the promise* [covenant] *that he would inherit the world did not come to Abraham or to his descendants through the law* [God's literal Scriptural covenant] *but through the righteousness of faith*" (*Romans* 4.13). The "*righteousness of faith*" that Abraham presumably possessed **before** he was circumcised is St. Paul's new covenantal "*righteousness of God through faith in Jesus Christ*" (*Romans* 3.22). Unattainable to Abraham's circumcised descendants who follow the written "law," God's favor is thus now achieved by uncircumcised Gentiles "*who believe in Him who raised Jesus our Lord from the dead, who was handed over to death for our trespasses, and was raised for our justification*" (*Romans* 4.24–25). "*Gentiles, who did not strive for righteousness, have attained it, that is righteousness through faith; but Israel ... did not strive for it on the basis of faith, but as if it were based on works*" (*Romans* 9.30–32). [I]*f you belong to Christ, then you are Abraham's offspring, heirs according to the promise*" (*Galatians* 3.29). "*If it is the adherents to the law* [Jews] *who are to be the heirs, faith is null and the promise is void*: (*Romans* 13.14).

By shifting Abraham's "promise" from Jews to Gentiles: *"Paul's allegory is intended to make the Torah itself indorse this very message — to set the **theological message** of the Torah against its own **commandments**"* (Levenson p. 218, his emphasis). For example, in the *Epistle of Barnabas* (ca. 100 C.E.): *"circumcision was not of the flesh, but they [Jews] transgressed because an evil angel [Satan] deluded them"* (ANF vol. 1, p. 142). Such "exegesis" attempted to cloth any fancied theological claim with antique Scriptural authority. Christian "hermeneutics" thus became a Christian clerical vocation, in which one can pull imagined threads out of any Scriptural passage to create a labyrinthine theological world involving Jesus Christ in events from the birth of Adam to the tribal patriarchy of Abraham to the divine guidance of Moses, and even to the creation of the universe: *"He was in the beginning with God. All things came into being with him, and without him not one thing came into being"* (St. John's Gospel 1.2–3).

According to Dunn (2012, p. 212), St. Paul's claim for the presumed Christian "promise to Abraham" is *"the primary root of continuity between Christianity and Judaism."* This notion is surprisingly offered despite there being no semblance of Christianity— in name, practice, or "continuity" — during the more than millennial history between Abraham's presumed "primary root" and St. Paul's Jesus Christ. As noted earlier, prior to St. Paul's first century C.E. letters and the imaginations of later Christian theologians, there is no existing or historical sign of a divine worshipful Jesus Christ, Only Son of God, Savior of Mankind; nor any sign of a believer in Christianity's Jesus Christ, Jewish or Gentile.

In sum, although claiming Jewish Scriptural antiquity was designed to make Gentile Christianity acceptable to the Gentile world, it made no sense to Jews. It seemed quite bizarre that documents written by and for Jews, recounting their beliefs, laws, and history, were presumably written so they could have quite opposite meanings for future Gentile Christians.

Sadly, even modern Christian theologians, although lamenting Christian antisemitism, appear unable to grant Jews Biblical authority to reject Christian claims. Worthen (p. 5), for example, vindicates this stance with the common Christian Patristic charge that Jews are "*disobedient children liable to God's wrath and judgment*" for not accepting "*Jesus as Lord and Messiah*," and that "*the covenant made at Sinai with Moses has come to an end with the coming of Christ*."

In a similar self-vindicating fashion, a recent book of elaborate Biblical hermeneutics (Lucass) claims that Jesus, sacrificed to atone for human sin, is really no different from the kind of Messiah that Jews would expect if they properly read their own Scriptures: "*it is no longer possible to claim that the* [Christian] *messiahship of Jesus is 'un-Jewish' because he suffered died and was resurrected*" (Lucass, p. 198). Even "*the Eucharist, the injunction to eat Jesus' body and drink his blood, an injunction which is considered so alien by the Jewish writers, becomes once again a Judaic concept*" (Ibid. p. 201). Such views reflect the recurrent claim that because of their theological and exegetical blindness and obtuseness, Jews have no warrant to object to Christian conceptions and distortions of Jewish Scriptures.

However, the matter can be seen differently. It may well be that some or even many Jews may have considered a coming Messiah as a divinely-sent savior (Note #15), the Jewish majority at the time of Jesus certainly did not believe a Messiah can be killed without achieving some success in the struggle to relieve Jews from indigenous and Roman oppression (Note #11.*g*). Similarly, drinking blood and eating human flesh, promulgated (even symbolically) by St. Paul and New Testament writers, was an abomination in Jewish culture and Scriptures (Note #11.*f*). A. L. Williams (p. 417): "*Their* [Christian] *weakness lies in estimating the Jewish use of the Scripture wrongly. They never understood the mind of the Jews. Christian writers ... blamed the obstinate Jews for not accepting the evidence which seemed to them so strong. But, in reality, this was only because they themselves misconceived the case."* In Foster's words (p. 98): Christian theologians *"find scriptural allusions or echoes of the Jewish scriptures behind every key Pauline concept, instead of recognizing that some ideas may be truly innovative, and others may draw upon Gentile thought."*

Unfortunately, blaming Jews for rejecting Jesus and contesting Christian Scriptural misinterpretations, was used by Christian Fathers, such as St. John Chrysostom, to condemn Pagans or even fellow Christians who doubted Jesus Christ's equality with God, as suffering from the "Jewish disease" (Nirenberg, p. 113). Anti-Jewish hostility could be exercised in disputes between Christians even in the absence of Jews (Note #17).

8
LABELLING JEWS AS "CHRIST KILLERS"

"At the heart of Christian mistreatment of Jews over the centuries lay a simplistic and false syllogism: 'The Jews rejected and killed Jesus. Therefore, God must want to punish them, to make them suffer for this crime. Therefore, we Christians should help God by increasing the sufferings of the Jews '" (Fisher 1993, p. 105). Jewish deicide *"gained universal acceptance and lived on as a sort of socio-theological corollary of the Church's Christology"* (Flannery, p. 63).

Probably the earliest of New Testament writings, St. Paul's first letter to the Thessalonians (2.14–15) launched the litany of millennial vituperation: "…*the Jews, who killed both the Lord and the prophets.*" According to many scholars (for example, Vermes 2005) spurious narratives in the Gospels then followed, blaming Jews, born and unborn, for Jesus' crucifixion; an unrelenting mantra of Christian anti-Jewishness. St. Matthew 27.24–25: "*So when Pilate saw that he could do nothing, but rather that a riot was beginning, he took some water and washed his hands before the crowd, saying, 'I am innocent of this man's* [Jesus'] *blood; see to it yourselves.' Then the people as a whole answered, 'His blood be on us and on our children!'*" St. Luke 23.20–21: "*Pilate, wanting to release Jesus, addressed them again; but they kept shouting, 'Crucify, crucify him!'*" St. Mark 15.14: "*Pilate asked them, 'Why, what evil has he done?' But they shouted all the more, 'Crucify him!'*" St. John 19.6: "*When the chief priests and the police saw him they shouted 'Crucify him! Crucify him!' Pilate said to them, 'Take him yourselves and crucify him; I find no case against him.'*"

Such tales, in which a people verging on a nationwide revolt against abusive Roman rule (Note #15) clamor for the crucifixion of a popular compatriot, should certainly arouse incredulity if not censure for falsehood and slander. The response *"We have no King but the* [Roman] *emperor"* to Pontius Pilate's question *"Shall I crucify your King?"* "(St. John 19.15) seems also as deceitful an invention of Jewish love for their Roman rulers as the Jewish crowd's cry for Jesus' crucifixion. There is no hint that any of Jesus' disciples corroborated these malicious anti-Jewish accounts, nor does it accord with the large Jewish crowds that welcomed Jesus to Jerusalem (St. Mark 11.8–10, St. Matthew 21.8–11, St. Luke 19.36–38, St. John 12.12–13), or with the reverential attitude toward Jesus of the Galilean countrymen who supported him, or with documented open Jewish hostility toward the Roman army and Roman occupation (Josephus *Wars of the Jews*, Book II) leading to the impending war with Rome.

Conciliatory sentiments attributed to Pontius Pilate are also quite contrary to all that was known of this Roman Procurator. In one report of his governance, as related by a Jewish contemporary (Philo, p.784): Pilate feared "*they* [Jews] *might in reality go on an embassy to the emperor, and might impeach him with respect to other particulars of his government, in respect of his corruption, and his acts of insolence, and his rapine, and his habit of insulting people, and his cruelty, and his continual murders of people untried and uncondemned, and his never ending, and gratuitous, and most grievous inhumanity.*" According to Josephus (*Antiquities of the Jews*, XVIII:III-IV), Pilate set off protests and demonstrations causing "great slaughter" of both Jews and Samaritans. He was eventually sent for trial to Rome for extreme cruelty.

It is obvious that Jesus was not crucified by Romans for religious reasons, to which he offered no essential change (Note #16), but for an act of seditious insurrection in the Jerusalem Temple. Romans employed crucifixion as provincial punishment for sedition, and Pontius Pilate had no qualms in sardonically titling Jesus' cross "King of the Jews." This was hardly a religious title, but deprecates a provincial's attempt to challenge the "peace and order" of Roman rule (Notes #15, p. 185; #21, p. 232.). Had Jewish condemnation of Jesus been present, it would have extended no further than the aristocrats and priests who participated with Rome in Israel's subjugation and exploitation. According to St. Mark's Gospel (12.12), the antagonists to Jesus and his supporting "crowds" in the Temple disturbance were the Temple hierarchs who *"wanted to arrest him, but they feared the crowd."* Blaming *all* Jews for Jesus' murder, and absolving Pontius Pilate of any responsibility, served Christian leaders in appeasing both Roman authority and Roman Gentile society. It also helped justify Gentile Christianity's claim to being God's "True Israelites," replacing "Christ-killing" Jews as inheritors of the Jewish Scriptures (Notes ##7, #18, #19).

Modern historians such as Vermes (2005, pp. 82, 94ff); and Ehrman (2016, pp. 151–159) list significant discrepancies between the Gospel accounts of Jesus' execution.

- St. Mark's story (15) is apparently simple: Pontius Pilate expresses concern that Jesus is a usurper of authority (*"Are you the King of the Jews?"*), and then asks the Jewish crowd to choose which malfeasants they would release, Jesus or Barabbas the insurrectionist. The Jews respond by demanding Barabbas' release and Jesus' execution.

- In St. Matthew (27.19): faced by the Jewish crowds unrelenting demands for Jesus' execution, Pilate's wife pleads Jesus' innocence to Pilate, who then washes his hands of Jesus' "blood" (27.24).

- In St. Luke: Pilate (uncounseled by his wife) finds Jesus innocent of all charges (23.4). He then sends Jesus off to Herod Antipas, Roman-appointed Jewish ruler of Galilee (23.7), who is also convinced of Jesus' innocence, and who then returns Jesus to Pilate and the Romans. Pilate insists again that Jesus' is blameless, but the Jewish crowd nevertheless continues to demand Jesus' execution. Pilate then accedes to their demands, releasing Barabbas, *"and handed Jesus over as they wished"* (23.5).

- In St. John: contrary to the other Gospels, Jesus is sent to Pilate before the Passover Seder ("Last Supper") by Jews who refuse to enter Pilate's headquarters (Praetorium) in order to escape defilement (18.28). Pilate refuses to judge Jesus, and sends him back to the Jews, who then return him to Pilate because they say they are not permitted to engage in capital punishment. Jesus and Pilate then have a somewhat lengthy private conversation in the Praetorium (18.33–38) in which Jesus pleads his case, "*My kingdom is not from this world. If my kingdom were from this world, my followers would keep me from being handed over to the Jews. But as it is, my kingdom is not from here.*" (Who could have devised this private conversation, if not the writers/redactors of St. John's Gospel?) Pilate then exits to tell the Jews "*I find no case against him,*" and then engages in a succession of entries and exits to and from the Praetorium trying to convince the waiting Jews that Jesus should be released. The Jews insist "*We have no king but the emperor,*" and Pilate then "*handed him over **to them** to be crucified*" (St. John 19.16, my emphasis).

St. John's narrative prompted Casey (1996, pp. 197–198) to conclude that it: "*has been rewritten to avoid serious problems and to affirm serious falsehoods. The crucifixion has been put on the wrong day, with the result that the Last Supper is no longer a celebration of the Jewish Passover. The account is hostile to 'the Jews' from beginning to end. They demand Jesus' crucifixion, but give no plausible reason for demanding that he undergo this horrific punishment. The* [Roman] *charge that Jesus was king of the Jews has been reinterpreted, replaced with the assertion that he declared his kingdom not of this world. Pilate has been rewritten as an unconvincing figure who tries to have Jesus released.... The resulting stories are untrue from beginning to end. Thus the fourth evangelist has quite rewritten the central part of the myth of Christian origins. We must conclude that his work is a presentation of falsehood.*" By contrast, a modern New Testament scholar's statement (Klassen, p. 19n) that *"it is simply wrong to claim that there is anti-Semitism or anti-Judaism in the New Testament,"* is itself *"simply wrong."*

It is essential to recognize that New Testament stories, like many others, are not innocent of their effects: stories generate beliefs, beliefs generate emotions, and emotions generate actions. Labeling Jews as "Christ killers" turned out to be as terrible and as endlessly lethal a condemnation as the Christian Fathers could devise. Acts of the Apostles (7.52): *"They* [Jews] *killed those who foretold the coming of the Righteous One, and now you have become his betrayer and murderers."* St. Aristides (ca. 130 C.E.): [T]*hey* [Jews] *proved stubborn and ungrateful, and often served the idols of the nations and put to death the prophets and just men who were sent to them. Then when the Son of God was pleased to come upon the earth, they received him with wanton violence and betrayed him into the hands of Pilate the Roman governor; and paying no respect to his good deeds and the countless miracles he wrought among them, they demanded a sentence of death by the cross.... So much for the Jews."* (*Apology* XIV, ANF vol. 9, pp. 275–276).

St Justin Martyr (ca. 150 C.E.): *"The highest pitch of your wickedness lies in this, that you [Jews] hate the Righteous One and slew Him; and so treat those who have received from Him all that they are, and who are pious, righteous and humane"* (*Dialogue with Trypho, a Jew* CXXXVI, ANF vol. 1, p. 268). The prime physical evidence of Jewishness — circumcision, the covenantal bond between Jews and their God — was explained by St. Justin Martyr as the trait God designed to make it easier to condemn Jews in the Last Judgment *"for you have slain the Just One and His Prophets before Him"* (Ibid. XVI, ANF vol. 1, p. 202). To St. Irenaeus (ca. 180), Christian salvation depends on sustaining illusions of Jewish guilt: *"Unless, then, the Jews had become slayers of the Lord ... and by killing the apostles and persecuting the Church, had fallen into an abyss of wrath, we could not have been saved"* (*Adversus Haeresis*, ANF vol. 1, p. 501).

St. Melito of Sardis (*"On the Passover"* ca. 170): *"This is He who was put to death. And where was He put to death? In the midst of Jerusalem. By whom? By Israel: because he cured their lame and cleansed their lepers, and gave light to their blind, and raised their dead! ... O Israel, transgressor of the law, why hast thou committed this new iniquity, subjecting the Lord to new sufferings? ... He that hung up the earth in space was Himself hanged up; He that fixed the heavens was fixed with nails; He that bore up the earth was borne up on a tree; the Lord of all was subjected to ignominy in a naked body — God put to death! The King of Israel slain with Israel's right hand!"* (ANF vol. 8, p. 757). Tertullian (ca. 198): *"Albeit Israel washed daily all his limbs over, yet is he never clean. His hands, at all events, are ever unclean, eternally dyed with the blood of the prophets, and of the Lord Himself ...hereditary culprits from their privity to their father's crimes"* (ANF vol. 3, p. 685).

St. Hippolytus (ca. 200): *"Why was the [Jewish] temple made desolate?...It was because they killed the Son [Jesus] of their Bene-factor [God], for He is coeternal with the Father"* (ANF vol. 5, p. 220). Origen (ca. 240): *"One fact, then, which proves that Jesus was something divine and sacred, is this, that Jews should have suffered on His account now for a lengthened time calamities of such sever-ity.... For they committed a crime of the most unhallowed kind, in conspiring against the Saviour of the human race"* (ANF vol. 4, p. 506). St. Cyprian (ca. 250): *"[T]he Jews who not only unbelievingly despised Christ, who had been announced to them by the prophets, and sent first to them, but also cruelly put him to death"* (ANF vol. 5, p. 450).

Among the "chief matters" in Eusebius' *Ecclesiastical History* (1.1) are the misfortunes that *"overwhelmed the entire Jewish race"* because of their *"conspiracy against our Savior."* *Didascalia Apos-tolorum* (ca. 300, XLVII): *"It is evident that no hope remains to the Jews, unless, turning themselves to repentance, and being cleansed from the blood with which they polluted themselves, they shall begin to hope in Him whom they denied"* (ANF vol 7, p. 242). St. Aphrahat (ca. 330): "[Jesus'] *accusers and they* [Jews] *that crucified Him shall be burned in flames at the end"* (NPNF Series 2, vol. 13, p. 406). St. Hilary of Poitiers (ca. 350): Judaism was *"mighty in wickedness ... when it killed the prophets, and finally when it betrayed to the Praetor and crucified our God Himself and Lord"* (Michael, p. 20).

St. Ephraim (ca. 362): *"Israel crucified our Lord, on the plea that verily he was seducing us from the One God"* (NPNF Series 2, vol. 13, p. 307). *Dialogue of Athanasius and Zacchaeus* (ca. 385): *"Oh, that you would not have burned the books — you* [Jews] *who crucified the master* [Jesus] *and stoned His preachers"* (Varner 2004, p. 41). St. John Chrysostom (ca. 386): *"You* [Jews] *did slay Christ ... you did spill his precious blood. This is why you have no chance for atonement, excuse, or defense. ... Your mad rage against Christ, the Anointed One, left no way for anyone to surpass your sin. ... you dared a deed much worse and much greater than any sacrifice of children or transgression of the Law when you slew Christ"* (Harkins, p. 154).

St. Augustine (ca. 400) to Christian converts: *"The Jews hold Him, the Jews insult Him, the Jews bind Him, crown Him with thorns, dishonor Him with spitting, scourge Him, overwhelm Him with revilings, hang Him upon the tree, pierce Him with a spear, last of all bury Him"* (*On the Creed*, NPNF Series 1, vol. 3, p. 373). *"What a Dreadful thing it is to kill Christ! Yet the Jews killed Him"* (Ibid. p. 374).

Punishment of the Jews for the death of Jesus did not mean complete extinction. The Jews must continue to exist as testimony to Christians of the consequences of evil. St. Augustine (*Reply to Faustus* XII.12): *"To the end of the seven days of time, the continued preservation of the Jews will be a proof to believing Christians of the subjection merited by those who, in the pride of their kingdom, put the Lord to death"* (NPNF Series 1, vol. 4, pp. 187–188).

To New Testament writers and Christian Fathers, Jews are supposed to have been well aware of Jesus' special divinity, since only a truly evil people would conspire to kill a God. That is, Jews must have always recognized the "truth" of Christianity and rejected it because of their inherent wickedness (Acts of the Apostles 7.51–52). Christian "truth" thus attempted to gain validity by ascribing Jewish opposition against it, justifying both antisemitism and Christianity to Christians. St. Augustine: "*They* [Jews] *testify to the* [Christian] *truth by their not understanding it. By not understanding the books which predict that they would not understand* [!], *they prove these books to be true*" (*Reply to Faustus* XVI.21, NPNF Series 1, vol. 4, p. 227). The notion seems to be that opposition by non-believers is a proof of "truth," like a theological notion that opposition by the "unorthodox" is a proof of "orthodoxy." This strange logic also explains allegations that the Jews ritually desecrated the consecrated host of the Eucharist because they recognized its supernatural value and tortured Jesus once again.

Another apparent fallacy is blaming Jews for Jesus' death, yet insisting that Jesus' death was purposed by Jesus himself (not Jews!) "to save mankind from its sins": "*The Lord Jesus Christ who gave himself for our sins*" (St. Paul's *Galatians* 1.3–4, see Note #11.*c*)

9
JEWISH REBELLIOUSNESS AND
ROMAN DESTRUCTION

Roman defeat of the 66–72 C.E. Jewish rebellion coupled with Roman destruction of Jerusalem and its Temple had profound effects. Hundreds of thousands of Jews were killed (Josephus, *Wars of the Jews* VI:IX, claims more than one million) and many thousands sold into slavery. Roman spoils funded what is now known as the Roman Colosseum, the largest and most magnificent amphitheater of the time; and elevated Jerusalem's conquering generals (Vespasian and his son Titus) to Roman emperors, founders of the Flavian dynasty. "[F]*or Vespasian and Titus to use their manubiae* [booty] *to build the Colosseum was not only the best means to finance this enormous project but also a way to advertise their military achievements*" (Feldman 2001, p. 60).

To the Christian Fathers, all this destruction — Jerusalem, Temple, and much of Israeli countryside — was caused, not by Jewish rebellion against Roman oppression (Note #15) but by Jewish opposition to Gentile Christianity. In St. Justin Martyr's fictional *Dialogue with Trypho, a Jew* (ca. 150), violence against Jews results from their rejection of Jesus, and comes not from "Rome," which is never mentioned. According to Tertullian (ca. 200, *An Answer to the Jews* 13), "*Since, therefore, the Jews were predicted as destined to suffer these calamities on Christ's account, and we find that they have suffered them, and we see them sent into dispersion and abiding in it, manifest it is that it is on Christ's account that these things have befallen the Jews*" (ANF vol. 3, pp. 171–172).

Origen (ca. 240, *Contra Celsum* 4.22): "*One fact which proves that Jesus was something divine and sacred, is this, that Jews should have suffered on His account now for a lengthened time, calamities of such severity.*" Lactantius (ca. 300) has St. Peter and St. Paul prophecy that "*God would send ... a king who would subdue the Jews, and level their cities to the ground, and besiege the people, worn out with hunger and thirst. ... everything laid waste with fire and sword, the captives banished forever from their own lands, because they had exulted over the well-beloved and most approved Son of God*" (*The Divine Institutes* 3.21, ANF vol. 7, p. 123).

In *The Constitutions of the Holy Apostles* (VI.1), a series of early treatises on Christian doctrine: "*For the wicked synagogue is now cast off by the Lord God ... He has also left His temple desolate and rent the veil of the temple, and took from them the Holy Spirit ... For God has taken away all the power and efficacy of His word, and such like visitations from that people, and has transferred it to you, the converted of Gentiles*" (ANF vol. 7, pp. 451–452).

St Matthew's Gospel (24.2) preceded the above pronouncements, and placed Jewish destruction prophetically in Jesus' mouth: "*You see all these* [Temple buildings], *do you not? Truly I tell you, not one stone will be left upon another; all will be thrown down.*" Nirenberg observes that the Gentile Christian strategy of blaming Jews for their own destruction was to heighten "*the blindness of the Jews in the prophetic past and the misery of the Jews in the political present*" (p. 103).

For Jews, Roman destruction was a terrible calamity yet not fatal to their survival. More than relying on a specific geographical institution — the Jerusalem Temple — "Jewishness" could now be seen (as it commonly was) as membership in a cultural group associated with Scripturally-prescribed practices. Simon (p. 35): "*In destroying Jerusalem, the Romans forcibly dissociated the Jewish religion from the Jewish state, for manifestly the former continued to exist whereas the latter did not.*" Barclay (1996, p. 310): "[I]*t was more possible now for outsiders to understand the Jewish way of life in religious and cultural rather than mainly national terms.*" Although dispersion separated the Jews from their original "nationhood," Jewishness, like other religions, became a matter of personal beliefs, and (if governments allowed) one could be a Jew and still be a citizen-member of a non-Israelite nationality.

Characteristics that made Jewishness distinctive were therefore (1) membership by descent or conversion in a people who share an ancient Biblical Yahweh-worshipping religion based on a common literature and history — the Jewish Scriptures, (2) male circumcision, (3) dietary restrictions, (4) Sabbath, Festival, and Holy Day observances (e.g., Passover, Rosh Hashanah). These features run through all of Jewish history, whether "First Temple," "Second Temple," "Rabbinical," and so forth. That is, however Jews were described by themselves or others, their common culture, traditions, literature, and insular religion based on an invisible God, surpassed geography as defining elements of Jewish identity.

Note that as far back as the Babylonian exile in 587 B.C.E., more than six hundred years before the Romans destroyed the Jerusalem Temple, Jews developed modes of maintaining religious and cultural uniqueness outside Israel. By middle of the first century (ca. 50 C.E.), permanent Jewish communities already existed throughout the Roman Empire, not from forcible exile from Israel, but because of livelihood opportunities beyond the Jewish homeland. Whether in Europe, Africa, or Asia, Jewishness was sustained in assemblies/synagogues by sharing a common ethnic, social, and cultural identity through the "portability" of Jewishness — *"the Scriptures, the symbols, and the synagogue community itself. The Diaspora was not Exile, in some cases it became a Holy Land too"* (Kraabel 1992b, p. 30).

"That Diaspora Judaism survived the destruction of the temple indicates the strength of its other resources; and that it continued in most respects unchanged suggests that the temple had always been of greater symbolic than practical significance. Few if any aspects of Diaspora Jewish life had been governed by Jerusalem priests, and the symbolic functions of the temple could be continued in nostalgia" (Barclay 1996, pp. 420–421). *"When the sanctuary [Temple] was destroyed by the Romans in 70 C.E., the synagogue was assured of the divine presence, or any place where ten, or as few as two, men*

were gathered to study Scripture (Mishnah Abot 3.2, 6). Thus post-Destruction Judaism reactualized the law that originally sanctioned the plurality of temples (Exodus 20.24): 'In every place where I cause my name to be remembered, I will come to you and bless you.'" (Vermes 2010, p. 94).

As a replacement of Temple worship and sacrifice, synagogue practices included *"torah and haftarah readings, targumin, sermons, communal prayer, and religious poetry ... [T]he Passover celebrations now focused on the Seder in a domestic setting, rather than on the paschal sacrifice in the Temple precincts ... [P]rayer replaced sacrifice as the means of atonement, and holidays such as Hanukah, Purim, Tish'ah b'Av, and Simhat Torah were now introduced into the Jewish calendar"* (L. I. Levine 2009, p. 15). Also, honoring Priests as hereditary religious celebrants gave way to honoring Rabbis as teachers of religious and worldly knowledge. *"It is not priestly descent, as such, but rather one's mastery of Torah, which confers authority on one's teaching"* (Schremer 2010, p. 10).

To gain atonement without Temple sacrifices, *"Zion gave way to Sinai, sacrifice as a key form of communicating with God gave way to prayer, torah-study and holy living (as at Qumran), priest gave way to rabbi, temple gave way to synagogue, and the furniture of the temple became the furniture of the mind and heart"* (Barton, p. 375). This follows a prophetic tradition that goes back about eight centuries B.C.E. to the words of Hosea (6.6): *"For I* [Yahweh] *desire steadfast love and not sacrifice, the knowledge of God rather than burnt offerings."* As declared in Proverbs (21.3): *"To do righteousness and justice is more acceptable to Yahweh than sacrifice."* After the Temple was destroyed, Rabbi Yochanan ben Zakkai states: *"We possess another source of expiation, equal in importance to the Temple itself, and that is 'acts of kindness'"* (Abrabanel, p. 29).

The Rabbinical tradition which then gained influence and authority *"developed a comprehensive system of civil law that overtly addressed secular and communal matters as part of its religious system*" (Edrei and Mendels 2013, p. 270). Thus, in spite of Gentile Christianity's claim that destruction of the Temple was the sign of replacing the Jews in God's favor, there were "*increasing numbers of synagogue worshipping both in the Land of Israel and in the Diaspora*" (Fraade, p. 263). According to Herr (p. 232): "*The very identity and essence of the Jewish nation was sustained and remained unchanged.*" Gruen points out (p. 233) that "*Vast numbers of Jews dwelled outside Palestine in the roughly four centuries that stretched from Alexander [356–323 B.C.E.] to Titus [66 C.E.] ... The Jews of the Diaspora, from Italy to Iran, far outnumbered those in the homeland.*" It is quite clear that Jewish migration from Israel/Palestine awaited neither first century Roman destruction of the Temple (70 C.E) or second century defeat of the Bar Kochba rebellion (132–135 C.E.; Note #15, p. 189).

To Gentile Christian leaders and theologians, however, destruction of the Jewish Temple was not only evidence of God's reproof for rejecting Jesus as Savior, but also marked the replacement of all Temple sacrifices with a single propitiatory event, the killing of Jesus (St. John 2.21) — an atoning sacrifice absolving Gentile Jesus-believers from sin (Note #11.*c*). Also as fundamental: disastrous defeat of Israel's national structure provided St. Paul's Gentile Churches an unparalleled opportunity to further distance themselves, through diatribes and Gospels from the now discredited nation, and assume the pose of a Roman institution (Notes #21, #22).

10

MYTHS USED TO JUSTIFY CHRISTIAN ANTI-JEWISHNESS

Among Christian myths to explain Christian anti-Jewishness are the following:

1. Jewish institutions such as synagogues persecuted or expelled Messiah believers, thereby accounting for Christian anti-Jewishness (Evans and Hagner).

Note however, neither Messiah believers nor Jerusalem Temple critics were considered Jewish heretics subject to persecution. *"Temple and cult criticisms were in vogue everywhere in Judaism and even in its holy scriptures"* (Schmithals, p. 107). *"[I]f confessing Jesus had resulted in expulsion from the synagogue, the disciples would have been expelled from the synagogue. Of this, however, there is no trace, not even in [St.] John, let alone in the synoptics [St. Mark, St. Matthew, St. Luke]"* (Casey 1991, p. 3; see also Kaylor, p. 100). *"Deuteronomy 21. 22–23* ['anyone hanging on a tree is under God's curse' — Jesus' crucifixion] *is an unlikely basis for early Jewish rejection and persecution of Christianity, and other causes should be sought"* (O'Brien, p. 55, see also Note #21). *"Given the range of people, Jew and Gentile, accommodated in Greco-Roman synagogues, and the variety of attitudes apparent among the rabbis, tolerance might have been the most common Jewish response to early Jesus followers"* (Setzer, p. 579).

Note #16 makes clear that Jews tolerated considerable religious diversity between individuals and between groups— Pharisees, Sadducees, Essenes, etc. *"In light of the Dead Sea Scrolls ... differences over what was central in Israelite tradition, or scathing critiques of the Second Temple and Jerusalem elites, were nothing new or extraordinary at the time"* (Oakman 2012, p. 154). *"Despite all the sectarian animus found in the various texts from or about the*

Second Commonwealth period, even the most virulent never accuse the members of other groups of having left the Jewish community. Sinners they were but Jews all the same" (Schiffman, p. 116).

It was not Jesus' messianic message that Jews considered blasphemous and unacceptable, but the post-Jesus anti-Jewish creeds expressed by St. Paul, writers of the New Testament, and Gentile Christian leaders; namely that Jesus-believers must abandon Jewish laws, festival, rituals, practices, and elevate Jesus to divine status far beyond the stature of Jewish prophet or sage, paralleling the powers of Yahweh (Notes #11.*b*, #22). St. Paul's denunciations of Jewish Mosaic "Law" launched the quickly widening gap between Jews and Gentile Christians (Note #18). An early Gentile Christian letter (*Epistle to Diognetus*), perhaps of the first century C.E. or early second, characterizes Jewish practices as "*utterly ridiculous and unworthy of notice.*" Included in "*useless and redundant customs*" are Jewish holidays and Temple observances, and "*their scrupulosity concerning meats, and their superstition as respects the Sabbaths, and their boasting about circumcision, and their fancies about fasting and new moons*" (ANF vol. 1, p. 26).

To St. Paul and his adherents, Jewish Christian "Judaizers" from St. James' Jerusalem synagogues stood far outside the newly-seeded identity of the Gentile Christian Church. Later Jewish Christian movements, whether "Judaizers" or not, were declared "heretics" by "orthodox" Christians. Even more religiously and ethnically distant from Gentile Christianity were, of course, non-Christian Jewish synagogues. It seems reasonable to ask: if Gentile Christian leaders were concerned about expulsion, why join Jewish synagogues they held in contempt:

- for non-belief in the divinity of Jesus Christ;
- for engaging in culturally "repellant" and ethnically "alien" (non-Gentile) Jewish practices;
- for sustaining archaic Biblical laws abandoned by the Gentile Christian Church;

* for their Jewish "Christ-killing" heritage?

Christians may seek self-justification in blaming Jew-hatred on Jewish disregard or antipathy, but such arguments conceal Gentile Christianity's need to denigrate Jews to defend its displacement of Jews in God's favor and wrest possession of the Jewish Scriptures (Notes #7, #18, #19). *"It seems probable that from the time of Justin* [ca. 150 C.E.], *if not from the time of Acts* [questionably dated between 80–115 C.E.], *the proposition that Jewish hostility was primarily responsible for the Church's sufferings was a theological convention requiring little or no evidence in its support"* (Hare, p. 456). *"For Christianity, anti-Judaism was not merely a defense against attack, but an intrinsic need of Christian self-affirmation"* (Ruether 1974, p. 181).

2. Jews drove the Christians out of Jewish synagogues by a special liturgical curse (Birkat Haminin).

Whatever *Jewish* heretical groups "minim" covered ("epikursum"/epicureans, etc.), Boyarin points out (2004, pp. 67–69) this curse probably did not appear before the end of the second century C.E., pertaining to those *Jews* who opposed early Rabbis (*Tannaim*). In S. J. D. Cohen's (2013) analysis, all eight *minim* sayings in a second century Rabbinical document (the Mishnah) aim at *Jews* dissenting on matters such as the shape of the phylacteries or methods of Temple sacrifice. Not a single *minim* saying implies a Christian Jesus-believer, Jewish or Gentile. *"[T]he Mishnah alludes to the proscribed practices or beliefs of the minim, but does not define the groups or the individuals involved. It provides no details on who they are or how they fit (or don't fit) into rabbinic society, or what they otherwise believe or don't believe, do or don't do. ... The miscreants are not cursed; they are not threatened with excommunication or any other form of communal discipline. ... In this world we do nothing to them except express our disapproval"* (Ibid., pp. 219–220). Applied later to Jesus-believers, *minim* still does not mean

Gentiles but only Jews whose *"Torah scrolls are written in Hebrew and contain the divine name in Hebrew"* (Ibid. p. 222).

Thus, for Rabbis, the term *minim* did not specify a singular particular group but targeted countrymen of any persuasion who departed from fundamental Jewish communal beliefs and practices. Schremer (2010) notes that a prime source of Rabbinical censure arose from threats to the Jewish community's ethnic and religious integrity by those who "denied God" because of Israel's terrible defeats in its' 70 C. E. and 135 C.E. rebellions (Note #9). *"Rome's power was conceived by the rabbis theologically; that is, it was considered a threat to the fundamental belief in God's omnipotency and His very divinity. It is not a coincidence, therefore, that various midrashic sources attribute to Rome some of the stances that are ascribed to the 'minim' ... thus constructing Rome as the emblem of these theological assertions"* (Schremer., p. 53).

Nevertheless, despite Rabbinic discomfort, castigating anyone with the term *minim* in early Rabbinic Judaism would not have excluded them from the Jewish community: *"There is no evidence that it* [minim] *served to hound out of the fold particular deviants whose continued presence was believed to threaten the health of the body politic. Nor is there evidence that it served to define correct behavior for rabbinic Jews by clarifying what was forbidden in thought or deed"* (Goodman 2007b, p. 171). *"[Rabbi] Yohanan would seem to have reckoned that there were at least twenty-five types of Judaism before the destruction of the Temple in 70 CE — one acceptable variety and twenty-four others* [minim]*"* (Ibid., p. 46).

In respect to Jewish Christians, first and second century C.E. Rabbis *"did not see the earliest Christians as constituting a separate religious community. ... Even if we were to accept many of the polemical statements in our sources at face value and assume the violations of 'halakha'* [Jewish law] *in the early Christian community to be more extensive, the early Christians would still be considered Jews. Nor should we assume that the claims that Jesus was a miracle*

80

worker or magician ... would have in any way reflected on the Jewish
status of his followers. Even the belief in the divinity or messiahship
of Jesus ... would not in view of the Tannaim have read the early
Christians out of the Jewish community" (Schiffman 1985, pp. 51–
52). Jewish Messiahs such as Bar Kochba may have been deluded
and deluding but were still considered Jews.

Even in the later post-Mishnah "Talmud" (Rabbinical discussions and debates on Jewish laws and rituals) compiled in the third
to fifth centuries C.E., "*the term minim (heretics) is invariably applied to **Jewish** heretics (among whom, of course the Jewish Christians* [Nazoreans/"Notzrim"] *were counted) ... 'Among the Gentiles
there are no minim' says the Talmud*" (Schoeps, p. 14, my emphasis).
The term *minim* would therefore have meant little to Gentile Christians, nor borne them any religious threat; any more than religious
Jews would have felt *religiously* threatened by mainstream Gentile
Church pronouncements against Christian heresies.

It seems clear that whenever *Birkat Ha-minim* was instituted,
a liturgical boundary between Jews and Pauline Christians would
have long been in place. "[W]*e cannot presume that the term notzrim*
[Jewish Jesus-believer] *existed in the blessing before the fourth century C.E.*" (Teppler, p. 72). (See also Reinhartz, pp. 349–353;
Hakola 2005, pp. 45–55; Kimelman; and J. T. Sanders 2002, p. 369.)

In contrast to the marked early separation between Jews and
Gentile Christianity, Horbury, (p. 12) emphasizes Gentile Christian
feelings of "rejection" and "disappointment" at being excluded from
Jewish (and Jewish Christian?) synagogues. However, feelings of
"rejection and disappointment" hardly coincide with Gentile Christian leaders' fundamental opposition to Jews in customs, beliefs, or
rituals (Note #11); nor with Christianity's compelling need to convince Romans that Gentile Christianity is "not new" but "true,"
claiming Gentiles, not Jews are heirs to the antique Jewish Scriptures
(Notes #7, #18, #19). It is difficult to believe that Gentile Christian
leaders would attempt to join Jewish synagogues while: (1) regarding

Jews as condemned by God in favor of Gentile Christians (Note #6); (2) claiming Jewish assemblies, and Jewish "Law" as sinful anachronisms (Note #18); (3) denouncing adoption of Jewish concepts and Jewish practices as satanic "Judaizing" (Note #17).

Note that the earliest written curse between Christians and Jews came not from Jews but from St. Paul. In a letter to his Galatian converts (1.7–9, ca. 50 C.E.), he warns of "Judaizers" (Jews and Jewish Christians) "*who are confusing you and want to pervert the gospel of Christ. But even if we or an angel from heaven should proclaim to you a gospel contrary to what we proclaimed to you, let that one be accursed! As we have said before, so now I repeat, if anyone proclaims to you a gospel contrary to what you received* [from me], *let that one be accursed!*" St. Paul's curse obviously derives from opposition to competing Jewish religious teachings (St. James' Jesus-believing "Judaizers"), and not from reaction to a Jewish "curse."

St. Paul's claim for seeking acceptance in synagogues and then being (unfairly?) censured and punished five times as a "sinner" (*2 Corinthians* 11.24) also seems inconsistent with his non-Jewish mission and his non-Jewish covenantal ideology. Why would a self-proclaimed "Apostle to the Gentiles"; who changed his name from Hebrew "Saul" to Greek "Pavlos"; who preached the need to abandon Jewish Biblical "Law" which he compared to "excrement"; who declared that his Gentile followers rather than Jews were the true heirs of Abraham; and who vehemently denounced proponents of Jewish Law ("Judaizers"); repeatedly insist on membership in a Jewish synagogue? One can also question why observant Jews — regarded by Romans as members of an "alien" religion — had legal authority to punish a Roman citizen engaged in establishing non-Jewish beliefs and practices for Gentiles. St. Paul's claim to be as "Jewish" as his Jewish Christian competitors was patently to gain competitive status in proselytizing Gentiles who had attended Jewish synagogues.

82

Posing as self-sanctified non-Jewish "True Israelites" (Notes #14, #19), there is no evidence that leaders of St. Paul's Christian churches ever defined themselves as religious Jews, or attempted membership in Jewish synagogues, or sought any form of Jewish identification even when it would have benefited them (Note #3, p. 28). As we have seen, throughout its first centuries Gentile Christianity's universal theme is that the Jews are inherently evil, and Gentiles supplanted the Jews in God's favor. Attaching a "Jewish" label to opposing Christian factions sufficed for their condemnation by Christian theologians as "heretics" (Note #17). By contrast, *the rabbis of the period were interested neither in heresy nor in Christianity. We may be sure that* [Jewish] *heretics and Christian Jews were out there in the second century, but the rabbis paid them little attention*" (S. J. D. Cohen 1992, p. 216; also p. 94 below).

In commenting on a detailed study of Jewish rabbinical writings, Lasker states (pp. xxii-xxiv) *"most Jews were apathetic vis-à-vis this emerging* [Christian] *faith which eventually would have such an impact on Judaism. There is no recognition in rabbinic literature of such major Christian authorities as Justin Martyr (second century), Origen (third century) or Jerome (late fourth century). ... The sparse number of texts accumulated by Hereford* [in a book entitled '*Christianity in Talmud and Midrash*'] *would indicate that Jesus himself and his Jewish followers (let alone Gentile Christians) were not at the center of rabbinic concern.*" Since the Rabbis showed little response to Gentile Christianity until its fourth century rise in power, there is no sure evidence that the curse against minim applied to Gentile Christians and Gentile Christianity — all outside the Jewish communal fold from St. Paul's first century's churches onward.

In about fifty pages analyzing how the term *minim* was used by second and third century C.E. Palestinian Rabbis ("Tannaim") who wrote the Mishnah and Tosefta, Burns (2016) makes the following statements. *"Rather than singling them out for specific criticism, the rabbinic sages evidently saw* [Jewish] *Christians as part of an undifferentiated mass of Jews whose standards of practice and belief fell short of their own"* (p. 165). *The rare* [Jewish] *Christians who found their ways into the rhetorical crosshairs of the 'Tannaim' represented just one Jewish type of the variety whom the latter believed stood to impede their own collective enterprise. Christianity, therefore, did play a role in their conception of 'minuit'* [deviation] *only in the abstract sense that followers of Jesus were among those Jews whom they deemed to call heretics"* (p. 181). *"Although aware that the Roman authorities had outlawed* [Gentile] *Christianity, they appeared neither to have known or cared why that was the case. Perhaps most significantly, they seem completely unaware of the state of the Christian enterprise beyond their local Jewish communities. ... The Tannaim characterized the Christian as a Jew because the only Christians whom they knew actually were Jews"* (p. 208). *"[I]t seems reasonable to surmise that the invention of the 'birkat ha-minim' accomplished very little by way of actually driving* [Gentile] *Christians from Palestinian Jewish society"* (p. 207).

"The drive for new [Christian] *identity was not the final outcome of pressure from external* [Jewish] *forces but the prime mover in the process of self-definition"* (Hakola 2007, p. 192).

3. Christian anti-Jewishness was no different from, or no more virulent than, common Pagan anti-Jewishness of the time.

Pagan attitudes toward Jews ranged from dislike to respect and adoption of Jewish practices (Gager 1985). According to Sevenster (p. 56), *"the Jews were judged not as a race, but as a people, as a given community of faith and morals, in the same way as any other peoples ... not a single indication is to be found in ancient literature that anti-Semitism in the ancient world use the theory of race as a weapon of attack."*

Nevertheless, whatever Pagan dislike of Jews existed, Christianity added its own form of virulent long-lasting hatred. Contrary to

Meagher (p. 22) who insists that that Gentile Christian theology is not the agent that "*brought Christians to their unconscionable treatment of Jews,*" Simon (p. 223) points out, "*there was a fundamental difference between the anti-Semitism of Pagans and that of Christians. ... Christian anti-Semitism, insofar as it was officially espoused by the Church, did have a sanction as well as a coherence the Pagan sort always lacked. It did not base its arguments on ascertainable facts, not even, for that matter, on the hearsay evidence of popular gossip, but on a particular kind of exegesis of the biblical writings, an exegesis that interpreted them in the light of the death of Christ as a long indictment of the chosen people. Where Pagan anti-Semitism was, for the most part, spontaneous and unorganized, that of the Christians was devoted to a well-conceived end. Its aim was to make the Jews abhorrent to all, to sustain the dislike of those in whom the Jews already aroused dislike, and to turn the affections of those who were well disposed.*"

Thus, despite claims that pre-Christian antisemitism accounted for much of Christian anti-Jewishness, the antisemitism that became embedded in Christianity was quite unique. This is not to say that Pagan antisemitic sentiment did not continue into Christian times — Christian proselytizers certainly made use of it — but Christianity added completely new features, both religious and secular, that made Jew-hatred interminable and unremitting. Jews on every social level were presented to the Christian world, and to all who would listen, as an evil despicable people condemned by God, the New Testament, and the Christian Fathers.

According to Ruether (1979, p. 233): "*The heart of the conflict between Jew and Christian ... lies in the Christian claim to be the 'true Israel' which defines the old Israel as apostate and 'divorced' by God. This sets Christian anti-Judaism fundamentally apart from pagan antisemitism. ... Between a pagan who objects to Jews because they are funny-smelling orientals who refuse to assimilate into Greek ways ... and the Christian who rejects Jews as the apostate Israel who has refused to recognize her messiah, there is a gulf that is more than rhetoric. ... The Jew, for the Christian of the New Testament, is not primarily the puzzling stranger, but the rejecting elder brother who refuses to bend to the claims of the younger. ... It is a relation that demands reprobation, but also hankers for Jewish conversion, that decrees punishment."*

4. *Attacks on Jews in the New Testament and Christian literature arose from occasional extenuating circumstances ("just a product of the times"! "a family fight"! "sibling rivalry"!) and should not be taken seriously. There are, for example, ambiguities in St. Paul, expressing not only a preponderance of hate but also some signs of remorseful respect towards Jews (Romans 9.4–5). (See also Simon, pp. 230–231.) One can also find some Christians, such as St. Clement of Rome and Theophilus of Antioch who wrote some kind words about Judaism.*

It is not uncommon for harsh New Testament polemics against Jews to be claimed as arguments between Jews themselves — a *"Jewish issue."* Efroymson et al (Introduction, p. x): "[T]*he New Testament documents arose among Jews who followed Jesus (or their Gentile converts). When they argued — and these writings frequently argue — they argued either against other Jews who also followed Jesus (with their Gentile converts), or against Jews who did not. But the issues were nearly always Jewish issues."*

However, as we have seen, contrary to acting like Jewish "siblings," St. Paul's Gentile Christians defined their identity quite differently from Jews early on: not only in respect to ethnic distinction, but in claiming novel theology, beliefs, and practices (Note #11). These differences, added to the anti-Jewish pitch of New Testament documents condemning Jews as enemies of Jesus and "Christ-killers," certainly distanced Gentile Christians from identifying themselves as Jews. Even Jews who joined Rome's early Church suffered hostility from their Gentile colleagues, with St. Paul asking that Jewish Church members be pardoned as "weak/sickly in faith" (*Romans*, Chapters 14–15).

"The picture that emerges from this [St. Paul's *Romans*] *letter ... is of a community now dominated by confident gentiles, immensely proud of the Torah-lite lifestyle that they have developed for themselves. For these people, their sights set firmly on the new age that is about to dawn, the Temple, Sabbath observance and food restrictions enjoined by the law of Moses are an irrelevance, and fellow Christians still in thrall to the Torah were almost beneath contempt"* (H. M. Williams, pp. 156–157).

Despite St. Paul's presumed conciliatory wishes, there is no evidence that conflict between Rome's Jesus-believing Gentiles and Jesus-believing Jews receded. To the "strong in faith" Gentiles, "weak in faith" foreigners were people *"who still retained the appearance of Jewish piety"* (Reasoner, p. 223). Beyond St. Paul's *Romans* letter, there is also no indication of practicing Jews in any other Gentile Christian Church. Jewish Christians who followed Jewish practices in their own synagogues remained condemned as "Judaizers" or heretics, as we see in repeated castigations by St. Paul and Christian Fathers (Note #17).

It is therefore apparent that anti-Jewish invectives in the New Testament were not merely to distinguish "bad Jews" (non-Jesus-believing Jews) from "good Jews" (Jesus-believing Jews), but were fashioned as a more fundamental conflict between "Christians" and "Jews" —conflict made to have begun between Jesus on one side and "Jews" on the other. St John's Gospel (Note #12) expresses this in its most acrimonious form. In the Book of Revelation (2.9), *"synagogue of Satan,"* originally applied by its author to St. Paul's Gentile Christian churches (Pagels, p. 59), was later converted to *"synagogue of Jews"* (Note #17), also including Jewish Christians (see Galambush, pp. 307–309). Christian intemperate ranting against Jews began with the New Testament and was carried forth without limit by early Christian Fathers (Notes #14, #17).

Claims that derogatory comments about Jews and the Jewish religion by New Testament writers and Patristic Fathers were erroneously interpreted would be welcome, but do not explain their continual use and ongoing impact. Varner (2004, p. 564), states that the anti-Jewish Christian hostility in the many *Adversus Judaeos* documents are "*past mistakes,*" and one should not "*associate past writers with crimes of which they are simply not guilty.*" However, calling anti-Jewish indoctrination a "*mistake*" is plainly exculpatory. Are two thousand years of anti-Jewishness imbibed by Christian readers and audiences the result of mistaken understanding of misconstrued documents from misinterpreted Christian leaders?

We do know that vituperative Christian anti-Jewishness, however and whenever expressed, had much greater import than mere bluster, and, as shown here and by others (e.g., Efroymson, Parkes, Nicholls, Ruether, M. S. Taylor), served essential functions in Christian development. That is, Jews were not used like pagans as a mere contrast to Christian beliefs, nor was Christian antisemitism the result of an unfortunate misunderstanding. Rather, among other motivations, Christian leaders used the "teaching of contempt" of Jews as a theological necessity to justify Christianity to both its members and Roman society to gain antique support from highly contested Jewish Scriptures (Notes #7, #18, #19).

Being the satanic "other" to Christians, Jewishness became a divinely condemned status exemplified in St. John's Gospel. "*The Jews are other than those who believe; they are other than those aligned with Jesus and hence God; they are other than the Johannine community out of which and for whom this Gospel was written.... They are so strongly marked out as 'other,' and spoken of in such insulting language, that the Gospel does not hold out any hope of bringing them into belief*" (Tanzer, p. 109). Gospel canonization of anti-Jewishness and its augmentation by the Patristic Fathers, thus firmly embedded prejudice and Jew-hatred in Christianity and helped "*to affirm the identity of the Church, which could only be done by invalidating the identity of the Jews*" (Reuther 1974, p. 181).

Supported by state and civic power from the time of Emperor Constantine (313 C.E.) onward, made the Christian legacy of anti-Jewish hostility and rhetoric highly potent and dangerous despite politically powerless Jewish rejoinders and complaints.

5. *Some Christian scholars claim that Christian anti-Jewish attacks were not really against Jews but primarily against Christian "Judaizers" attempting to foist Jewish rituals or customs on Gentile Christianity (Murray).*

This argument has some substance in the sense that it was Jewish-Christian "Judaizers," sent out to early Christian communities by St. James and other Jesus' disciples, who elicited most of St. Paul's anger. Nevertheless, although Gentile Christians were warned against "Judaizers," the merciless hostility against "Jews" for their perceived crimes against Jesus and their rejection of Christianity's claim to Biblical "godliness" became the mainstay of Gentile Christian anti-Jewish polemics.

- It was "Jews" who were responsible for killing Jesus (Note #8).
- It was "Jews" who persecuted Gentile Christians (Note #10.6).
- It was "Jews" who disputed Gentile Christian reinterpretation of the Jewish Scriptures (Notes #7, #18).
- It was "Jews" who opposed Gentile Christian antiquarian claims to being the "True Israelites" (Note #19).

Interestingly, in accusing "Judaizing" emissaries for following "a different Gospel" — the Jewish "Law" (e.g., *Galatians* 1.6–9, 2.4, 3.10–12, 4.9–10, 5.2, 6.13, also Notes #17, #18) — St. Paul never seeks support from sayings of Jesus himself. One can only assume that Jesus the Jew (Note #4) and Jesus the Jewish Messiah (Note #15) did not share St. Paul's anti-"Law" views that were later sanctioned in the New Testament Gospels. Nor did Jesus' disciples oppose the Jewish "Law," as evidenced by:

- St. Peter's confrontation with St. Paul (*Galatians* 2.11–13,);
- persistence of the "Law"-abiding Temple worshipping congregation led by St. James after Jesus' death;
- the continued presence of St. James' Jesus-believing "Judaizers" who advocated that all Christians should obey the "Law."

"These problems suggest…that Jesus' ultimate followers vigorously opposed Paul — perceiving him as distancing himself from what they remember as Jesus' fidelity to the Law and to the Jewish people" (Cook, pp. 101–102). *"Yeshua* [Jesus] *was a Jew, and an observant one, that is, he was committed to the keeping of the Law in the way that seemed best to him. Since he was a 'Rabbi,' he taught others to do likewise. In brief, he did not come to dispense with or do away with the Torah, the Law. He came to carry it out"* (Swidler, p. 44). *"To propose to Jesus that Jews cannot be saved apart from faith in Christ or, for that matter, that Gentiles are saved in this way, would probably produce in Jesus either puzzlement or laughter or a simply resounding* **no** *(or all three together). For from the standpoint both of the ever-impinging reign of God and of needed moral norms, any Christian abandonment of the law is wrong and Jesus' retention of the Torah is right"* (Eckardt 1992, p. 85). *"The pro-Gentile sayings in the Gospels are unlikely to have originated with Jesus and do not belong to his authentic teaching"* (Vermes 2010, p. 32). In St. Paul's Gentile churches, would not Jesus the Jew have been a "Judaizer"?

The theological notion that the "Christ-event" was a gift from God, separating Gentile Christians from Jewish practices (Barclay 2010), would not have made sense to Jesus and his disciples. It is therefore plainly misleading that Christianity was just a straightforward slide from Jesus to St. Paul. Strongly disputed are claims in Acts of the Apostles (Chapter 15) and St. Paul's *Galatians* (Chapter 2) that a supposed "Jerusalem Conference" with Jesus' Jewish disciples (led by St. James) granted St. Paul license to convert Gentiles without demanding they observe Jewish Scriptural commandments. The terms of such presumed agreement seem unclear and ambiguous (Donaldson 2006, p. 127), and St. Peter's baptism of Gentiles as Christians (Acts 10.48) is an apparent invention of St. Luke designed "*to choke at source every conceivable objection to the Gentile mission*" (Klauck, p. 32).

"*The setting in Acts, according to which Paul met the apostles in Jerusalem a few days after his conversion (9.19, 26) is ... not trustworthy: Luke wants to show that Paul received legitimacy from the Church of Jerusalem*" (Moreschini and Norelli, p. 5; also Kee 2013a, p. 11). "*Acts of the Apostles, a source on which many historians have heavily depended, is a myth of Christian origins*" (Tyson, p. 17, also Note #11 p. 126).

In Acts (11.1–18), St. Luke depicts St. Peter recruiting *uncircumcised* male Gentiles as though such practice was traditionally sanctioned by Jesus' disciples. Only later in Acts (15.1–5), when supposedly bad-mannered "Pharisaic" Jews joined the Christian movement, does St. Luke indicate that the demand for Gentile circumcision first appeared. "*Numerous details in Luke's presentation of the Jerusalem council vis-à-vis the Cornelius affair combine to depict the movement to circumcise Gentile converts as belated, extrinsic, and pernicious*" (Garroway, p. 27, also Vermes 2012, pp. 67–68). St. Luke's strategy "*is to a great extent simply stamping the pattern of church life he wants to inculcate in the* [Gentile] *Hellenistic communities of his time on the image of the* [Jewish Christian] *community of their origin*" (Crowe, p. 66).

Moreover, St. James' "Judaizers" from Jerusalem never act as though they are aware of the so-called "Jerusalem Conference" when they confront St. Peter for dining with Gentile Jesus-believers who do not obey Jewish dietary laws (*Galatians* 2.12). Similarly, St. Paul never admonishes any of the "Judaizers" for ignoring the supposed agreement, nor does St. Paul act as though aware of the presumed Conference's prohibition to eat foods sacrificed to idols. *"Nothing is unclean in itself; but it is unclean for anyone who thinks it unclean"* (*Romans* 14.14). *"[Eating]* *Food will not bring us close to God"* (*1 Corinthians* 8.8). *"Eat whatever is sold in the meat market without raising any question on the ground of conscience"* (*1 Corinthians* 10.27). The only dietary counsel St. Paul offers is not to confront "weak" Christians who observe Jewish kosher dietary laws. (See also J. Becker, p. 194, Hubbard, p. 155.)

Most significant, as noted earlier, St. Paul discloses that his decision to preach Jesus Christ "among the Gentiles" did not come from any "Jerusalem agreement": *"I did not confer with any human being, nor did I go up to Jerusalem to those who were already apostles before me"* (Galatians 1.16–17). Nowhere in his *Galatians* letter, in which he vehemently opposes Gentile circumcision fostered by his "Jewish Christian" adversaries, does St. Paul claim license for this view from a "Jerusalem Conference."

It is also evident, that from the time of his Christian conversion (fourteen or more years before the supposed "Jerusalem Conference") and throughout remainder of his life, St. Paul's Gentile preachments would have engendered adamant opposition from Jerusalem's Jesus-followers:

- that the coming of Jesus negates the Jewish Torah, which now fades away (*Galatians* 3.24–26);
- that the Jewish Torah is not from God but from *"weak and beggarly spirits"* (*Galatians* 4.9);
- that the Torah is *"the ministry of death, chiseled in letters on stone tablets"* (*2 Corinthians* 3.7);
- that observing Torah commandments generates sin *"for all who rely on the works of the law are under a curse"* (*Galatians* 3.10).

Jesus' disciples would hardly have conferred "apostolic authority" on St. Paul for an anti-Jewish program denigrating Jewish law, rituals, and practices (see also Notes #2, #14). Moreover, in his *Romans* letter St. Paul never claims he received either St. James' or St. Peter's sanction for special apostleship to the Gentiles. Since the Roman "Church" was organized by Jesus-believers from Jerusalem and not by St. Paul, Rome would have had Jewish Christian members (the "weak" Christians of *Romans* 14.1–2, 15.1) who would have known there was no such "Jerusalem Conference" agreement.

Mack (1999, p. 134) points out that St. Luke's Acts of the Apostles is "*an imaginary reconstruction in the interest of aggrandizing an amalgam view of Christianity early in the second century. Luke did this by painting over the messy history of conflictual movements throughout the first century and in his own time. He cleverly depicted Peter and Paul as preachers of an identical gospel* [to Gentiles], *and he wrote as a philosopher-historian, saying in effect to the Romans, 'We Christians could be very good for you.' That is myth-making in the genre of epic. There is not the slightest reason to take it seriously as history.*"

Prominent among Acts of the Apostles' early Christian narratives is St. Stephen's mythical speech before his alleged martyrdom by Jews (6.8–7.60). According to Shelly Matthews (pp. 131–132), St. Luke's purpose in fabricating this episode is to portray "*Christians as a legitimate social-religious group distinct from Jews*" by "*(1)appropriating Jewish prestige markers, while simultaneously denigrating actual Jews (insofar as they refuse to accept Jesus as messiah) as subversive and murderous subjects of empire; (2) engaging in the daunting task of demonstrating that followers of the Way* [Christians] *are innocent of any charges of subversion they face and that Rome's preferred stance toward these followers is to do them no harm. He does this in the face of widespread traditions of Roman involvement in the crucifixion of Jesus and the execution of Paul, to say nothing of the devastation of Judea as a consequence of*

Roman military conquest. … [O]ne could, with justification, argue that the story, from beginning to end, is the fictional creation of the author." (See also M. Grant, p. 218–219.)

Gratuitously added to St. Stephen's presumed execution is the presence of St. Paul, then known only as "Saul," a non-Jesus-believing Jew persecuting innocent Jesus believers. In St. Paul's own accounts of that time, there is no mention of any persecuted "St. Stephen," and St. Paul states that he himself "*was still unknown by sight*" to Jerusalem's Jewish Christians (*Galatians* 1.21). According to Löning (p. 113), "*the impressive dramatic intertwining of the Stephen tradition with the conversion story of Paul is clearly the work of the author of Acts.*"

St. Luke's "theological agenda" (Ehrman 2003, p. 172), firmly rooted in St. Paul's Gentile Christianity, shows how assiduously Christian leaders distanced themselves from Jews though forced to use Jewish Scriptures for religious respectability. That is, while commandeering the Jewish Bible to demonstrate Christian antiquity, they claimed to supplant Jews in God's favor and fashioned Jews into models of anti-Christian violence through devices such as the killing of Christ and St. Stephen's martyrdom. Presence of Jewish Christians, the first witnesses to Jesus' messianism, had little pacifying effect on Gentile Christianity's denigration of Jews and opposition to Jewish Torah observances. "*The rhetorical effect of Acts is to persuade readers that Jews are the mortal enemies of Christians and that they are to be vigorously opposed, despised, and treated with contempt*" (Smith and Tyson, p. 340).

6. Jews instigated political persecution of Christians thereby causing anti-Jewish backlash.

This claim is unfounded since Jews never gained political power to seriously threaten Christianity, nor would Roman authorities before Constantine have stepped in to favor either group in whatever disputes they may have engaged. The massive Jewish rebellions against Rome in the first and second centuries would hardly have given Jews permission to persecute Gentiles, whether or not Christian. Note that although some scholars suggest that reported first century quarrels (ca. 49 C.E.) about a man named "Chrestus" was really between Jews and Christians, the edict expelling the disputants from Rome favored neither, making no distinction between them (Hvalvik, pp. 180–184). In the fourth century when Christians gained imperial status and Roman authorities began to intervene between Jews and Christians, it was in favor of Christians, marking the beginning of direct threats to Jews (Note #23).

According to unprejudiced scholars, "*actual evidence of Jewish instigation of persecution ('stirring up trouble') is hardly to be found*" (Lieu 1996, p. 91). Fredriksen (2003, p. 59) points out that "*anti-Christian actions focused on the issue of public cult* [worship of the Emperor and the civic gods]. *Were Jews on these volatile occasions to have made themselves so conspicuous, they would have risked emphasizing, on precisely the same issue, their own degree of religious difference from majority culture.*" Furthermore, Pagan converts of St. Paul's Gentile churches and Jews of local synagogues would have been so separated by differences in custom and culture to make improbable any rivalrous Jewish mission to foment political persecution. (See, for example, Donfried, p. 44.)

It is also likely that although Christianity's early experiences were of considerable importance to Christians, they were of little significance to Jews more concerned with Roman oppression and Roman destruction of Jerusalem and their Temple. The Jewish "Mishnah", a post-Temple rabbinical extension of Jewish Biblical laws (forerunner of the Jewish Talmud), whose writings were finalized about the end of the second century C.E., shows no clear hint of Christian existence.

"*Prior to the time of Constantine* (305–337 C.E.) *the documents of Judaism that evidently reached closure — the Mishnah, Pirqué Abot, the Tosefta — scarcely took cognizance of Christianity and did not deem the new faith to be much of a challenge. If the unsystematic and scattered allusions are meant to refer to Christianity at all, then the sages regarded Christianity as an irritant, an exasperating heresy among Jews who should have known better"* (Neusner 1987, p. 7). *"Expressed hope for the destruction of the oppressive Roman empire is indeed a recurrent theme throughout classical rabbinic literature ... [T]he need to respond to Christianity was not a major concern of Palestinian rabbis of Late Antiquity"* (Schremer 2009, p. 364). *"The Mishnah does not establish strong borders around its community, it is not interested in defining orthodoxy, suppressing deviance, or establishing the limits of dissent"* (S. J. D. Cohen 2013, p. 220). *"Even when the Jews could have avenged themselves against the Christians with the tacit support of the government, as in the time of Julian [361–363 C.E.] they nonetheless refrained from initiating or participating in such a move"* (Irshai, p. 415).

The examples that Josephus, Jewish historian writing at the end of the first century, gives of Jewish assimilation or "apostasy" (abandoning Judaism) are always of Jews turning to one or another form of Paganism, the dominant society, but never to Christianity. The Tosefta, third century commentary and elaboration of the Mishnah, makes distinctions between Jews and Samaritans and between Jews and idolatrous Gentiles, but makes no mention of "Christians" (Lightstone, pp. 100—101). According to J. T. Sanders (2000, p. 144), *"There is little evidence of Jewish conversion to Christianity after the first formation of Christian congregations in the Jewish homeland, whereas there is quite a bit of evidence elsewhere that early Christian congregations were at least predominantly Gentile."*

Although some scholars claim that Gentile Christian anti-Jewish polemics were measures of "self-defense" against Jewish attacks (Horbury; Ludlow, p. 33) and blame Jewish hostility as the primary cause for "Parting of the Ways" between Jews and Christians (Geraty), such arguments discount the following:

96

- Although Jews may have verbally contested Christian claims of Jesus' virginal birth and resurrection, there are no Jewish literary anti-Christian counterparts to Christian anti-Jewish (*Adversus Judaeos*) texts that began from the second century onward. The first known Jewish anti-Christian document, *Toledoth Yeshu*, probably appeared no earlier than the eighth century (Newman 1999, p. 62).

- The six claimed "disputations" between Jews and Christians, flanked by the second and sixth centuries (Varner 2013, p. 563), were all written by Christians with ostensible Jewish opponents who were persistently defeated. Real Jewish disagreement never entered the arena of Christian literary dispute since there are no known "disputations" against Gentile Christianity written by Jews. Nor are there Christian "disputations" that record the many valid long-standing reasons why Jews did not adopt Gentile Christianity (Note #11). For example, Jewish opposition to worshipping a human such as Jesus Christ (Note 11.*b*) did not await St. Paul and his movement: "*Can mortals make for themselves gods? Such are no Gods!*" (Jeremiah 16.20).

- As shown above, the rabbinical movement of the first few centuries made no discernible mention of Gentile Christianity, considering it of no more interest than Paganism. "*The rabbinic sources treat all pagans as essentially faceless, and Christianity not at all, except as part of that same blank wall of hostility to God (and by the way, to Israel)*" (Neusner 2004, p. 461). "*Israel's sages did not find they had to take seriously the presence or claims of Christianity*" (Ibid. p. 444). Only after Christianity became an authoritatively supported Roman antagonist, was there notable Jewish concern.

- It was not Jewish opposition to Jesus as Messiah that prompted Gentile Christian *Adversus Judaeos* literature. Although isolated from mainstream Judaism, Jewish Christian movements persisted throughout the first five centuries without rabbinical tracts against them being at all comparable to Gentile Christianity's numerous, caustic, and continuing *Adversus Judaeos* tracts.

- Christian Jew-hatred did not depend on the local presence of Jewish antagonists. Jews were denigrated even in localities where they were absent (Notes #20, #23).

- Although some Jews may have expressed hostile sentiments during the development of early Christianity, they left no visible signs other than the possible liturgical curse *Birkat Haminim*. As noted above (#10.2), this curse did not appear before the end of the second century, and most probably applied to **Jews** who opposed Rabbinic authority, not Gentiles. As also noted, the earliest recorded curse between Jews and Christians is not from Jews but from St. Paul (*Galatians* 1.7–9) against Jewish Christian "Judaizers" who oppose Gentile Christian abandonment of Jewish laws. Unrestrained, St. Paul's curse in *Galatians* 3.10–11 extends beyond Jewish Christian "Judaizers" to Torah-observant Jews: "*For all who rely on the works of the law are under a curse ... [N]o one is justified before God by the law; for the one who is righteous will live by faith.*"

- If Jewish aggression was the agent responsible for Gentile Christianity's virulent antisemitism, anti-Jewish polemic should have faded from the fourth century onward. Christianity then became the official imperial religion, and Jews could neither attack or question Christian beliefs and practices (Note #23). However, as we know, defamation of Jews as evil "Christ Killers" rejected by God (Notes #6, #8, #18, #19, #23) continued endlessly despite a politically silenced Jewish community.

- Given Gentile Christianity's need to claim Biblical antiquity by supplanting Jews as the "True Israel" (Note #19), the mere existence of Jews who followed Scriptural laws abandoned by Gentile Christianity threatened its antique façade (Notes #7, #18, #19, #23). Jewish hostility, modest or imagined, became a foil to justify denigrating Jews in gaining antique religious credibility for Gentile Christianity. *"The statement of Jewish hostility in general terms is based on theological exegesis and not on historical memory"* (Parkes, p. 148). *"Antijudaism was ... an intrinsic need of Christian self-affirmation. ... a part of Christian exegesis ... to affirm the identity of the Church, which could only be done by invalidating the identity of the Jews"* (Ruether 1974, p. 181).

Belief in Gentile Christianity's Jesus Christ was easily extended from belief in Jewish responsibility for his murder to belief in Jewish responsibility for persecuting Christians. Absurd transpositions of Jewish Scriptures were enlisted in the Christian cause to show (future!) Jewish persecution. Lieu notes (2002 pp. 141–142): "[St.] *Irenaeus uses the well-known theme of brotherly rivalry. Esau representing the Jews, Jacob the Christians: 'Jacob took the blessings of Esau as the latter people* [Jacob's Christians] *has snatched the blessings of the former* [Esau's Jews]. *For which cause his brother suffered the plots and persecutions of a brother, just as the Church suffers this self-same thing from the Jews'* (Irenaeus, Adv. Haer. IV.21.3). *For* [St.] *Hippolytus the two elders who spied on Susannah represent 'the two peoples, one from the circumcision* [Jews], *the other from the nations* [Pagans]', *who still seek false witness against Christians in the hope of stirring up destructive persecution* (Hippolytus, ad Danielem I. 13-15). Christian self-interest sanctified misuse of any Biblical narrative, reading "Jacob" ("Israel") as a Christian (!) and the spying elders as Jews and Pagans. (See also Notes #7, #18.)

The artificial introduction of Jews as "inciters" of Pagan hostility encountered by St. Paul in St. Luke's Acts of the Apostles (Chapt. 14) dismays even some Christian theologians. *"There can be no doubt that this is a very problematic aspect of the way he* [St. Luke] *works, and we cannot simply accept this from him without any critical objection*" (Klauck, p. 61). As M. S. Taylor (pp. 102–104) shows, presuming persecution by Jews became a measure of "*true Christian*" experience; and, among other arguments, a Christian group (Montanists) was impugned heretical by claiming that the group lacked the experience of Jewish persecution. "*Is there one person, my good sirs, among those from Montanus ... who was persecuted by the Jews or killed by the wicked?*" (Eusebius, ca. 330, *Ecclesiastical History* 5.16.3). It is quite incongruous that Jewish refusal to accept Christian doctrine (Note #11) was interpreted as a physical threat engendering vituperative unremitting hatred, whereas three centuries of sporadic but lethal persecution by Romans engendered only plaintive Christian claims of mistreatment and a conciliatory attitude (Notes #3, #21, #22).

As expected, Jewish relationship with Christianity changed radically after Christianity reached official Roman imperial status in the fourth century. To the Christians, major political concerns were establishing dominance over Pagans and Jews; and Christian religious concerns centered on the God/nature of Christ (Note #11.*b*). To the Rabbis, open ideological confrontation against Christianity was imprudent since Jewish survival depended upon the now-theocratic Christian state. Jewish religious concerns then centered on continued development of the "Oral Torah," via the Talmud and so forth, that would serve and conserve Judaism in the gray days ahead.

7. Anti-Jewishness arose because of competitive Jewish missionary activity to convert the same Gentiles to Judaism that Gentile Christianity was proselytizing.

Simple as it sounds, this notion falls flat because there are few, if any, known events to support active Jewish proselytization among Romans. Fredriksen (1995, pp. 321–322): "[A] *supposed market competition between these two communities, Jewish and Catholic,*

100

cannot account for anti-Jewish polemic for the simple reason that we have little evidence for actual Jewish missions in antiquity generally. Jews in principle welcomed converts, but do not seem to have mounted missions to attract them." Feldman (2006, pp. 205–206) finds no evidence *"of missionary activity, let alone organized missionary activity, by Jews in the Hellenistic-Roman period (in fact, we do not know the name of a single Jewish missionary who systematically sought converts to classical Judaism during this period, nor do we know the title of a single tract that has as its goal the conversion of non-Jews to Judaism)."*

Edrei and Mendels (2013, p. 271): *"[T]he rabbis rejected a missionary approach, they had no aspiration to proselytize others. They fashioned the Torah as a **national** Torah without universalist goals"* (their emphasis). Since Gentiles would hardly be concerned about Pharisaic disputes with Sadducees and other Jews on the degree to which Mosaic Law was to be followed, St. Matthew's Gospel's claim (23.15) that Pharisees "cross sea and land to make a single convert" really refers to converting Jews to Pharisaism, not Gentiles.

Goodman (1992, pp. 53–55): *"I do not doubt either that Jews firmly believed in their role as religious mentors of the Gentile world or that Jews expected that in the last days the Gentiles would in fact come to recognize the glory of God and divine rule on earth. But the desire to encourage admiration of the Jewish way of life or respect for the Jewish God, or to inculcate ethical behavior in other peoples, or such pious hope for the future, should be clearly distinguished from an impulse to draw non-Jews into Judaism. ...It is likely enough, then, that Jews welcomed sincere proselytes in the first century. But passive acceptance is quite different from active mission."* ... *"[T]exts of the early church which appear to attack Jews as competitors for the souls of converts refer in fact to followers of Jesus* [Jewish Christian "Judaizers"] *who, in the eyes of their opponents, clung too hard to Jewish customs."* (See also Vaage 2006a, pp. 14–15.)

Josephus, whose writings were probably more widely read than those of any other Jewish writer of the first century, actively defended Judaism, presenting it as an attractive alternative to idolatrous religions (Mason). However, although noting that some Gentiles adopted Jewish customs, Josephus took care never to claim that Gentiles must adopt Judaism to be "saved." In Isaiah (66.23), Gentiles will receive salvation only in the final days when "*all flesh shall come to worship before me, says Yahweh.*" According to Levinskaya (p. 33), "*the defense of Judaism and polemics against polytheists which are definitely present in Jewish literature, are markedly different from signs of missionary zeal. Simple comparison with Christian literature shows the difference in approach.*" McKnight (p. 77): "*Judaism was not a missionary religion.*"

11
WHY DID JEWS FIND CHRISTIANITY UNACCEPTABLE?

A common Christian accusation against Jews was their failure to relinquish their religious beliefs and practices in favor of Christianity. *"Christian anti-Semitism is in the first instance an expression aroused by Israel's resistance to the Gospel"* (Simon, p. 207).

Although Christian polemicists used this argument to condemn the "stiff-necked" "hard-heartedness" of the Jews, it is difficult to give it more than rhetorical value. Unwilling to recognize that Gentile Christian doctrines and practices imperiled Jewish identity, Christian leaders acted as though Jews had no reason to resist conversion. Jews presumably had so few ties to their religion, they would unquestionably adopt Christian versions of highly questionable beliefs and customs, among which are the following:

a) That a human (Jesus) was born of a virgin (St. Matthew 1.23, St. Luke 1.27). *"He was born of a virgin. A virgin conceived, a virgin bore, and after the birth was a virgin still"* (St. Augustine, *On the Creed* 6, NPNF Series 1, vol. 3, p. 371; see also Horner, p.313).

In the Gospels, Jesus' status progresses from "Son of Mary" (St. Mark 6.3), an epithet used contemptuously by his "hometown" opponents that *"focuses on Jesus' lack of legitimacy"* (Lüdemann 1998, p. 53), to adoption by "Joseph" (St. Matthew 1.19–21, St. Luke 1.27), a supposed descendant of King David. Levin shows that "adoption" by Joseph, Jesus' alleged nonbiological father — a claim offered by Christians to explain Jesus' Davidic ancestry — would not have given Jesus kingly rights among Jews.

Virginal birth of a divine-human figure was a feature of Greco-Roman "mystery religions" (Note #22) and was also attributed to Roman emperors (Freke and Gandy, pp. 29–31). In proselytizing Pagans, such claims would not have appeared unusual — the Roman religious world encompassed not only many Gods but also many "mysteries" and "miracles."

"The world of the evangelists was a world in which magic, thaumaturgy, divination, augury, astrology, and a variety of other superstitions commanded widespread belief. Miracle was no problem, in a sense, for the ancients since they had no developed concept of the laws of nature. Nature was not a closed system, operating in response to laws that could not be violated. Nature, history, human experience were the arena for the action of supernatural forces, gods, angels, divine men, spirits and demons" (Telford, p. 89).

For example, legendary Romulus, born of a Vestal Virgin from intercourse with Mars, God of War, was believed to have founded Rome on Palatine Hill. After many battles, Romulus disappeared from Earth and was transformed into the God Quirinus, worshipped by Romans along with Father God Jupiter. Even more like Gospel legends of Jesus is the Pagan Apollonius story (Ehrman 2014, pp. 11ff). Births of both men were announced to their virginal mothers by a divine messenger; both performed miracles of healing the sick, exorcising demons, and reviving the dead; both preached spiritual values to a material world; both were denounced as societal enemies; and both were believed to ascend to heaven in god-like form and then reappear on Earth. What Apollonius lacked was Jesus' presumed antique Jewish Scriptural history and his elevation to "Redeemer of Sins" and "Savior of Mankind."

St. Justin Martyr (ca. 150): *"When we say that the Word who is the first-born of God was produced without sexual union, and that He, Jesus Christ, our Teacher, was crucified and died, and rose again, and ascended into heaven, we propound nothing different from what you believe regarding those whom you esteem sons of Jupiter"* (*First Apology*, XXI, ANF vol. 1, p. 170). *"And if we even affirm that He was born of a virgin, accept this in common with what you accept of Perseus"* (Ibid. XXII).

Interestingly, a modern Christian theologian suggests that since some vertebrates are known to produce offspring by parthenogenesis (asexual reproduction), *"Why not God"* to account for Mother Mary's "parthenogenesis" (Bird 2008, p. 21). For humans, the problem would be that a fertile female has two X sex chromosomes but no Y chromosome, and a male has both an X and a Y. How did Mother Mary's parthenogenetically produced male child get a Y chromosome?

b) That this human Savior is also a Demigod or even a God. "[A]t *the name of Jesus every knee should bend, in heaven and on earth and under the earth, and every tongue should confess that Jesus Christ is Lord"* (St. Paul, *Philippians* 2.10–11). Although St. Paul's letters equivocated, his concept of Jesus as a heavenly ruler and divine savior in the pattern of other Greco-Roman deities is certainly "God-like": "[H]*e is a preexistent immortal being (Philippians 2.6) with tremendous power who produces benefaction (i.e. salvation) for those who worship him"* (Litwa, p. 5). If we combine Jesus Christ's sublime power with his immortality in defeating death through resurrection (*Romans* 6.9, *"death no longer has dominion over him"*), we have, by most concepts of divinity, a preternatural immortal who can judge and affect the entire world and its events. That is, a visual Jesus Christ more worshipful than the invisible Jewish/Israelite God Yahweh. R. N. Longenecker (1970, p. 141) proposes that St. Paul did not use his god-like concept of Jesus Christ as an additional polytheistic entity, but as another face of monotheism: St. Paul's "God the Father" and "Lord Jesus Christ" *"were roughly equivalent,"* both being somehow human-like and invisible.

Later Christian documents and Christian Fathers soon showed few doubts of Jesus Christ as a God. Since Jesus' mother was believed a virgin, she could only have been impregnated by a God or God-like emissary. *"For our God, Jesus Christ, was according to the appointment of God, conceived in the womb of Mary, of the seed of David, but by the Holy Ghost"* (St. Ignatius, *Letter to the Ephesians* XVIII, ANF vol.1, p. 57). *"In the beginning was the Word, and the Word was with God, and the Word was God ... And the Word became flesh* [Jesus Christ] *and lived among us"* (St. John 1.1–14). *"Long ago God spoke to our ancestors in many and various ways by the prophets, but in these last days he has spoken to us by a Son* [Jesus Christ], *whom he appointed heir of all things, through whom he also created the worlds"* (*Letter to the Hebrews* 1.1–2).

"He [Jesus Christ] *is the image of the invisible God, the firstborn of all creation, for in him all things in heaven and on earth were created"* (*Colossians* 1.15–16). *"Brethren, it is fitting that you should think of Jesus as of God — as the judge of the living and the dead"* (*Second Epistle of Clement* 1, ANF vol. 9, p. 251). *"As a king sends his son, who is also a king, so sent He* [God] *Him* [Jesus Christ]*; as God"* (*Epistle to Diognetus* 7, ANF vol. 1, p. 27). *"He* [Jesus Christ] *manifested Himself to be the Son of God. For if He had not come in the flesh, how could men have been saved by beholding Him?* (*Epistle of Barnabas* 5, ANF vol. 1, p. 139).

St. Irenaeus (ca. 180, *Against Heresies* 3, Payton, pp. 18–19): *"God recapitulated in himself the ancient formation of man, so that he might kill sin, deprive death of its power, and give life again to humankind. This was why the savior had to be formed with the same physical body as Adam had, which would enable the last Adam to suffer pain and death in the place of the fallen humanity, in order to bring them to eternal life with God."*

For many Christians, Jesus Christ replaced the Jewish God, Yahweh, with the title "Lord" ("Kyrios"), a Greek title given only to Yahweh in the Greek ("Septuagint") translation of the Jewish Bible. (In the Hebrew Bible there is no "Lord-God" only

"Yahweh-our God.") Once this Greek mark of divinity was conferred (St. Paul, *Romans* 1.4, "*Jesus Christ our Lord*" [Kyrios]), it did not take long to further change the meaning of the Greek "Christ" (anointed) from that given to a Jewish Messiah ("anointed political/military leader") to that given to a deity — "*God's Son from Heaven*" (St. Paul, *1 Thessalonians* 1.10), "*Jesus Christ, the Son of God*" (e.g., St. Mark 1.1) — in which "*Son of God*" is now meant literally, not metaphorically. "*Behold again: Jesus who was manifested, both by type and in the flesh, is not the Son of man but the Son of God*" (*Epistle of Barnabas* XII, ANF vol. 1, p. 145).

"*The Father of the universe has a Son; who also, being the first-begotten Word of God, is even God. And of old He appeared in the shape of fire and in the likeness of an angel to Moses and to other prophets, but now in the times of your reign, having, as before said, become Man by a virgin*" (St. Justin Martyr, *First Apology* 63, ANF vol. 1, p. 184). "*Thou hast not known, O Israel, that* [Jesus Christ] *was the first-born of God, who was begotten before the sun, who made the light to shine forth, who lighted up the darkness, who fixed the first foundations, who poised the earth, who collected the ocean, who stretched out the firmament, who adorned the world*" (St. Melito of Sardis, ANF vol. 8, p. 757).

The Apostles' Creed ("The Summary of Christian Faith") states: "*I believe in Jesus Christ, God's only Son, our Lord,*" as does the Nicene Creed: "*We believe in one Lord, Jesus Christ, the only Son of God.*" St. John (10.30) has Jesus say, "*The Father and I are one,*" and later (20.28), "*Thomas answered him, my Lord and my God.*" On his way to martyrdom, St. Ignatius (ca. 100) asks Rome's Christians "*Pray Christ for me, that by these instruments* [teeth of the wild beasts] *I may be found a sacrifice*" (ANF vol. 1, p. 75). St. Augustine (ca. 400): "*He* [Jesus] *is prayed to by us, as our God*" (*On the Psalms* LXXXVI.1., NPNF Series 1, vol. 8, p. 410). "*It could not be that God's only son should not be God ...*

For it is impossible for the will of the Son to be any whit parted from the Father's will. God and God; both One God: Almighty and Almighty; both One Almighty" (Ibid. *On the Creed*.3, NPNF Series 1, vol. 3, p. 370).

In Jewish history, "Son of God" had various meanings, from depicting Israel itself (Exodus 4.22, Deuteronomy 32.18, Hosea 11.1) to characterizing a pious Jew, a saintly miracle-worker, or a charismatic Hasid, King, or Messiah (Vermes 2012, p. 49), but never a worshipful deity (Vermes 2013, p. 15). Although accepted in Gentile society for emperors and heroes, elevation of humans to the rank of God ("apotheosis") was rejected in Judaism, and worship was ascribed monotheistically to the invisible Yahweh. *"I am Yahweh your God who brought you out of the land of Egypt, out of the house of slavery; you shall have no other gods before me"* (Exodus 20.2). *"Hear, O Israel: Yahweh is our God, Yahweh alone"* (Deuteronomy 6.4). *"I am Yahweh who made all things, who alone stretched out the heavens, who by myself spread out the earth; who frustrates the omens of liars, and makes fools of diviners"* (Isaiah 44.24–25).

Ehrman (2014, pp.127–128) points out that claims for Jesus Christ's God-like divinity *"do not derive from the life of the historical Jesus but represent embellishments made by storytellers who were trying to convert people by convincing them of Jesus' superiority and to instruct those who were converted. ... He* [Jesus] *believed and taught that he was the future king of the coming kingdom of God, the messiah of God yet to be revealed."*

To Jews, worshipping Jesus Christ as God fell into Paganism's pantheon of idolatry, and opposition never waned. *"You shall not make for yourself an idol, whether in the form of anything that is in heaven above, or that is on the earth beneath, or that is in water under the earth. You shall not bow down to them or worship them"* (Deuteronomy 5.8–9). A fifteenth century Jewish manuscript argued that a dying god is not a god: "[I]*f they say, Why do you not believe that Jesus is God? Reply to them, Why did he accept death? ... 'So you see that he is not God, for he was slain'"* (Horbury, p. 255).

Detachment from monotheistic Jews *"was the decisive step which ensured that Jesus was hailed as God, and genuinely treated as different in nature from the rest of us"* (Casey 1991, p. 37). Thus, as Young (2006, p. 15) points out, *"only the spread of Christianity to the Gentiles could have enabled a Jewish rabbi to have become the Lord Jesus Christ, Son of God."* St. Aphrahat: *"He who came from God is the Son of God and is God"* (*Select Demonstrations*, NPNF Series 2, vol. 13, p. 387). The notion of a new Christian filial divinity in name and form also led Pagan critics, such as Celsus (ca. 180), to ask how can Christians denounce Pagans for polytheism *"if they themselves worship Jesus as a second god?"* (Trigg, p. 219).

Christian debate on the extent of Jesus Christ's divinity became a consuming issue for centuries. Was Jesus Christ born divine? Was Jesus Christ born human and became divine? Was Jesus Christ simultaneously human and divine, and became more divine upon his resurrection? Was it from birth, teaching, or crucifixion that Jesus' role as Christianity's Savior began? Compared to "God the Father," does Jesus Christ's proclamation (St. John 10.30) *"The Father and I are One,"* mean that Jesus Christ and God are the same entity, or does the plural "are" mean two separate entities but somehow united?

Was Jesus Christ like God? Same as God? Subordinate to God? Was there a divine "Holy Trinity" in which the "Holy Spirit" is equal to Jesus Christ? Subordinate to Jesus Christ? Is there a simple 1-2-3 ranking in the Trinity? ("[W]*e reasonably worship Him* [Jesus Christ] *having learned that He is the Son of the true God Himself, and hold Him in second place, and the prophetic* [Holy] *Spirit in the third"* (St. Justin Martyr, *First Apology* 13, ANF vol. 1, pp. 166–167.)

Decisions on these matters fluctuated among various Christian orthodoxies and heresies (Lössl, pp. 155–191), with venomous disputes, excommunications, and historic executions — quarrels which still go on today (Erickson). *"[T]he concept of orthodoxy gave rise to a kind of discourse that was authoritarian and intolerant in the extreme, ... emperors in Late Antiquity resorted at times to actual persecution and ... heresy became a crime, just like paganism. ... the concept of orthodoxy implies not only intolerance but also violence"* (Cameron, pp. 113–114). *"It is no wonder that a tolerant pagan like Ammianus should say that 'wild beasts are not such enemies to mankind as are most Christians ... in their deadly hatred of one another'"* (Ste. Croix 2006, p. 222).

"Orthodox" Gentile Christian theologians insisted that Jesus Christ represented a unique "hypostatic" union, being God and human at the same time — one person with two natures. Mirroring St. Paul's image of Jesus Christ transforming himself from God to man (*Philippians* 2.7), is Origen's later declaration (ca 240): *"Christ Jesus, he who came to earth...in these last times he emptied himself and was made man, was made flesh, although he was God, and being made man, he still remained what he was, namely God"* (*De Prinicipiis*, Stevenson, p. 149).

In order to preserve a monotheistic element in Christianity, many theologians used the "Holy Trinity" as a way of tying Jesus to God as being of "one substance" (*homoiousios*) partitioned into three entities. However, to other theologians, if Jesus Christ was the Son of God, then God the Father must have existed before Jesus Christ. How could Jesus Christ not be different from the Father — lesser than, or perhaps even greater than? Moreover, if both Jesus Christ and God was one God —one divinity — how could one divinity be both "Son" and "Father"? In the words of Tertullian (ca. 200, *Against Praxeas* XI), *"For He* [God] *calls Him* [Jesus Christ] *Son, and if the Son is none other than He who has proceeded from the Father himself, He will then be the Son, and not Himself from whom He proceeded.... If you want me to believe Him to be both the Father and the Son, show me some other* [Scriptural] *passage where it is declared, 'The Lord Said unto Himself, I am my own Son, today have I begotten myself'"* (ANF vol. 3, p. 605).

For most Christian believers the Jesus Christ-God relationship did not follow the theology of separate but equal members of a trinity. Enthronement of Jesus Christ as Lord (St. Paul: *Philippians* 2.6–11, *Colossians* 1.15–20, *Ephesians* 1.20–23) results *"in the reign of Christ as Lord of the entire cosmos"* (Scroggs, p. 14). *"And if he is Cosmocrator, he has in effect become God. Simply stated, the structure implies a replacement theme. Yahweh as God* [of the Jews] *has been replaced by Kyrios Iesous Christos* [Lord God of Christian prayer] (Ibid. p. 17; also Note #22). According to Lamb: Yahweh, the "badly behaving" God of the Old Testament was replaced by Jesus Christ, the "better behaving" God of the New Testament. In St. Justin Martyr (*Dialogue with Trypho, a Jew* LXXV), the name of God *"not revealed to Abraham or Jacob was Jesus ... he who led your father into the land* [Israel] *is called by the name Jesus'* (ANF vol. 1, p. 236).

To justify these and other imaginative concepts, the Christian Fathers claimed that Christian "faith" in Jesus Christ provides "knowledge." *"Knowledge is characterized by* [Christian] *faith, as faith becomes characterized by knowledge. ... As without the four elements it is not possible to live, so neither can knowledge be attained without faith. Faith is then the support of truth"* (St. Clement of Alexandria, ca. 200, *The Stromates* 2.6, ANF Vol. 2, pp. 350, 354). More modern theologians follow apace, and Rauser (p. 232) suggests that faith provides as much knowledge as the natural sciences. According to Karl Barth, an esteemed theologian, when one *"confesses"* the Apostle's Creed, one creates knowledge, and the *"Creed of Christian faith"* is *"rational in the proper sense"* (Ibid. p. 224). However, since there is no way of testing whether such "theological knowledge" corresponds to the "true" nature of God and Jesus Christ, it is easy to see that any "faithful" theological notion on this matter can be proclaimed, and many were. If we consider historical "knowledge" as based on material physical events, faith in miracles such as immaculate conception, multiplying loaves and fishes, walking on water, and raising the dead, is not "knowledge" without acceptable evidence that such events can and did occur. The only "knowledge" we have of these supposed events is that there were/are believers in such miracles.

The ease with which any theological belief about God and Jesus Christ could be advanced and the inability of any one theological belief to disprove another, thus led to an overabundance of unprovable theological doctrines and dogmas. A small sampling of these includes Gnostics, Valentinians, Basilideans, Theodotians, Monarchians, Marcionites, Arians, Anomoeans, Nestorians (Edwards 2009). Which beliefs, by consensus or coercion, were then declared "orthodox" and which "heresy," were based on which group of Christian Fathers and political sovereigns attended and prevailed in Church councils (Ehrman 2011a, and also Jenkins). St. Epiphanius (ca. 315–403 C.E.), Bishop of Salamis, compiled a list of some 80 Christian heresies, of which many, including those listed above, turn on different views of the God/human nature of Jesus. Filaster, Bishop of Brescia (ca. 385) extended Epiphanius's list to 156 heresies (Pritz, p. 71).

In a modern critique of "faith-based" scholarly explanations for the many novel claims in St. John's Gospel, Dunderberg (2013a, p. 349) offers: *"The obvious risk with them is that, once you start arguing supernaturally, there is no limit to, or control of it. Anything is arguable in this case. ... [S]ome scholars already tap into the potentialities inherent in supernatural argumentation without constraints."*

Interestingly, not only "faith" and "orthodoxy," but controvertible "truth" was forcibly injected into creating and judging Christian theology, beginning with St. Paul's *"I am speaking the truth in Christ"* (*Romans* 9.1). "Orthodox" versions of Jesus Christ's divinity devised by clerical councils were then positioned as "true", while beliefs held by other sects and religions were ranked "untrue." Unexplained was: can a particular sect's description of divine mythology be "truer" than all other beliefs when there is no way of showing how any theological belief can be tested. In all such contentions, Gentile Christian self-sanctified believers in "faithful orthodoxy" stood fast in proclaiming they alone knew the "true" divine nature of Jesus Christ, and remained unconcerned that worshipping a human divinity, however explained, is idolatry to Jews.

c) That this innocent God/human figure was most cruelly sacrificed in compliance with the wishes of an all-merciful all-just God as a scapegoat to atone for Christians' sins against this all-merciful all-just God. Seeking divine propitiation of sin, disease, and misfortune through blood sacrifices was common in ancient society, used also as a means to provide food for participants. Human sacrifice, however, had long been abandoned in Jewish culture marked by the Biblical story of the "Aqedah" in which Abraham offers a ram as a sacrificial substitute for his son Isaac (Genesis 22.13).

St. Paul theologically resumed this defunct practice by having God offer crucified Jesus (*"His own Son," Romans* 8.3) to absolve Christian sins. *"Christ Jesus, whom God put forward as a sacrifice of atonement by his blood"* (*Romans* 3.25). *"The Lord Jesus Christ, who gave himself for our sins"* (*Galatians* 1.3-4). *"I live by faith in the Son of God who loved me and gave himself for me"* (*Galatians* 2.20). *"In him we have redemption through His blood, the forgiveness of our trespasses"* (*Ephesians* 1.7). Like the Jewish Passover lamb sacrificed for Israel's redemption from Egyptian slavery, St. John's Gospel (1.29) declares Jesus *"the* [sacrificial] *Lamb of God who takes away the sins of the world"* (also St. Paul, *1 Corinthians* 5.7). The sacrifice of God's son Jesus also emulates Abraham's planned sacrifice of his son Isaac, since *"Christian allegorists* [exegsists] *read Isaac as one of the prefigurations of Christ"* (Schoenfeld, p. 2).

Christians exchanged their disdain for animal sacrifice in the Jewish Temple by endlessly repeating claims for the validity of Jesus' human sacrifice. In the New Testament's *Letter to the Hebrews*: *"Nor was* [Jesus] *to offer himself again and again, as the high priest enters the* [Temple] *year after year with blood that is not his own ... But as it is, He has appeared once for all at the end of the age to remove sin by the sacrifice of himself"* (9.25–26). *"We have confidence to enter the* [heavenly] *sanctuary by the blood of Jesus'* (Ibid. 10.19). In the New Testament's first letter of *John* (1.7): *"The blood of Jesus his Son cleanses all from sin."* In St. Clement of Rome's *First Epistle to the Corinthians* (XLIX, ca. 60–80): *"Jesus Christ our Lord gave His blood for us by the will of God; His flesh for our flesh, and His soul for our souls"* (ANF vol. 1, p. 18).

Epistle of Barnabas (ca. 100): *"He was wounded for our transgressions, and buried for our iniquities, with His stripes we are healed"* (V, ANF vol. 1, p. 139). *"The Son of God could not have suffered except for our sakes"* (Ibid. VII, p.141). In St. Ignatius' *Epistle to the Trallians* (8.7, ca. 100): *"He gave Himself a ransom for us, that He might cleanse us by His blood from our old ungodliness"* (ANF vol.1, p. 69). In St. Justin Martyr's *First Apology* (ca. 150): *"He was numbered with the transgressors and He bare the sins of many, and was delivered up for their transgressions"* (ANF vol.1, p. 180).

In St. Irenaeus' *Against Heresies* (Book 5.2, ca. 180): *"By His own blood He redeemed us, as also His apostle* [St. Paul] *declares 'In whom we have redemption through His blood, even the redemption of sins'"* (ANF vol.1, p. 528). The *Gloria* in the liturgy of the Roman Catholic Mass echoes this notion in the prayer, *"Lord Jesus Christ, Only Begotten Son, Lord God, Lamb of God, Son of the Father, You take away the sins of the World."*

In contrast, Jewish prophets taught that one can only atone for one's own sins. *"In those days they shall no longer say: 'The parents have eaten sour grapes* [indulged in lewd behavior], *and the children's teeth are on edge* [guilty].' *But all shall die for their own sins; the teeth of everyone who eats sour grapes shall be set on edge"* (Jeremiah 31.29–30). *"A child shall not suffer for the iniquity of a parent, nor a parent suffer for the iniquity of a child; The righteousness of the righteous shall be his own, and the wickedness of the wicked shall be his own"* (Ezekiel 18.20). *"What to me is the multitude of your sacrifices? says Yahweh. ... Wash yourselves; make yourselves clean; remove the evil of your doings from before my eyes; cease to do evil, learn to do good; seek justice, rescue the oppressed, defend the orphan, plead for the widow"* (Isaiah 1.11–17). *"Will Yahweh be pleased with thousands of rams? ... Shall I give my firstborn for my transgression, the fruits of my body for the sin of my soul? ... He has told you, O mortal, what is good; ...to do justice, and to love kindness, and to walk humbly with your God"* (Micah 6. 7–8). In *Aristeas*, a Jewish document probably dating to the second century B.C.E., honoring God *"is not done with gifts or sacrifices, but with purity of heart and of devout disposition"* (Shutt, p. 28).

As Horsley (1994, p. 168) points out: *"There is little or no evidence that the Jesus* [Jewish Christian] *movement in Palestine believed that 'Jesus had to die for our sins.'"* That St. Paul and the Gentile Christian movement reintroduced human blood sacrifice, never rationally answered questions of how such a dastardly inhuman deed can expiate human sins, or why Jesus' crucifixion is more expiatory of sin than Roman crucifixion of many, many, thousands of others. If, according to St. Paul (*Romans* 3.25), *"He* [God] *did this to show his righteousness,"* how does crucifixion of an innocent show righteousness, and how does punishment of an innocent absolve punishment of the guilty? *"For Christ also suffered for sins once for all, the righteous for the unrighteous"* (*1 Peter* 3.18). Thus, despite theological sanction for Jesus' crucifixion, the question remains: Why did a loving God horribly punish Jesus Christ, his son, for sinful crimes he did not commit?

If we accept that the "core element" of the Christian Holy Trinity embodies the belief *"Father, Son, and Holy Spirit act inseparably"* (K. Johnson, p. 54), a conundrum arises: *"Did God the Father punish **himself** as the Son?"* According to Johnson (Ibid. p. 67), the theological answer offers a further conundrum: that Jesus Christ is simultaneously both a divinity and human creation, and therefore *"both object and subject of the events that constitute his passion* [death on the cross]. *He is the subject from the standpoint of his divine nature (as the one who willed his death), while he is the object from the standpoint of his human nature (as the one who suffered on our behalf)."*

One can also question, why do theologians, New Testament writers, and Christian Fathers claim that Jesus was crucified primarily, if not only, because of Jewish culpability (Note #8) yet insist that he merited a God-given motivated execution *"to save us from our sins."* That is, how are Jews guilty for a divinely purposed sacrifice to save mankind? As Fisher (1993, p. 105) points out: blaming the Jews for Jesus' crucifixion dodges Christian responsibility *"that Christ died freely because of the sins of all, so that all* [Christian sinners] *might attain salvation."*

To Christian theologians, atonement through the killing of Jesus is crucial to Christianity. *"Deny the vicarious nature of the atonement — deny that our guilt was transferred to Christ and He bore its penalty — and you in effect have denied the ground of our justification. If our guilt was not transferred to Christ and paid for on the cross, how can His righteousness be imputed to us for our justification?"* (MacArthur, p. 9). *"For in His death alone our forgiveness from sin and guilt and therefore our liberation from death is accomplished*" (Barth, vol. 3, p. 615). *"If Christ had not 'delivered us from death' (2 Corinthians 1.10), he would have accomplished nothing, neither releasing the chains of sin nor overcoming death's obstruction*" (Falque, p. 22). *"What validated Jesus' message and delivered his followers was not the specific content of his ethical teaching, nor his great deeds, but the offering of his own life on the cross*" (Pervo 2010, p. 238).

According to Schröter (p. 62), the ignominy of Jesus' execution is countered by the theological belief that *"through the death of Jesus God has shown his power toward him and explicitly vindicated his claim."* Or, as described by Riches (p. xvii), crucified Jesus *"is in fact a king and more than a king, he is the one Lord of Israel, unus Dominus. ... to behold the man Jesus ... is to behold the true God."*

However, to Jews seeking freedom from oppression, unanswered questions would have remained:

- How does execution of a Messiah show "power"?
- How does Jesus' execution "vindicate his claim"?
- How does Jesus' execution exemplify the "true God"?

More likely, the existential impetus for turning Jesus' death into a pious sacrifice was for Gentile Christians to overlook his militancy as a popular leader and activist (St. Matthew 21.8–12) executed as a political agitator. *"Jesus, King of the Jews"* (Ibid. 27.37) was hardly a spiritual titular motif.

d) That this God/human figure was then resurrected from the dead. To St. Paul and Christian leaders since, belief in Jesus' resurrection provides an essential foundation for Christianity's religion and theology. *1 Corinthians* (15.14): *"If Christ has not been raised, then our proclamation has been in vain, and your faith has been in vain."* Fitzmyer, (p. 86): *"The resurrection of Jesus is the cardinal affirmation of Christian faith found in the New Testament and passed on by early Christians. To confess that 'Jesus is Lord' one has to admit that 'God raised him from the dead' (Romans 10.9). ... Not to admit the resurrection of Jesus means that one is not a Christian.*" Ehrman (2014, pp. 131–132): "*Without the belief in the resurrection, Jesus would have been a mere footnote in the annals of Jewish history. ... Belief in the resurrection is what eventually led his followers to the claim that Jesus was God.*" Hoffmann (2010, p. 180): "*It was belief in the extraordinary triumph over death and not the facts of his life that saved Jesus from obscurity.*" (See also Note #22, p. 243.)

In contrast to Christian belief that Jesus' resurrection gave him divine glory, Jews believed that neither Jesus' crucifixion nor resurrection manifested a conquering Messiah engaged in liberating Israel and establishing world peace. To Jews who believed in resurrection, it was to occur in a universal "end-time/apocalypse" when all the dead are restored (Vermes 2008). Being raised from the dead does not make a human divine, but subject to divine judgment. "*At that time your people shall be delivered, everyone who is in the book. Many of those who sleep in the dust of the earth shall awake, some to everlasting life, and some to shame and everlasting contempt*" (Daniel 12.1–2).

To Pagans, human resurrection of a divinity may not have appeared far-fetched. According to Klauck (p. 6), Romulus, legendary founder of Rome, may have served as the Pagan model for Jesus' rapture, having disappeared from Earth to become a God-like figure. However, to a more skeptic non-believer, resurrection appears as an attempt to glorify a terrible event (Jesus' crucifixion) sadly marked by the divine indifference shown in Jesus' last statement. "*My God, my God, why have you forsaken me*" (St. Mark 15.34, St. Matthew 27.46). Interestingly, St. Luke (23.46) changes Jesus' dying statement to "*Father, into your hands I commend my spirit,*" which is then reduced to a three-word announcement in St. John (19.30) "*It is finished.*"

The Gospel sequence thus amends Jesus' view of death from the complaint of an ordinary mortal against providential apathy (St. Mark, St. Matthew), to passive acceptance (St. Luke), to personal involvement or choice (St. John) in order to satisfy the god-like concept that Jesus foresaw the nature of his own death. Schelle (p.5), quotes an earlier commentary (by E. Schwartz) that the editors/redactors of St. John's Gospel have Jesus act as "*a hero who courageously seeks out the enemy (the Jews) and goes heroically to his death, freely renouncing the protection of his followers.*" In contrast, Jesus' complaint of abandonment and the obvious confusion of his disciples on his arrest and crucifixion marked by St. Peter's trifold "denial" (St. Mark 14.68ff, St. Matthew 26.70ff, St. Luke 22.57ff) shows that Jesus did not anticipate his execution, but may have expected his Temple protest to somehow inaugurate his new "Kingdom of God." Charlesworth (1988, p. 144) suggests Gospel statements that Jesus foresaw his crucifixion were "*shaped and created after the fact.*"

Gospel inconsistencies on resurrection include the "short ending" of St. Mark (Chapter 16) who makes no mention at all of a revived vision of Jesus, except for a supposed "empty tomb," and later Gospels who go from resurrected Jesus first appearing to his disciples in Galilee (St. Matthew 28) to claiming a first appearance near or in Jerusalem (St. Luke 24, St. John 20). In one case, he is merely a vision on a mountain top (St. Matthew); in another, he bears an entirely new body and new clothing (St. Luke); and in still another, he has the material body and wounds of his crucifixion (St. John). As Tabor notes (p. 87): "*What we have here is a series of theologically motivated traditions written decades after the event, removed from both place and time, battling out competing stories of what happened after Jesus died. They cannot be harmonized.*"

Some theologians suggest that "*theologized history*" is the proper way to explain events such as Jesus' resurrection or his resurrection of dead Lazarus (St. John 11.1–44); that is, to bring *"theological explanations to bear upon the account of the life of a historical person"* (Tovey, p.222). However, from a less theological view, a mordant question presents itself (O'Collins, p. 16): *"What are we to make of the moral probity of Mark in creating such a fictional narrative (and one that touches on an utterly central theme in the original Christian proclamation) and of the gullibility of the early Christians (including Matthew and Luke) in believing and repeating his fiction as if it were basically factual narrative?"* As also posed by Crossley (2006, p. 25): *"would another discipline in the humanities* [other than theologians] *seriously consider as historically reliable something as spectacular as someone literally rising from the dead?"*

C. A. Evans (2016) suggests that since Jesus was no more than a mild-mannered religious dissident, unthreatening to Roman governing authorities, he would have received proper burial in order to fulfill the New Testament story that he arose from an empty tomb, However, from what we know of the historical Jesus, his acclaim among Jews was much more political than religious: a Jewish Messiah seeking to liberate his fellowmen from exploitation and tyranny (Note #15). His execution was therefore as an insurrectionist promoting a "Kingdom of God" (Note #21, pp. 232ff), and his burial was most likely in accord with all those who threatened the Roman state — not in a tomb but a common grave. According to Ehrman (2014, pp. 161–168), the prevailing Roman practice of keeping crucified bodies on the cross for scavenging dogs and vultures as a further deterrent for rebellion, would have made it highly unlikely that Jesus' body was placed in a tomb to be found later miraculously emptied. There is no evidence that Jesus' family had the status to prevent routine Roman wretched treatment of crucified corpses, or that Roman Governors such as Pontius Pilate ever showed compassion for victims they crucified.

e) That without **belief** in Jesus' God/human figure (and his resurrection) one cannot attain salvation from sin. *"God gave his only Son, so that everyone who believes in Him may not perish but may have eternal life"* (St. John 3.16). *"[T]hose who do not believe are condemned already because they have not believed in the name of the only Son of God"* (Ibid. 3.18). St. Justin Martyr (ca. 150) *"The blood of Christ will deliver from death those who have believed"* (*Dialogue with Trypho, a Jew* CXI, ANF vol. 1, p. 201). Tertullian (ca. 198): *"We want no curious disputation after possessing Christ Jesus, no inquisition after enjoying the gospel! With our faith we desire no further belief. For this is our palmary faith that there is nothing which we ought to believe besides"* (*Praescriptionibus Adversus*, ANF vol. 3, p. 246). Also, *"After we have believed, search should cease; otherwise it must end in a denial of what we have believed"* (Ibid. p. 248).

Christian "belief" not only encompasses faith in events recounted in New Testament narratives, but also in further mystical phenomena. As pointed out previously, St. John's Gospel transforms Jesus from the charismatic Jew from Galilee, to the mystical "Logos," the first creation of God, who then made life and the universe. *"He* [Jesus Christ] *was in the beginning with God. All things came into being through him, and without him not one thing came into being"* (1.2–3). St. Clement of Alexandria (ca. 200), places belief in Jesus Christ as belief in God. *"He who has believed the Logos knows the matter to be true, for the Logos is truth, but he who has disbelieved Him that speaks* [Christ] *has disbelieved God"* (*The Stromates* 2.4, ANF vol. 2, pp. 349–350).

Propounded often by St. Paul onward, redemption from sin (*"Justification"*) occurs only through Christian belief (*"Only Faith," sola fide*), not through deeds (*"Works"*). Acts of the Apostles (4.12): *"There is salvation in no one else, for there is no other name* [Jesus Christ] *under heaven given among mortals by which we must be saved." 2 Timothy* (3.15): *"The sacred writings instruct you for salvation through faith in Jesus Christ." Letter to the Hebrews* (5.9): "*He* [Jesus Christ] *became the source of eternal salvation." 1 Peter* (1.9): "*Even though you have not seen him* [Jesus Christ] *now, you believe in him — for you are receiving the outcome of your faith, the salvation of your souls.*" Belief emerges as the primary determinant of redemption: "good beliefs" are rewarded by salvation, and "disbeliefs" punished. To the Christian Fathers, lack of belief in Jesus Christ, whether purposeful or through ignorance, was as much deserving of punishment as heresy. Belief in Jesus Christ is to be saved by Jesus Christ.

Contrary to emphasizing salvation through "belief," the Jews placed emphasis on active remediation. "*Turn now, all of you from your evil way, and amend your ways and your doings*" (Jeremiah 18.11). Turning back from evil ways — operative behavioral repentance — became a common Jewish theme, known as "Teshuvah": reforming oneself through amendment. "*Among all the proscriptions and ordinances of the Mosaic law, there is not a single one which says: You shall believe or not believe. They all say: You shall do or not do. Faith is not commanded, for it accepts no other commands than those come to it by way of conviction. All the commands of the divine law are addressed to man's will, to his power to act. ... Whenever it is a question of the eternal truth of reason, it does not say **believe**, but **understand** and **know**. ... Nowhere does it say: Believe, O Israel and you will be blessed; do not doubt, O Israel, or this or that punishment will befall you*" (Mendelssohn, p. 100, his emphasis).

f) That by eating the bread and wine in a Christian ritual (the "Eucharist," "Holy Communion," "Sacrifice of the Mass," "The Lord's Supper") one eats (literally or symbolically) the flesh and blood of the God/human figure. St. Paul, *1 Corinthians* 10.16: "*The cup of blessing that we bless, is it not a sharing in the blood of Christ? The bread that we break, is it not a sharing in the body of Christ?* As previously noted (#7, p. 51), St. Paul's authorization for this concept did not come from a known event in Jesus' "Last Supper," but from information he received in an imagined conversation with the resurrected Jesus (*1 Corinthians* 11.23–26).

Remarkably, St. Paul's imaginative dream is repeated almost verbatim by later Gospel writers (St. Mark 14.22–24; St. Matthew 26.26–28; St. Luke 22.19–20), and became a primary sacrament of Christianity as though Jesus, a Torah-respecting Jew, would actually have made statements asking followers to share his blood and flesh. *"We have every reason to believe that Mark got his tradition of the words of Jesus at the Last Supper from Paul. Matthew and Luke, who then used Mark as a source, also repeat what Paul had said decades earlier"* (Tabor, p. 147). In St. John (6.52–57), dating perhaps early in the second century, St. Paul's invention is even further embellished: *"The Jews then disputed among themselves saying, 'How can this man give us his flesh to eat?' So Jesus said to them, 'Very truly, I tell you, unless you eat the flesh of the Son of Man and drink his blood, you have no life in you. Those who eat my flesh and drink my blood have eternal life, and I will raise them up on the last day, for my flesh is true food and my blood is true drink. Those who eat my flesh and drink my blood abide in me and I in them. Just as the living Father sent me, and I live because of the Father, so whoever eats me will live because of me.'"*

Council of Trent: *"Therefore has it ever been a firm belief in the Church of God, and this Holy Synod doth declare it anew, that, by the consecration of the bread and of the wine, a conversion is made of the whole substance of the bread into the substance of the body of Christ our Lord, and of the whole substance of His blood."* The "Mystery of Faith" in the liturgy of the Roman Catholic Mass declares *"When we eat this Bread and drink this Cup, we proclaim your Death, O Lord."* Even more "Eucharistic" is the third century prayer in The Acts of Thomas (158): *"Your holy body which was crucified for our sake we eat, and your life-giving blood which was shed for our sake we drink. Let your body be to us for life, and your blood for the remission of sins*" (Klijn, p. 242). Blood-drinking was a rite found in the "mystery" religions (Note #22) and common in idolatrous sacrifices.

Maccoby points out (1991, p. 125): "*The whole notion of 'eating the god' is familiar in a Hellenistic* [Pagan] *setting, but bizarre in a Jewish one.*" The Biblical restriction in Leviticus (7. 26–27) is quite clear: "*You must not drink any blood whatever, either of bird or animal....Any one of you who drinks any blood shall be cut from your kin.*" Lüdemann (2010, p. 203): "*Can one seriously imagine a pious Jewish teacher of righteousness inviting his followers to partake, even symbolically, of his flesh and blood.*"

g) That Jews must accept this God/human figure as a Messiah who did not deliver the Jews from oppression, nor eliminate the horrors of war (Note #15). "*In Jewish belief...Jesus was not the Messiah precisely because he did not bring about the full restoration of the Jewish people in the Land of Israel and God's universal reign of peace*" (Novak, p. 222). Triumphant Messiahs do not die before they battle Israel's oppressors and lead their followers to victory, universal peace, and termination of evil.

"*Messianism has to do with that category which Christians talk about but have so little ability to grasp; namely history; real visible history; endemic human sinfulness that still goes on long after 'Christ has come'; wars, famines, unjust oppression, murder; the riddle of history and the human condition that goes on unresolved. Judaism alone among the human religions takes this seriously. Christianity, on the other hand, typically uses its christology to deny the question. Messianism has to do with the hope that someday this question will be resolved. ... [I]t has to do with setting history to rights, settling the score of unrequited evil. God intervenes, judges the good and the evil and makes appropriate retribution between them. God changes the human condition so that it sins no more. ... Things become 'very good,' as they were*

124

*intended to be at the beginning. ... One can reject this hope, but one cannot claim that it has already happened in the last two thousand years. ... It has been the great disservice of Christianity to this messianic question that it has either rejected the need for messianic hope or denied that it will ever happen by claiming that it has **already** happened 'spiritually'"* Reuther (1979, p. 244, her emphasis).

h) That Jews do not understand their Scriptures (Notes #7, #18) which, Christians insist, displaced God's favor from Jews to Christians, who now supplant Jews as the "True Israel" (Note #19).

i) That the laws of Moses were abrogated by Christianity. Jews should therefore reject Scriptural commandments and their understanding of Jewish history, and abandon the cultural and religious traditions tied to their identity (Note #18).

j) That Jews accept the Christian view of Jewish guilt, deicide, and demonization embodied in the New Testament. *"His* [Jesus'] *blood be on us and our children"* (St. Matthew 27.25). *"You* [Jews] *are from your father the Devil"* (St. John 8.44).

k) That Jewish suffering from Roman domination and injustice stemmed from God's punishment for refusal to accept Jesus Christ as Savior — a myth that Jews were presumably too sinful to believe.

l) That the Christian Church proposing all these objectionable ideas represents the "Kingdom of God" on earth.

Given that Christian leaders and theologians could not have escaped awareness that Jews would find many or all these conditions unacceptable, one can only conclude that Christian insistence on Jewish conversion was not a real expectation but a phantom designed to further show Jewish sinful obstinacy and "hard-heartedness." *"[T]he perpetual statement of the Gentile leaders that the Jews continued to reject Christ was fundamentally untrue, because they were being offered Him only upon conditions which were false and impossible for a loyal Jew to accept — in other words, an attitude to the whole of Jewish history and to the Law which was based upon Gentile ignorance and misunderstanding, and was quite unsupported by the conduct of Jesus himself"* (Parkes, p. 93).

Even when Christian Fathers, such as St. Irenaeus, wrote some nice things about the Jews (*Against Heresies*, 4.24, ANF vol. 1, p. 495), they were motivated by the notion that Jews, with their long observance of Scriptural commandments, would easily accept Christian reinterpretations. Neusner insists the question posed by the Christian church *"turns on why the Jews do not believe, rather than on what they do believe. The upshot is that there really is no interest at all in 'Judaism' in any form"* (2001, p. 103). Even knowledge that Jesus and his disciples followed Jewish practices (Notes #4, #16), did not diminish Gentile Christianity' hostility to Jews and Judaism.

It is clear that on the religious grounds presented to them, Jews would have found very little to their liking in Gentile Christianity. As Mack points out (1999, p. 134): *"No Jew worth his salt would have been converted when being told that he was guilty of killing the Messiah."* The first unambiguous evidence of Jews defecting to Gentile Christianity comes from three fourth century epitaphs (S. G. Wilson 2006), a time when Gentile Christianity had become the official religion of the Roman Empire and could offer advantages on a large social and political scale.

Taking these points into account, we can see that for many Christians, myths associated with Jesus (stories that are *"neither true nor probable"* — Meggitt 2010, p. 62) became central to their beliefs. *"Without any doubt, the mystery of our religion is great. He was revealed* [as Son of God] *in flesh, vindicated in spirit, seen by angels, proclaimed among Gentiles, believed in throughout the world, taken up* [to Heaven] *in glory"* (*1 Timothy* 3.16).

Mythic themes prevail in many documents about Jesus during the first few centuries, ranging from stories about his infancy to his appearances after resurrection. (White, for example, lists more than 30 different discovered Gospels or Gospel-like materials.) *"It is an open question whether a historical Jesus had anything to do with any of these Jesuses, much less the Jesuses of the* [New Testament] *Gospels"* (Price, p. 266; also Meggitt 2010, p. 73). To paraphrase Crossan (1995, p. 10), *"Gospels are not history remembered but mythology historicized."*

In the world of Acts of the Apostles (written in the end of the first or early second century, and commonly ascribed to St. Luke), rampant mythology was quite acceptable. "[W]*e read of divine intervention in the choice of a successor apostle* [St. Paul], *of tongues of fire coming down and causing people to speak clearly in languages that are foreign to them, of healings by mean of a passing shadow, of death seemingly caused by speech, of an angelic release from prison, of voices from the sky, of scale-like substances falling from formerly blind eyes, of multiple visions with divine messages, of inexplicable survivals of shipwrecks and snake bite, and on and on"* (Tyson (p. 15).

Abounding in Acts of the Apostles are fabricated speeches, imagined voyages, theistic illusions, and inventive prophecies designed to connect Jesus' life with the apostolic expansion of Gentile Christianity. As noted earlier (Note 10.5), among Acts' spurious stories are:

- Authorization of St. Paul's Gentile recruiting mission by presumed agreement with Jesus' Galilean disciples.
- Claims that it is Jews rather than Romans who are the prime enemies of emergent Gentile Christianity.

"For many the chief obstacle to viewing Acts as a work of history arises from its content rather than its style and form. After all excuses have been made for the presumed lack of ancient concern for strict truth, Acts is still lacking. More than a few incidents appear

to have been invented, good sources were not used even if available, and the characterization of both people and events can often be shown to be either highly improbable or contrary to known facts" (Pervo 1987, p. 8).

The shift from "faith" to "history" — to seek actual rather than theological factors in explaining the course of history — is uncomfortable for theologians who have *"the need to make sure that Christianity is not explained in purely human terms"* (Crossley 2006, p. 17). As summarized by Young (2006, p. 12), *"At the heart of the Christian cult lay worship of the Son of God, who preexisted with God, was incarnate in Jesus, is risen from the dead, and now lives and reigns with the Father in Glory."*

The insistence on Christian "faith" over "history" applies even to modern *"apologetic writers [who] do not seem to be aiming for intellectual honesty — they seek to defend Christianity, not the historical method"* (Burke, p. 410). For example, an article by Tàrrech begins with the statement, *"Examination of the historical Jesus cannot leave to one side the question of God's Spirit in his life and work"* (p. 365). Jesus' spiritual experiences are then described (p. 392): *"God's Spirit which 'descends upon him' (Mark 1:10) and immediately 'drives him into the desert' (v. 12). There, the wild beasts surround him in submission (v. 13). The wild beasts represent the evil spirits, who follow Satan but who are now subject to Jesus. ... Jesus sees Satan falling from the heavens 'like lightning' (Luke 10:18)."*

For Jews, faced with imagined Gospel events presented as history, knowing Jesus is to search behind myth for whatever history can be uncovered. To paraphrase Ehrman (2014, p. 2), the issue is not the theology of how God was changed into man, but who was the man that Christian theology turned into God. That is, to search for the real Jesus behind the Gospel stories whose many myths obscure his history (Note #12). Compelling this search is the need to discard deceitful and lethally damaging Christian anti-Jewish fictions woven into the New Testament.

128

We can also see that many of Christianity's basic precepts listed above gave Jews no deeper understanding of Judaism, nor would they have made religious sense to Jesus and his disciples who followed the essentials of Jewish law (Notes #4, and #16, p. 195). For Gentile Christians, on the other hand, the Jewish Scriptures had to be transmogrified to justify Christianity as a "non-Jewish" divinely revealed religion. As discussed in Notes #7, #18–#19, Christian theologians engaged in an endless Biblical search for quotations that could in any way be reinterpreted to provide newly emergent Christianity with an antique façade. Unfortunately for Jews (Note #20), it was therefore Christianity that needed Judaism — that is, its documents and the crucified Jesus — to transform Jesus, a Jewish worshipper of Yahweh, into an object of Christian worship.

12
GOSPEL HISTORY

Scholarly interest in Gospel history has endured for centuries (see, for example, Metzger). Among general findings:

- We know of no writings by Jesus himself, or by any of his immediate disciples. Although Aramaic was the language of the Galilean countryside in which Jesus lived and preached, we have no Aramaic letters or documents from the Galilean Jesus movement. Because of Jesus' opposition to establishment scribes, some scholars claim it doubtful that Jesus himself was literate and capable of writing (Keith).

- The 70 C.E. Roman destruction of Jerusalem and most of its population caused the disappearance of the original Jesus-believing community in Israel, "*and with it perished all its records*" (Brandon 1968, p. 17).

- It has been proposed that early Jesus movement writings were in a lost collection of sayings called the "Q Gospel" (Kloppenborg, pp. 59–64). "Q" was supposedly formulated in Greek sometime after Jesus' death, and versions of "Q" can apparently be found in New Testament Greek Gospels of St. Matthew and St. Luke.

- Some scholars do not accept "Q" (Adamczewski); and of those who accept it, there is debate as to which of the "Q" sayings are authentically Jesus' or drawn secondarily from a Jesus-believing group after his death. (See, for example, Gregg.)

- Whatever their source, there is common agreement that sayings attributed to "Q" must have originated in the Jewish Christian movement, before the Roman destruction of the Jerusalem Temple.

- Koester (2007, p. 241) suggests: *"The people who began the collection of these words may or may not have been personally acquainted with Jesus' ministry during the time of his life. What they preserved were not extensive records of Jesus' teaching, but reformulated summaries of what they had learned. ... What is preserved ... is mostly prophetic sayings and instructions for the community, its organization, and its missionary activity. There is no recourse to Jesus' suffering, death, and resurrection."*

- In contrast to St. Paul's teachings, none of the "Q" sayings oppose Jewish Scriptural laws (Crossley 2006, pp. 102–116). Similarly, *"The Q speeches know nothing of a mission to other peoples ('Gentiles') beyond Jesus' mission to the people of Israel"* (Horsley 2012, p. 113).

- The six or seven "authentic" letters of St. Paul, and seven others that claim his authorship, comprise more than half the "books" of the New Testament (14/27; Vermes 2012, p. 106). In *Galatians* 1.11 he introduced the term "Gospel" as the message he privately received from the resurrected Jesus (Note #2, p. 12ff). St. Paul insisted the "Gospel" ordaining him to preach a new non-Jewish religious doctrine to Gentiles was his exclusive "Gospel of Christ" (*1 Corinthians* 9.12) or "Gospel of God" (*Romans* 1.1), as opposed to non-divine "Gospels" offered by Jesus' Jewish disciples. Note that "Gospel," or "Evangel" in Greek, means "Good News," and was also the term used for birthdays of Roman Emperors (Young 2006, p. 15), and for celebrating their ascension to imperial status (Byrskog, p. 2).

- Dozens of Gospels or Gospel-like documents succeeded St. Paul in the first few centuries, carrying varying histories of Jesus and his disciples with varying theological messages. According to Gamble (p. 24): *"Gospel writers not only used existing written sources but also exercised editorial freedom in adapting them. This makes it plain that the Gospel writers did not attach any special sanctity or even adequacy to their sources and that each meant to provide something better."*

- Decision as to which of these Gospels were "true" and which "untrue" were made by third and fourth century assemblies of Bishops from "orthodox" churches.

- Excluded from "orthodox" ranks were churches whose beliefs were considered "heresies."

- The four Gospels considered "true" first appeared in the interval between 70 C.E. and about 110 C.E. Towards end of the second century they were grouped together by St. Irenaeus (ca. 180) into his "fourfold" Gospel (*Adversus Haeresis*, ANF vol. 1, p. 426). Along with St. Paul's letters and other documents, these later became part of a 27-document New Testament "canon"; where "canon" is commonly understood as the anthology of Christian documents authorized as trustworthy by third and fourth century "Church Fathers."

- Eusebius, Church historian and Bishop of Caesarea, formulated the canonization procedure at the time of the Council of Nicaea (ca. 325 C.E.). He claimed "orthodox" churches inherited their authority for each Gospel's "truth" from Jesus' own apostles who presumably founded these churches three hundred years earlier. These apostles then presumably passed on their "apostolic authority" to succeeding Bishops in a continuous line of "apostolic succession."

- Essentially, what became "authorized," then became "canonized," then became "sacred," and so it remained. The New Testament, according to L. T. Johnson (2007, p. 63) *"draws its authority from the decision of the Christian community to canonize these ancient writings as its sacred texts."*

Notwithstanding Eusebius' claims, we know that concepts of "apostolic origin" and "apostolic succession" were conjectural: neither Gospel authors, nor Gospel editors ("redactors") had been recorded. "[T]*he concept of 'apostolic' was very much broader and could connote, beyond direct apostolic authorship, authorship by followers of apostles, derivation from the general time of the apostles, or even simply an agreement of content with what the church took to be apostolic teaching. ... no N[ew] T[estament] writing secured canonical standing on the basis of apostolicity alone*" (Gamble, p. 68).

Appearing generations after Jesus, at times when even his disciples were probably long dead, in a language he never preached, by writers and "redactors" who were most probably Gentiles, the New Testament Gospels were hardly the product of Galilean eyewitnesses who expected an imminent Kingdom of God. "*Jesus' disciples were lower-class, illiterate peasants from remote rural areas of Galilee, where very few people could read, let alone write, and let alone create full-scale compositions. We don't know of a single author from that time and place, Jewish or Christian, who was capable of producing a Gospel even had she or he thought of doing so. ... They, like Jesus, anticipated that the end of the age was imminent ... These people had no thought of recording the events of Jesus' life for posterity because in a very real sense, there was not going to be a posterity*" (Ehrman 2014, p. 244).

Quoting an array of writers on literacy in Roman Palestine, Hezser offers the following:

- "]N]*obody has so far been able to demonstrate that a school system which aimed at educating the broad public in reading and writing existed in ancient Israel, or even that the knowledge of reading and writing was important by the populace*" (p. 32).
- "[A]*lmost all ancient education 'was purely vocational'*" (p. 33).

- *"We cannot assume that anyone except professional scribes was able to read and write unless the evidence points strongly to the literacy of another group, which ... it does not"* (p. 33).
- *"[I]n some rural town and settlements the literacy rate will have been below one percent, and some villages may not even have had one single individual who could read"* (p. 35).

Gospel authenticity hangs on very little hard information. We do not know who among Jesus' audiences heard and transmitted Jesus' sayings; nor who observed or reported his actions and associated events; nor how accurate the communication from person to person; nor for how long a period oral transmission prevailed; nor where, when, and by whom scribal literacy entered into the sequence of transmission. Nor do we know of any original Aramaic reports; nor how faithful the transcription from Aramaic, oral or written, to New Testament Greek; nor how many manuscripts were written and revised before the final "canonical" selection process in the fourth century.

That different Gospels use similar sayings or describe similar events, can derive from copying from a common source such as the first Greek Gospel (St. Mark); or from St. Matthew and St. Luke sharing Greek "Q" sayings or other sources whose dates are unknown; or from nameless Gospel writers, editors, and transcribers copying one from another. Throughout this process, we should keep in mind that some or many changes were made during transcriptions to suit the recorders' specific concepts and shaped to form their audiences' beliefs. In St. John's Gospel, many of Jesus' sayings and events are quite different from other Gospels, reflecting the author's agenda to enhance Jesus' divinity and undo Jesus from his Jewish heritage.

Since the identity of all those involved in Gospel writing were unknown, the need to present an "apostolic" source was fulfilled by giving each Gospel a single "apostolic" name: St. Mark, St. Matthew, St. Luke, and St. John. Other than six or seven of St. Paul's letters, authorship of the remaining New Testament books also had no recorded information; nor were there founding records of the many "orthodox" churches; nor reliable registries of past Bishops for each such church. To fill gaps of "apostolic succession," lists of Jesus" apostles and "orthodox" Bishops had to be augmented to the point where the meaning of "apostle" became ambiguous. Jesus' presumed original twelve "disciples" were expanded in St. Luke's Gospel into 70 unnamed presumed "apostles" (10.1), and by fourth century Eusebius into even more unknowns.

Eusebius admits "*I confess that it is beyond my power to produce a perfect and complete history*" (*Ecclesiastical History*, Dungan 1999, p. 102). Gospels to be canonized were therefore selected by churches who "*in the present time are held in honor*" (Ibid. p. 103). Gospels of churches not "held in honor" were eliminated, and Gospels disputed by "orthodox" churches were not considered canonical but "apocryphal." A single vote by one of the orthodox churches could place a document into the disputed apocryphal class or reject it entirely; such as the ill-fated Gospel of Peter, rejected because of the negative vote by Bishop Serapion of the Antioch "orthodox" Church (Maier, p. 216). In Eusebius' terms, "orthodoxy," variously understood as "right belief" or "true faith," served as a loose criterion to reject writings "*whose opinions and thrusts of their contents are so dissonant from true orthodoxy*" (Ibid. p. 115).

According to Gamble: "*scripture helped to mold the tradition of faith, and the tradition of faith helped to shape the canon of scripture. In practice, therefore, the criterion of orthodoxy resulted in a circular argument: writings were accepted as authoritative if they conformed to the rule of faith, and the rule of faith was validated by appealing, among other things, to the authority of some of the same writings*" (pp. 69–70). "*Historical criticism has shown that the ancient church was most often mistaken in its claims that the canonical writings were written by apostles, while the history of the canon makes it doubtful that the theoretical criteria (apostolicity, catholicity, etc.) were effective means for canonization"* (Ibid. p. 83).

Among many Christian documents circulating at the time were "Infancy Gospels," "Ministry Gospels," "Sayings Gospels," "Passion Gospels," "Resurrection Gospels," Gospels attributed to different "Holy Women," as well as "Acts" and "Letters" ascribed to different apostles. (See Schneemelcher; Ehrman and Pleŝe; J. K. Elliot; Miller 1992.) The fictitious ascription of such documents to presumed apostles and even to Jesus are traditionally called "pseudonymous" — a scholarly euphemism for "forgeries" — intentional deceptions meant to gain attention and establish "apostolic truths" by counterfeit authority. According to Ehrman (2011b, p. 19), *"At present we know of over **a hundred** writings from the first centuries that were claimed by one Christian author or another to have been forged by fellow Christians."* *"Even apostles of Jesus who, in real life, could not have written a paragraph in Greek had their souls depended on it — Simon Peter, James the brother of Jesus, and John the son of Zebedee, for example — had writings attributed to them"* (Ehrman 2013, p. 532). About half the New Testament (13 of its 27 items) has counterfeit ascriptions (Ibid. p. 529). Ironically, a posture of "truth" and prohibition against "lies" can be professed by forgers themselves, as one finds in New Testament letters that many scholars believe were falsely ascribed to St. Paul, such as letters to the *Ephesians* and *Colossians* (Ibid. p. 541).

As mentioned in Note #4, the four Greek language New Testament Gospels appeared in periods after the 70 C.E. destruction of the Jewish Jerusalem Temple. Until about 150 C.E. most Christian communities used only a single Gospel (Schneemelcher Vol. 1, pp. 20–21), anonymously authored and revised by their individual churches and copyists. For example, the original ending of St. Mark, the earliest of the four New Testament Gospels, ignored or showed no awareness of Jesus' resurrection, a serious omission of later

Christian belief. By the second century we know this defect was corrected by material added from St. Matthew, St. Luke, and St. John (Trobisch, pp. 134–136).

What the original Gospel authors actually wrote remains therefore conjectural since we have no Gospel manuscripts that can be examined earlier than the year 200 C.E.. According to Koester (2007, p. 53), the illusion that the New Testament Gospels accepted by the Christian Fathers in the third and fourth centuries "*are almost identical with the* [original] *autographs cannot be confirmed by any external evidence. On the contrary, whatever evidence there is indicates that not only minor, but also substantial revisions of the original texts have occurred during the first hundred years of the transmission.*"

In many details each Gospel was unique, modified to fit religious views and needs of its individual community, or as Rousseau states (p. 58), "*designed to steer its audience through a labyrinth of choices*" — to establish what is to be believed. None of the Gospel texts were "*considered inviolable. On the contrary, their texts could be reused freely in new forms of writing, be expanded by new materials, and be shaped otherwise according to the demands of the community. All these gospels were primarily produced not as 'literature' but as writings destined for oral performance; memory of texts heard and interpreted could also find its way into the copying of texts*" (Koester 2005, p. 43).

Removed from Jesus' Aramaic-speaking followers in Israel-Palestine by language, time, and distance, transmission of Jesus" sayings and acts into "Gospels" thus became quite detached from their original environs. Condemned as "Judaizers" (Note #17), Jesus' immediate Galilean followers had little influence on St. Paul's Gentile Greek-speaking Christian congregations with their different backgrounds and concerns. Other than in their imaginations, neither St. Paul, nor the Gentiles he converted, nor the Gentiles whom they converted, nor those who wrote the Gospels, ever saw or heard the

Galilean Jesus. The stories that St. Paul, Gentile Christian converts, and Gospel writers told about Jesus *"in virtually every case were not people who accompanied Jesus during his public ministry"* (Ehrman 2016, p. 83). For example, the oldest Gospel, St. Mark's, whose many elements were later incorporated into St. Matthew's and St. Luke's Gospels, *"shows unfamiliarity with the geography of Palestine (e.g. 5.1; 6.45; 7,31; 8.22; 10.1; 11.1), Jewish customs (7.2–4; 10.2; 14.1; 14.64) and even the Jewish leadership groups (e.g. 3.6; 6.17; 8.15; 12.13). ... The Gospel is a product of a long process of* [non-Israel] *community tradition and not of direct eyewitness testimony."* (Telford, pp. 11–12).

As many studies have shown, conversations and events passed on orally from one to another, even over short periods of time — let alone over long periods — are not faithful to their origin (Ehrman 2016). Not only are details distorted but even their "gist" can be notably modified. Oral cultures can not only invent imagined events and sayings, but can restate and modify actual events or sayings in entirely new ways relevant to their new context. *"Whoever performs the* [oral] *tradition alters it in light of his own context"* (Ibid. p. 186). "Memories" of the past easily change to fit needs of the present.

In Allison's study (pp. 2-7): *"Remembering is not like reading a book but rather like writing a book. If there are blanks, we fill them in. If the plot thins, we fill it out. ... [W]e may well recollect what we assume was the case rather than what was in fact the case. ... We are apt to project present circumstances and biases onto our past experiences. ... Output does not match input. ... [I]ndividuals transmute memories into meaningful patterns that advance their agendas. Collectives do likewise. ... Just as we take on different roles for different occasions, so too do we shape our memories according to the varied settings in which we find ourselves. ... Utilizing the past to promote current interests — the classical form critics saw this in every page of the canonical Gospels — leads to alterations.*

... When, as in the canonical Gospels, memory becomes story, narrative conventions inescapingly sculpt the result."

Telford (p. 22) points out that detailed analyses of St. Mark's Gospel *"uncovered the extent to which the evangelist selected, arranged, linked altered, modified, reshaped, expanded and in some cases even created the material of which his Gospel is composed. Where the traditions needed to be woven together into a connected presentation, for example, it was he who provided the seams which link the individual sayings or stories together or the summary passages linking sections of the narrative. ... Where individual traditions lacked indications of time or place, it was he who frequently supplied them with a chronological, topographical or geographical setting. ... Where such traditions required comment or explanation, he introduced parenthetical statements. ... [T]he evangelist was motivated by literary and theological concerns than by purely historical ones."*

In Schröter's words (pp. 18–19), *"the Gospels are witnesses that narratively rework and theologically interpret the events of Jesus' activity and fate."* Luz, in a review of St. Matthew's Gospel (p. 57), describes a sampling of Jesus stories as "narrative fiction": instances of *"created versions of orally transmitted texts"*, as well as (pp. 59–60) *"fictional devices to present his readers with the definitive separation of the community from the Jews. In this way, the narrative is subservient to the theological message"*.

Müller (p. 33) sums up the four Gospels in the following way: *"Because it is not history writing, what is related does not necessarily refer to real events, but stories as well as speeches and parables may well have been created as narrative expressions of proclamation. Thus the speeches in Matthew and John clearly are Matthean and Johannine respectively, and the same pertains to the parables unique to the Gospel of Matthew and the Gospel of Luke: they are wholly in accordance with the theology of each gospel respectively. The assumption that each gospel author has been highly creative in their presentation of the earthly Jesus is strengthened by the acknowledgement that they are written for internal use, that is, for use in congregational worship."*

Given their different origins in time and place, and the succession of "redactors" and copyists that transmitted them, it is no surprise that by the time the four Gospels began appearing (40 to 70 years after Jesus' death) and by the time their contents were fixed as "canonical" (more than two and a half centuries after his death), there were many narrative and prescriptive differences between them. These included varied accounts of Jesus' supposed genealogical descent from King David, (as fictional as King Herod's supposed Davidic descent); when Jesus cleansed the Temple; when he died; events in his professed resurrection; and whether he permitted exception to remarriage after divorce. Such differences *"could be multiplied several hundred-fold"* (Petersen 2004, p. 53). Focusing on proclaiming their religious message, Gospel writers and redactors were unable, or felt little need, to distinguish between actual and imagined events. (See also Ehrman 2003, pp. 169–170.)

In addition to editorial differences and inventions, many obvious copying errors in Gospel manuscript transcriptions also raise questions about textual reliability. Ehrman (2003, p. 219): *"We find that no two copies (except for the smallest fragments) agree in all their wording. There can only be one reason for this. The scribes who copied the texts changed them. Nobody knows for certain how often they changed them, because no one has been able yet to count all of the differences among the manuscripts. Some estimates put the number at around 200,000, others at around 300,000 or more. Perhaps it is simplest to express the figure in comparative terms: There are more differences among our manuscripts than there are words in the New Testament."* According to Curry (p. 113), there are *"about 500,000"* textual variants among the more than 5,600 archaic Greek New Testament manuscripts now available, none of which are yet established as non-error originals.

For example, a fourth century New Testament manuscript, the *Codex Sinaiticus*, discovered in Mount Sinai's St. Catherine's Monastery, is estimated to bear over 24,000 changes. *"There are insertions and deletions of single words or letters, minor substitutions, corrections and alterations to spelling, changes to accentuation and the modification of marks used to denote words which have been abbreviated. Substantial changes involving the substitution, deletion or addition of large changes of text are fewer. But there are still several hundreds of these, the count depending on where the cut-off point is chosen for the number of characters involved"* (Cresswell, p. 60).

How then can one be sure of what one reads? *"Is the text of the New Testament reliable? The reality is there is no way to know. If we had the originals, we could tell you. If we had the first copies, we could tell you. If we had copies of the copies, we could tell you. We don't have copies in many instances for hundreds of years after the originals. There are places where scholars continue to debate what the original text said, and there are places where we will never know"* (Ehrman 2011c, p. 27).

Since so many historical, editing, and transcriptional differences characterize the canonical books, the issue plaguing theologians (see, for example, Chapman) is how can secular language and transmission, with all their many limitations, preserve divine inspiration? That is, since canonization did not prevent a history of "revisions of revisions of revisions," how can one discern that the Biblical editors, redactors, and error-prone copyists were so "divinely inspired" that every (or even any) word in the Bible, inconsistencies and contradictions notwithstanding, comes directly from God? Other than assumed "faith," no theologian has ever shown that inspiration more "divine" than the "fleshly human" accounts for what we read in the Bible.

Nevertheless, questionable differences and origins were ignored, and the four New Testament Gospels were given the special status of "Apostolic Scriptures" in the third and fourth centuries. St. Augustine (ca. 400) rationalized they could not possibly contain any false or contradictory statements since they were divinely inspired by apostolic authors. *"The confirmation of the universal and unquestionable truth of the Divine Scriptures have been delivered to us ... by the apostles and have on this account been received as the authoritative canonical standard"* (*Letters* LXXXII.7, NPNF Series 1, vol. 1, p. 351). *"What is held by the whole Church, is rightly held to have been handed down by apostolic authority"* (Ibid. *On Baptism, Against the Donatists* IV.24, NPNF Series 1, vol. 4, p. 461). That none of these "Apostolic Scriptures" were written by a Jesus disciple was a lack conveniently amended, as noted above, by providing apostolic names to each of them.

C. S. Evans (p. 155), a modern theologian, suggests that official clerical approval was sufficient to confer divine origin: *"the fact that the Church recognized the books of the New Testament as canonical* [apostolic] *is itself a powerful reason to believe that these books are indeed the revelation God intended humans to have."* According to other theologians (e.g., Kruger), canonization of books in the New Testament were not determined by clerical choice but by their intrinsic "Holy Spirit," recognized by those possessing "Holy Spirit." However, which Holy-Spirited claimants were "orthodox" and which were not, was a contentious issue that required decision by conferences of the Christian Fathers. The criterion of divine inspiration thus really became a matter of clerical judgment and expediency. As Gamble put it (p. 72), New Testament writings *"were judged to be inspired because they had previously commended themselves to the church for other, more particular and practical reasons."*

As to their content, Charlesworth points out (1988, p. 59) there is a *"vast difference between the edited documents in the New Testament and the earlier traditions that lie behind them."* Some of these differences have been mentioned in Note #4, and others, along with

142

their effects, have been taken up throughout this monograph. Although a persistent quest of many historians has been to find the "Historical Jesus," reliable information obtained so far seems minimal and problematical (Zindler). As might be expected of writers unfamiliar with past unrecorded events, the New Testament reports little of who Jesus actually was: there is guesswork but no record of the years of his birth and death, and little, if anything, reliable about his development and personal history. Since we can so little depend upon historical accuracy in "Acts of the Apostles" (Smith and Tyson, and also pp. 90 and 126 above), we can only be sure of the existence of St. James the Just (Yakov) and St. Peter (Shimon), evidenced in St. Paul's letters. In general, we have negligible information about Jesus' other male disciples in terms of names, numbers, backgrounds, and histories — and even less information about his female followers.

Very little is given of the relationship between the Jesus movement and that of John the Baptist who baptized Jesus. Water immersion (the "Mikvah"), a rite used by Jews to expunge outer impurity, was employed by John the Baptist to achieve repentance and forgiveness of sin (St. Mark 1.4). That supposedly sinless Jesus would have sought forgiveness of sin was an uncomfortable embarrassment to Christians that Gospel writers tried to explain away (e.g., St. Matthew 3.13–15), and St. John's Gospel eliminated Jesus' baptism entirely. St. Paul used baptism to transcend mere "repentance," converting it into a mystical sacrament of being "*baptized **into** Christ Jesus ... so that, just as Christ was raised from the dead by the glory of the Father, so we might walk in newness of life. For if we have been united with him in a death like his, we will certainly be united with him in a resurrection like his*" (*Romans* 6.3–5)." Emulating magically dying and being reborn in contemporary "mystery" religions, Pauline baptism became the heart of Gentile Christian initiation.

Although there is no evidence that Jesus ever instituted baptism for his followers, we do know that Jesus' theme of an imminent "Kingdom of God," rewarding the righteous and condemning the wicked (St. Mark 1.15), was influenced by John the Baptist and most probably earlier Jewish prophets such as Isaiah (Note #15, p. 173). As time went on, and the anticipated Kingdom failed to appear, it was turned into a future expectation (St. Matthew 24.44, St. Luke 12.40) which St. John's Gospel (18.36) lengthened into something heavenly — "*not from this world.*"

In sum, the New Testament Gospels scaled down the twisted scramble of complex interacting events in first century Israel into a short tale about a man who lived in Israel's Galilee and preached a coming "Kingdom of God" to his fellow Jews. Other than a religious agenda, New Testament stories offer only bare hints of the social, economic, and political influences affecting Jesus and motivating his actions (Note #15). We learn little of the oppressive role Imperial Rome played in Israel, nor of the corruptions of Israel's aristocrats and leaders, nor of the stressful lives of Jesus' Galilean audience. When Jesus' ministry began and how long it lasted is also a mystery. Three of the New Testament Gospels shortened Jesus' public appearances to only a single year and St. John's to two years. What is mostly given in the Gospels is therefore what Christians were expected to believe about Jesus, framed in dutiful religious stories that lack credible evidence. "*The canonical gospels of the New Testament shifted Jesus' focus from social relations to relations between human beings and God. In this sense, the New Testament made an early contribution to obscuring the meaning of Jesus' resistance*" (Oakman 2008, p. 297).

Despite such failures, interspersed throughout these stories are bits of the historical Jesus that can be connected to the dynamic environment of the time — a prelude to the imminent Great Jewish Revolt of 66–72 C.E. (See Notes #4, #9, #15 and extensive reviews in Crossan 1991; Fredriksen 1999; Meier; Thiessen and Merz; Vermes

144

1973.) Theological myths about Jesus may obscure but do not completely hide *"his first century context as both an apocalyptic prophet and a champion of social and economic justice for an oppressed people"* (Gowler, p. 80).

As mentioned earlier (Note #4, p.38), contrary to what we might expect, St. Paul's letters, earliest of New Testament writings, say little of historical Jesus, and according to Lüdemann's analysis (2010, p. 212) *"cannot be considered a reliable witness to either the teachings, the life, or the historical existence of Jesus."* St. Paul records almost nothing of Jesus' sayings; nor anything of his earthly life; nor makes any mention of his trial, only that he was crucified; nor offers any hint that Jesus would have supported St. Paul in disputing Jewish notions of God, Mosaic Law, and Temple observances. To St. Paul, crucifixion transformed Jesus into a mystical occult figure *"I have been crucified with Christ, and it is no longer I who live but it is Christ who lives in me"* (*Galatians* 2.19–20). According to Scroggs, (p. 111), St. Paul's *"lack of interest in the earthly Jesus'* comes from the view that Jesus' primary importance to Christianity derives not from his life but from his believed resurrection, in which *"Jesus has become Lord of the Cosmos."* (See also Notes #14, #22.)

It is clear that "canonization" of the New Testament completely ignored synagogues of Jewish Christians whose "traditions" were certainly more closely derived from Jesus and his immediate Jewish disciples than the "apostolic" traditions of "orthodox" Gentile Christian Churches. Sadly, within less than a century of Jesus' death, Gospel writers attempted to turn the Jewishness of Jesus and his disciples into an unsanctified religion practiced by a demonical people (Notes #6, #8, #13).

In essence, New Testament writers transformed religious advocacy into biased dramatized history; in which Gospel "truth" became a distillation of Christian "faith" that far overshadowed historical "fact." To modern Christian theologians, such stories of "faith" are euphemized as "traditional" or "collective memory," and the "Divine Spirit" claimed to have guided the Gospels, is more important than Gospel reliability (Stewart, pp. 6–7). In the words of a notable Christian theologian: "*Not the historical Jesus, but Jesus Christ, the preached Christ, is the Lord*" (Bultmann, p. 208).

From all discussed so far, I believe it difficult to accept:

1. Jesus' illiterate Galilean Aramaic-speaking followers memorized — supposedly without fault or change — the events, interactions, and sayings ascribed to Jesus.

2. Notwithstanding evidence that information is easily modified between hearers and speakers in chains of transmission, these "memories" were passed on orally for four or more decades after Jesus died— again supposedly without fault or change.

3. Transmitted oral "memories" were then translated into the Greek language — again supposedly without fault or change —by later non-Galilean writers and editors who never saw or heard Aramaic-speaking Jesus.

4. The Greek writings about Jesus were then copied and recopied — again supposedly without fault or change —by different copyists and editors, until four "Gospels" (those of Saints Mark, Matthew, Luke, and John) were given a combined "orthodox" status in the last quarter of the second century (182–188 C.E.) by St. Irenaeus, and subsequent copies of these Gospels "canonized" as divinely inspired by clerical Councils from the fourth century onward.

5. The four "Gospels", with all their many variations and erraticisms, must therefore represent unquestionably faithful accounts of exactly what was said by Jesus, exactly what Jesus experienced, exactly how Jesus acted, and exactly why and how he died.

As egregious as these factors are in accepting overt anti-Jewishness in Synoptic Gospel accounts (St. Mark, St. Matthew, and St.

Luke), it is certainly even more egregious in accepting blatant Jew-hatred in St. John's Gospel, which uses the term "Jew" 70 times — more than four times their combined usage in the other three Gospels.

St. John 5.10: "*So* **the Jews** *said to the man who had been cured, 'It is the Sabbath; it is not lawful for you to carry your mat.'*" 5.15–16: "*The man went away and told* **the Jews** *that it was Jesus who had made him well. Therefore* **the Jews** *started persecuting Jesus because he was doing such things on the Sabbath.*" 10.19–20: "*Again* **the Jews** *were divided because of these words. Many of them were saying: 'He has a demon and is out of his mind. Why listen to him?'*" 10.24: "*So* **the Jews** *gathered around him and said to him,…'If you are the Messiah, tell us plainly.'*" 10.31–33: "**The Jews** *took up stones again to stone him…***The Jews** *answered, 'It is not for a good work we are going to stone you, but for blasphemy.'*"

In all of St. John, Jesus is not a "Jew" but an "Israelite." Only once — and that by a Samaritan woman used to characterize Jewish-Samaritan hostility— is Jesus called a "Jew" (4.9). Casey points out (2010, p. 28) that St. John divides Jesus' audience into two ethnic groups (2.6): "'*the Jews' and 'his disciples' even though all Jesus' disciples were Jewish.*" Some scholars claim that St. John's use of the Greek name *Ioudaioi* meant local inhabitants of Judea in southern Israel (as opposed to Galileans?). But Judeans were Jews, and such circumlocution does little to diminish its pejorative usage. In St. John, Jesus' sympathizers "fear Jews" from Galilee to Judea (17.13, 19.38, 20.19) including Israel's synagogues (12.42). Similarly, St. John's terms "King of the Jews" (18.33, 39; 19.3, 14, 15, 19, 21) and "Passover of the Jews" (2.13; 6.4, 11.35) obviously means all Jews, not just Jews in the Judean province (Tanzer, p. 113). Freyne (2014, p. 109) reports that "Judeans" was a literary term for all Jews by a second century B.C.E. author that refers to "*the twelve tribes of the Judeans.*" For Gospel readers and translators *Ioudaioi* remains "**Jews**" and, according to St. John, "**Jews**" are not merely ignorant but contemptible.

Reinhartz (p. 342): "*...the Fourth Evangelist was less concerned to present a historical conflict between Jesus and the Jews than to set them up as two opposing poles of his Christology* [Jesus' divine attributes]*, his Soteriology* [salvation through Jesus] *and his narrative. That is, while the evangelist may have believed that a conflict between Jesus and the Jews had occurred, his concerns were more literary and theological than historical.*" In St. John, not only is Jewish ancestry claimed to be of "the Devil," and "Jews" are unrelenting enemies who seek to kill Jesus, but Jewish ritual observances are also rejected by Jesus. Since parables were a common Jewish teaching method, Jesus' role as a Jewish teacher (Rabbi) is also denied by picturing him never uttering a single parable. It is also hard to imagine that St. John's Gospel's complex theological claims (e.g., 1.1-18) were supposedly written by one of Jesus' countrified Galilean Jewish disciples ("*the disciple whom Jesus loved*" (21.20-24)), all of whom may have expected an imminent "Kingdom of God," but none of whom displayed St. John's Gospel's theological sophistication, such as placing Jesus in Genesis.

"*In the Gospel of John, the philosophical incorporation of anti-Judaic midrash* [commentary] *reaches the highest development in the New Testament. ... we have two worlds: the spiritual world of light 'above'* [non-Jewish Gentile Christianity] *and the dark alienation from the divine 'below'* [Jews and Judaism]" (Ruether 1974, p. 111). "*By mythologizing the theological division between 'man in God' and 'man alienated from God' ... John gives the ultimate theological form to that diabolizing of 'the Jews' which is the root of anti-Semitism in the Christian tradition*" (Ibid., p. 116).

To Casey (1996, p. 228): "*The history of Christian anti-Semitism is not only horrifyingly wicked: it is also centrally deceitful. The fourth Gospel is at the centre of this deceit. Here Jesus is wrongfully represented as condemning 'the Jews.' Here grounds such as his deity are put forward which were never put forward by him, and which safely ensured that Jews who maintained their identity, the*

148

same identities as that of Jesus and the first apostles, would turn down the Gospel and therefore suffer persecution. ... This Gospel is a standing contradiction of the Jewish identity of Jesus and the first apostles. It is not a source of truth."

Summarizing studies by a large number of Biblical scholars, Miller (1999, p. 143) points out: *"The evangelists are interested in faith more than in facts. We also know that they felt free to invent facts by creating stories out of whole cloth if this would enhance their proclamation of faith."*

"Faith is the assurance of things hoped for, the conviction of things not seen" (*Letter to the Hebrews* 11.1).

13
CHRISTIAN JEW HATRED
AND ANTISEMITISM

Until Christianity's success, common ethno/racist prejudices did not lead to systematic ethno/racist persecutions (Note #5). *"An anti-Jewish 'movement' existed in antiquity only from time to time, and in certain localities. Thus there was no such thing as a continuing anti-Semitic stream"* (Conzelmann, p. 132). However, the picture for Jews changed radically in the fourth and fifth centuries C.E. when Rome adopted Christianity as its official religion (Note #23).

The more modern terms for Jew-hatred — "antisemite" and "antisemitism" — were coined by a nineteenth century German Jew-hater, Wilhelm Marr. Marr did not use "Semite" for Semitic people such as Arabs, but as formalism for "Jew," and so it remains understood. Marr's purpose was to deny Jews human rights, and in 1879 he helped found the international "Antisemitic League," an organization designed to foster political support for antisemitism. *"To bring all non-Jewish Germans of all confessions, all parties, all positions in life to one common and close union, that will strive towards one goal ... to save our German fatherland from complete Judaization"* (Katz, p. 261).

Among notable antisemites were Richard Wagner, composer, and Houston Stewart Chamberlain, historian and political philosopher. Chamberlain's theories, espoused by various influential Christian theologians and ideologues in Nazi Germany, included the concept that Israel's Galileans were really Aryans, as was Mary, Jesus' mother. Jesus was therefore not a Jew but an Aryan, and Christianity therefore had no Semitic origin or connection. This racist concept was then widely promoted by German Christian theologians during the Nazi period (Heschel 2008, also Spicer), and even Jewish converts to Christianity were not spared racist identification and persecution.

Karl Adam (Professor of Theology at Tübingen University): *"According to biological laws there can be no doubt that the Jew as Semite is racially foreign and will remain racially foreign. It will never be possible to integrate the Jew into the Aryan race: no 'mixing of blood' would ever permit this to happen. Blood is the physiological basis of our intellect (Geistigkeit), of the special way that we feel, think, and want; it has given definitive shape to the Germanic myth, and to German culture and history. Therefore German self-assertion demands that we protect the purity and the freshness of this blood, and secure this through force of law. This demand springs from our well-ordered love of self: the love of self that for Christian morality is the natural prerequisite for love of neighbor"* (Connelly, pp. 20–21).

German theologians used such "racist doctrines" to create a "Holy Reich" that would be acceptable to Nazi ideologues. *"Hitler's regime was so largely based on the myth of universal popular support that the official acquiescence of the churches was a vital factor sustaining the Third Reich and permitting it to work its wickedness freely"* (Allen, p. 123). When World War II began in 1939, *"95 percent of the eighty million people of the greater German Reich was still registered as members of the Catholic or Evangelical* [Protestant] *Churches, and even the majority of the three million Nazi Party members* [including Hitler!] *still paid the Church taxes and registered themselves as Christians. The united support of all these millions of German Christians was needed for the war effort if Hitler's plans for Germany were to be fulfilled"* (Conway, pp. 232–233). A small number of German clerics, often Protestant and fewer Catholic, individually opposed Hitler and Nazi persecution of Jews, but Christian churches were mostly silent. Among Catholic priests, more than 17,000 served in various capacities in the Nazi Wehrmacht during the War (Faulkner Rossi, p. 1). Since two-thirds of Germany's population was Protestant (Erickson, p. 24), the number of Lutheran and Reformist pastors serving Hitler's war machine probably exceeded or even doubled that number.

Even theologians willing to recognize Jesus' Jewish roots, persisted in claiming that Jesus discarded his "carnal" Jewish origin in order to establish "spiritual" non-Jewish Gentile Christianity. This attitude prevails long after the World War II defeat of Nazi Germany. Heschel (2009, p. 231): *"Jesus begins his life as a Jew, but ends his life as a Christian. Christianity itself is achieved ... through a process of emergence, a religious purification that attempts to rid the Jewish from the Christian."*

Antisemitism long shadowed Christian culture throughout Europe. The "Jewish Question" — how to contend with Jewish unwelcome presence —became a common political issue with "solutions" ranging from Jewish elimination through conversion or exile. Gerhard Kittel for example, like Karl Adam, Professor of Theology at Tübingen, author of the still-used *Theological Dictionary of the New Testament*, joined the Nazi Party on Hitler's ascension to power in 1933 to validate Hitler's antisemitism with religious Christian support. Kittel declared: *"It is not enough to base this battle* [against the Jews] *on racial points of view or current attitudes alone. The actual, complete answer can only be found when one succeeds in giving the Jewish question a religious foundation, giving the battle against the Jews a Christian interpretation"* (*Die Judenfrage*; Ericksen, p. 31). *"Kittel advocated the stripping of citizenship from German Jews, so that a special set of laws could be created to remove them from medicine, law, teaching, journalism — every important niche in German life — and forbid their marriage or sexual relations with non-Jews"* (Ibid., p. 32).

"Without the long history of Christian anti-Judaism and Christian violence against Jews, Nazi ideology could not have taken hold nor could it have been carried out" (*Dabru Emet, A Jewish Statement on Christians and Christianity*; Knowles, et al., p. 183). *"Antisemitism was the most predictable, most virulent hatred running through society. By feeding that hatred, whipping it into white heat, Hitler had, as it were, a supply of energy-hate that could be*

152

turned against anyone who stood in his way. ... In Hitler's totalitarian society every individual who for any reason acted against the interest of the people as defined by the Führer became in that moment a Jew" (Ryan, pp. 157–158). In Hitler's own words: "[T]he *art of all truly great national leaders in all ages consists primarily in this, not to scatter the attention of the people, but rather always to concentrate on a single enemy. It belongs to the genius of a great leader to make quite different enemies appear to belong to a single category"* (Ibid., p. 156, translated from *Mein Kampf*).

Antisemitism *"shaped the worldview of many people, both among those who came with more or less willingness under Hitler's rule and among those who successfully opposed and defeated him. Perhaps that commonality can help explain why the Germans found so many willing collaborators for their projects of extermination* [of Jews] *in many lands they occupied. Perhaps it explains as well why even some of the nations that most firmly resisted the German armies (the United Kingdom, the United States, and immediately after the war, the Soviet Union) nevertheless adopted important anti-Semitic measures of their own, such as closing their borders to Jews seeking to escape their executioners"* (Nirenberg, p. 458).

Although many Christian theologians have expressed concern and regret for the lethal persecution of European Jews, most avoid acknowledging the basic motivations that led Gentile Christianity to condemn Jews and the Jewishness of Jesus and his disciples. Can Christians deal with the notion that *"Christian beliefs contain an antisemitic principle that has warped the Christian mind on the subject of Jews since early times"*? (A. T. Davies 1979a, pp. XIV–XV). (See also Note #25.)

14

ST. PAUL AND "PARTING OF THE WAYS" (also Note #2)

Gentile Christian separation from Jews had its start in St. Paul's letters rejecting Jewish rituals and practices, leading to the first century C.E. split between his Gentile Christian churches and Jewish or Jewish Christian synagogues. *"If you let yourselves be circumcised, Christ will be of no benefit to you"* (*Galatians* 5.2). *"It is not the children of the flesh* [Jews] *who are the children of God, but the children of the promise* [spiritual Christians] *are counted as descendants"* (*Romans* 9.8). *"As regards the Gospel they* [Jews] *are enemies of God"* (*Romans* 11.28).

St. Paul's being *"in* Christ," a phrase he uses almost 50 times, transformed Jesus into a non-Jewish mystical divinity unrelated to the "fleshly" Jesus the Jew or Jesus the Jewish Messiah. Horrell (2002, p. 320): *"To describe an individual (e.g., 2 Cor 12.2) or a group (e.g., Rom 12.5; 1 Cor 3.1) as 'in Christ' is to articulate the core identity designation of the group, the boundary that defines insider* [Christian] *and outsider* [Jew, Pagan]." In St. Paul's Churches, a convert abandons one's previous religion, and joins the new *"in Christ"* Gentile group that overcomes *"the borders and uniqueness of the Jewish ethnic group. ...Only they* [Gentiles] *can fully separate themselves from* [Jewish] *ethnicity, the law, and the flesh"* (Rosen-Zvi and Ophid, pp. 137–139). Note that the more anger directed against an "outsider," the greater the increase in the "insider's" communal identity. *"To you has been given the secret of the Kingdom of God, but for those outside...they may indeed look, but not perceive, and may indeed listen, but not understand; so that they may not...be forgiven"* (St. Mark 4.11–12).

The group needs an enemy to bolster its own inner resources and maintain its own inner sense of value and purposiveness. The group sustains itself by idealizing its own values and setting them in conflict with the denigrated values of other groups. ... [T]he narcissistic basis on which the process operates demands a logic of extremes, in which there is a tendency for all value to be inherent in the in-group and no value or negative value to be inherent else-where" (Meissner, p. 233). *"The politics of othering permeates the discourses of Paul ... Its relentless othering engenders the strategies of marginalization and silencing* [others] *that are inscribed in the Pauline text and reinscribed by contemporary exegetical and theological scholarship"* (Schüssler-Fiorenza, p. 45).

To St. Paul, Jewish "flesh" and Christian "spirit" represented polar opposites of "profane" and "sacred" — akin to Jesus' change from earthly "flesh" to a resurrected divine "spirit." Jesus *"who was descended from David according to the flesh and was declared to be Son of God with power according to the Spirit of holiness by resurrection from the dead"* (*Romans* 1.3–4). Thus, ordinary Jews and Jesus' Jewish disciples saw no more than the "fleshly" Jesus, whereas St. Paul claims to have envisioned Jesus in a new "spiritual" sense that replaces Biblical Mosaic "fleshly Law." *"Even though we once knew Christ from a human* [fleshly] *point of view, we know him no longer in that way. So if anyone is in Christ, there is a new* [spiritual] *creation: everything old has passed away"* (*2 Corinthians* 5.16–17).

"Flesh" and "spirit" are forever in combat: *"For what the Flesh desires is opposed to the Spirit"* (*Galatians* 5.17). This dualism expresses the dualism in fealty to God between Jews and Christians. *"Those who are in the flesh cannot please God"* (*Romans* 8.8). *"All who are led by the spirit of God are children of God"* (*Romans* 8.14). The New Testament Gospels reflect this dualism, using narratives to place Jesus Christ on one side and Jews on the other. It reaches its apogee in St. John's Gospel (8.44–47) contrasting the devil and God: *"You* [Jews] *are from your father the devil, and you choose to do your father's desires. He was a murderer from the beginning and does not stand in truth, because there is no truth in him. When he lies, he speaks according to his own nature, for he is a liar and the father of lies. ... Whoever is from God hears the words of God* [Jesus Christ]. *The reason you* [Jews] *do not hear them is that you are not from God.*"

Behind St. Paul's distinction between "flesh" and "spirit" also lie behavioral and sexual overtones: "[N]*othing good dwells within me that is in my flesh*" (*Romans* 7.18). "[W]*ith my flesh I am a slave to the law of sin*" (Ibid. 7.25). Like other theological innovations, St. Paul's concept of "sin" was uniquely his own (Kelly), claiming that sin originated in Adam, and we, as his descendants, are therefore all sinners: "*sin came into the world through one man* [Adam], *and death came through sin, and so death spread to all because all have sinned*" (*Romans* 5.12).

Following St. Paul, "spirit" versus "flesh" offered Christian Fathers a moral contrast between "spiritual" Christians and "fleshly" Jews — "sexual purity" of Christians versus "carnal appetites" of Jews. Christian baptism is then the "spiritual" replacement for the "carnality" of Jewish penile circumcision. "*Those who belong to Christ Jesus have crucified the flesh with its passions and desires*" (*Galatians* 5.24).

According to S. Drake (pp. 102–103), such contrasts encouraged, if not initiated, "*the image of the sexually imperiled Christian. ...* [St. John Chrysostom] *conceived of Jewishness not merely as a disease but as a contagious epidemic that spread by means of illicit Judaizing men who preyed upon innocent Christian women. ...* [T]*he stereotypes of Jews in Origen's commentaries and Chrysostom's sermons contributed to a climate in which acts of violence against Jews were made thinkable, meaningful, and even endorsed.*" Depicting Jews as sexual predators, blasphemers, and "Christ Killers" set them apart from "moral" Christians as cast-off pariahs subject to social contempt and isolation; a status reinforced by Roman imperial disenfranchisement and Christian violence beginning in the fourth and fifth centuries (Note #23).

Gentile Christian leaders extended the disgrace of Jewishness even to Jewish Jesus-followers (Notes #13, #15), who, for the first few centuries, remained within Jewish identity (Note #16). According to Joan Taylor (p. 94), even after the failed Jewish 66–72 C.E. revolt against Rome, "*there is no reason to think that they* [Jewish Christians] *were considered separate from Judaism, even if other Jews thought they erred in their belief in Jesus as Messiah.*" In fact, archaeological evidence shows that Jews and Jewish Christians lived peacefully together in Trans-Jordan ("Golan") communities during the fourth to sixth centuries. "*This would tend to suggest that a parting of the ways was not deeply felt even here, from which we may extrapolate centuries of peaceful coexistence beforehand*" (Ibid. p. 103). According to S. J. D. Cohen (2013, p. 236) it was Rabbinical avoidance and neglect rather than confrontation that mostly parted the ways between Jews and Jewish Jesus-believers.

In contrast to such gradual "parting" between Jews and Jewish Christians, Gentile Christian leaders distinguished their churches and religious practices from Jews of all types early on. One has only to refer to St. Paul's letters proclaiming an imagined split of Abraham's descendants into Gentile Christians on one hand and Jews on the other — the "uncircumcised" faithful and the "circumcised" sinful, those tied to "the faith" and those tied to "the flesh," those who receive "the promise" and those "cursed by the Law."

As indicated earlier, among features St. Paul added to his division between Gentile Christians and Jews:

- Theology of a divine Jesus Christ as a Yahweh-substitute (*Philippians* 2.10–11, Note #11.*b*).
- Rants against "Judaizers" (*Philippians* 3.2, *Galatians* 1.6–9, Note #17).
- Claim that Jews were "Christ killers" (*1 Thessalonians* 2.14–15, Note #8).
- Claim that Jewish "blindness" prevents them from seeing the "*glory of Christ*" (*2 Corinthians* 4.4, Note #18).

- Claim that Gentile Christians replaced Jews in God's favor (*2 Corinthians* 3.5–6, Note #6).

Freed from obeying Jewish "Law" through faith in Jesus Christ (*Romans* 8.2, 10.4; *Galatians* 3.13, 3.24, 5.1), there is no evidence that St. Paul's Gentile Christians or their leaders joined or proposed to join the synagogues of either practicing Jews or Jewish Christians, or presented themselves to Romans as Jews, or that Romans considered Gentile Christians as Jews. "*Pauline groups were never a sect of Judaism. They organized their lives independently from the Jewish associations of the cities where they were founded, and apparently, so far as the evidence reveals, they had little or no interaction with the Jews*" (Meeks 1985, p. 106).

Given that it took only a single generation after Jesus' death for St. Paul to sanctify non-Jewish Gentile Christianity, "Parting of the Ways" from Judaism appears rapid rather than incremental. Once started, Gentile Christian Biblical exegesis quickly evolved, claiming that Jewish Scriptural writers really intended to provide the platform for an entirely unique Christian religion, appearing many centuries later than the Scriptures themselves — a self-elected inheritor of Scriptures whose rituals and commandments it vehemently denied, and which made no mention of Christians or Christianity. St. Justin Martyr: "[The Jewish Scriptures are] *rather not yours, but ours. For we believe them; but you, though you read them, do not catch the spirit that is in them*" (*Dialogue with Trypho, a Jew*, XXIX, ANF vol. 1, p. 209; also Notes #7, #18, #19).

Ruether (1974, p. 94): "*The anti-Judaic tradition in Christianity grew as a negative and alienated expression of a need to legitimate its revelation in Jewish terms* [Jewish Scriptures]. *… it continues on in the Church Fathers, and even to this day, as an ongoing expression of this same need by the Church to legitimate its Christological midrash by insisting that this actually represents the true meaning of the Jewish scriptures and is the divinely intended fulfillment of Moses, the Psalms, and the Prophets. It is not enough for* *the Christian tradition to hold this opinion. … As long as 'the Jews,' that is, the Jewish religious tradition itself, continues to reject this interpretation, the validity of the Christian view is in question."*

Continued claims to possess the Jewish Scriptures by Gentile Christian leaders were therefore not to maintain alliance with scorned Jews, but to convince Romans of Gentile Christianity's ancient origin by transferring Jewish Scriptural heritage from Jews to Gentiles. Thus, the novel notion that Gentile Christian churches resisted separating themselves from Jews because they felt *"inner-Christian resistance"* against separating Christianity from the Jewish Scriptures (Reed and Vuong, p. 122) ignores the Gentile Christian need to disparage Jews in order to appropriate for themselves the Jewish Scriptures.

It seems clear that in whatever categories we place Judaism and early Gentile Christianity; they should not obscure their essential differences. Multilevel distinctions in foundational documents, religious beliefs, rituals, liturgies, and ethnic backgrounds, are certainly greater than those between traditionally related "sects" and surely mark a significantly bordered religious separation. (See also Niehoff.)

Along with other scholars noted earlier (#10.6), Burns (2016, p. 56) points out that although ancient Rabbis ("Tannaim"), whose discourses are recounted in the third century C.E. Mishnah, may have been aware of Jewish believers in Jesus as a Messiah, they show no knowledge either of St. Paul or his Gentile Christian churches. This absence of early Rabbinical response to Gentile Christianity (Schremer 2009) shows that Jewish religious leaders had no desire to contact Christians, nor were they concerned about any Gentile Christian influence on Jews, nor did they deem St. Paul's churches an extension of Jewish beliefs, customs, and practices ("Judaism"). *"Christianity plays no role of consequence; no one takes the matter seriously. … Israel's sages did not find they had to take seriously the presence or claims of Christianity"* (Neusner 1986, p. 77). To the

Rabbis, St. Paul's Gentile Christianity was as much outside Judaism as idolatrous Paganism.

Charlesworth (2013, p. 293) and some other writers insist that because Jews and Christians share some "DNA" (Jewish Scriptures and some Jewish concepts of God), "*in a deep sense, no parting of the ways can occur universally and conceptually.*" Overlooked is that Gentile Christian and Jewish usage of Jewish Scriptures and its Scriptural deity does not mean common identity in cultural and religious traits, any more than different species sharing some DNA sequences mean they must be alike. Similarly, common anticipation of a divinely-sent apocalyptic figure offering messianic redemption — a Christian Jesus and a Jewish Messiah, a supernatural Son of God and a Son of Man — does not outweigh the multitude of differences that conferred separate social identities on Jews and Gentile Christians.

Thus, although Judaism and Christianity once shared some common features, there is no evidence that this supported further commonality. By the end of the first century or even earlier, whatever their use of Jewish Scriptural documents and apocalyptic beliefs, these two groups interpreted these documents and beliefs completely differently for different purposes; engaged in completely different religious/cultural/ethnic practices; and formed Jewish synagogues and Christian "ecclesia" (churches) recognized by Romans as completely different religious assemblies for different people. Sharing the Jewish Scriptures between Judaism and Christianity did not at all token religious camaraderie.

As we have seen, St. Paul's Gentile Christians and their communities were also judged distinctly unique by Roman Emperors such as Nero and Trajan, as well as by Pliny the Younger (Note #2). *Roman writers do not connect them* [Gentile Christians] *with Judaism in any respect*" (Judge, p. 359). Gospel writers (especially St. John, Note #12), as well as St. Ignatius and other early Christian Fathers similarly express distinctive separation from Jews and Judaism

(Note #5). "According to Dunn (2016, p. 4): "*What was at stake here, in Paul's view, was whether this new faith in/commitment to Jesus (the) Christ meant that gentile believers were converting to Judaism. Was belief in Jesus (the) Christ simply a first step to becoming a Jew? Paul was clear that the answer was no! ... Paul insisted that pisteuein eis Christon* [belief in Christ] *was a full response to the gospel of Christ. To insist on anything more as equally fundamental* [Jewish Scriptural "Law"] *was to diminish and deny the fundamental character and role of faith.*"

St. Paul made clear to his successors: "*a person is justified not by the works of the law but through faith in Jesus Christ ... because no one will be justified by the works of the law*" (*Galatians* 2.16). The "Law"-abiding "Old Covenant" with Yahweh is replaced by Gentile Christianity's "Faith"-abiding "New Covenant with Jesus Christ" (*2 Corinthians* 3.14). Hagner (p. 82) notes that "*the extent of newness makes it impossible to describe Christianity as merely a sect or reform movement within Judaism.*" Ruether (1974, p. 56): "*It was the raising up of faith in Messiah Jesus as a supersessionary covenantal principle — the view that one was not within the true people of God unless one adopted the faith in this form — that caused the break between the Church and Israel.*"

S. G. Wilson (1995, pp. 299–300): "*Most Christians, even before 70 CE, gathered in communities separate from Judaism. They met in churches, the Jews in synagogues (and the Pagans in temples). From the end of the first century they also increasingly worshipped on different days* [Sabbath/Sunday, Passover/Easter, etc.] *and in different ways* [rites, liturgies, sacraments]. *These two things alone would have given them a strong sense of distinct identity, as much publicly observable as privately felt. That these boundaries mattered, and from a very early stage, can be seen in the fierce reaction to those who transgressed them.*"

In Neusner's terms (2001, p. 28): "*Judaism and Christianity are completely different religions, not different versions of one religion. … The two faiths stand for different people talking about different things to different people*." Harlow, (p. 276): "*In sheer demographics, the Jesus movement was overwhelmingly non-Jewish in its constituency by the end of the first century, and in that sense was a largely Gentile religion.*" There are few Jewish Christians recognizable within St. Justin Martyr's new Christian society (ca. 150), and hardly any at all by the time of Tertullian (ca. 200).

Thus, to say that Gentile Christianity is another form of Judaism (Boccaccini) obscures the wide gulf between them that appeared quite early in the elements that define religion: beliefs, rituals, liturgies, customs, histories, festivals, theologies, priestly duties, and clerical hierarchies. Even in burial customs, Jewish and Christian catacombs outside Rome show "*two communities with different values and practices — a situation that had come about because their ways had parted such a long time before*" (M. H. Williams, p. 178). As we have seen throughout this monograph, Gentile Christian leaders' claims to possess the Jewish Scriptures had nothing to do with observing Scriptural "Jewish" conventions, but only to gain an antique history by their "reinterpretations," and convince Romans that these Scriptures were really written to provide "new" Christianity an "old" venerable identity.

Similarly, to say that "Judaism/Jewishness" never became a recognized religion until it was so identified by Roman restrictions in the fourth and fifth centuries C.E., or even centuries later (Boyarin 2012, pp. 2–3), "*neglects the copious evidence indicating that … 'Judaeans' sustained ideologies and behaviors conforming to the religious phenomenon today known as Judaism long before they knew to call their culture by that name. That ancient Jews, therefore, did not uniformly use the term 'Jew' and 'Judaism' is not a useful indicator of how those individuals functioned as a group. It merely indicates that they did not speak English*" (Burns 2016, p. 66). How could it not have been clear to Jews, their Rabbis, and even to

Gentiles, that St. Paul's Gentile Christians were neither "Jews" nor Jewish religion practitioners?

Some writers (e.g., Eisenbaum; Galambush, p. 22) consider the anti-Jewishness that accompanied "Parting of the Ways" as a regrettable interpretation of St. Paul's letters, and join a movement to replace the so-called "Old" version of St. Paul as an anti-Jew, with a "New" version of a "Jew at heart." They claim St. Paul did not really anticipate Gentile Christianity would separate itself from Judaism as extensively as it did (e.g., Gager 2000), but intended only to modify Judaism to include Gentiles. That Christian leaders and theologians long interpreted St. Paul's fulminations against "Judaizers" (Note #17) and Biblical "Law" (Note #18) as a condemnation of Jews was, according to their view, a misreading of his statements and intentions.

However, if we accept St. Paul's message as less anti-Jewish than it seems, serious questions arise.

- In their vituperations against Jews (Notes #6, #8, #12, #17, #18), did Christian leaders and theologians willfully ignore St. Paul's supposedly veiled Jewish/pro-Jewish message for two millennia, or were they so muddled as to inadvertently pervert a Jewish/pro-Jewish message now apparent to revisionist critics?
- Can this presumed misreading of St. Paul's letters be reversed by Christian agreement to discard the extensive development of Pauline Gentile Christian theology and its mythological anti-Jewish revision of Scriptural history going as far back as Abraham or even Adam?

Perhaps the attempt to enhance St. Paul's Jewish image is prompted by the belief that granting St. Paul a pro-Jewish "intent" would somehow diminish St. Paul's embarrassingly anti-Jewish "effect." Can a historic "effect" be ignored or minimized by claiming it had a different "intent"?

Whatever St. Paul's motives — whether we see St. Paul as true Jew, Greek non-Jew, Christian anti-Jew, or some combination thereof (Lüdemann 2002b) — anti-Jewish consequences of his letters spread widely and endured interminably. Two millennia of his readers were imbued with five fundamental notions used by generations of Christian theologians to demonize Jews and create sharp borders between Gentile Christianity and Judaism. To reiterate:

1. The Jews lost God's favor because they had a long history of disobedience and are guilty of the murder of Jesus (*1 Thessalonians* 2.14–15).

2. The Biblical Laws of Moses followed by Jews were negated by the coming of Jesus (*Galatians* 3.24). The Torah is a "*ministry of death*" (*2 Corinthians* 3.7) and prime source of sin that must be discarded by Gentile Christians (*Galatians* 3.10, 5.2). "*No human being*" is justified by "*deeds prescribed by the Law, for through the Law comes the knowledge of sin*" (*Romans* 3.20). Such statements apply both to Gentiles and Jews, since nowhere does St. Paul indicate that either Gentile or Jew can fulfill God's will by obeying the Law; righteousness comes only through faith in Jesus Christ and abandonment of the Law. "*For we hold that a person is justified by Faith* [in Jesus Christ] *apart from works prescribed by Law*" (*Romans* 3.28). "*If justification comes through the Law, then Christ died for nothing*" (*Galatians* 2.21).

3. Upon crucifixion, Jesus the human Jew became a superhuman Gentile savior. Since the Messiah title (Hebrew "Anointed," Greek "Christ") for a political/military leader fighting to liberate Jews from oppression meant little if anything to Gentiles, St. Paul transformed "Christ" into the surname of a divine mystical figure, "Jesus Christ/Christ Jesus Son of God," with transnational transethnic powers extending far beyond that of an alleged Jewish activist. "*Even though we once knew Christ from a human point of view, we know him no longer in*

164

that way" (*2 Corinthians* 5.16). "[A]*ccording to the flesh,* [out] *comes the Messiah* [Christ], *who is God overall, blessed forever*" (*Romans* 9.5). "[S]*cripture has imprisoned all things under the power of sin, so that what was promised through faith in Jesus Christ might be given to those who believe*" (*Galatians* 3.22). To a Gentile audience, the names that St. Paul used for Jesus throughout his letters — "Our Lord Jesus Christ," "Jesus Christ Our Lord," "Christ Jesus" — signified a resurrected God who arose from "*Christ crucified*" (*1 Corinthians* 1.23). To this imagined "Christ event," Jews are pictured as obtusely oblivious. "*The God of this world has blinded the minds of the* [Jewish] *unbelievers, to keep them from seeing the light of the glory of Christ, who is the image of God*" (*2 Corinthians* 4.4).

4. St. Paul's Gospel of "spirituality" enabled his followers to profess historical claims to ("spiritual"!) antiquity. Thus, Abraham, claimed by Jews as their ancestral patriarch because of the "Old Circumcision Covenant" with Yahweh (Note #7, p. 59), becomes the presumed father of Gentile Christianity by reason of his "spirituality." In St. Paul's "New Christian Covenant," circumcision is meaningless, since "spirituality" trumps "flesh," just as "faith" trumps "works" (*Romans* 3.11, 3.28, 4.13, 8.1–10, 9.8; *Galatians* 2.15–21, 3.2–5). The covenantal "Family of God" — St. Paul's Christian "Olive Tree" (*Romans* 11.17–20) — is thus pruned of its faithless Jewish branches and replaced with grafted wild olive shoots of faithful Gentile Christians: "*They* [Jews] *were broken off because of their unbelief, but you* [Gentiles] *stand only through faith*." "Spiritual" Christians from Abraham onward now replace Jews as the true "*Israel of God*" (*Galatians* 6.16) — transcending reality by magically transforming "spiritual" to "real"!

5. Jewish understanding of Biblical history must be amended to accommodate new Gentile Christian interpretations. To St. Paul's Gentile proselytes, it was **their** ancestors who were baptized by Moses "*in the cloud and in the sea*" and of drinking "*from the spiritual rock that followed them, and the rock was Christ*" (*1 Corinthians* 10.1–5). According to a modern Christian theologian (Dunn 1998, p. 508), it is *necessary* for Gentile Christianity to call itself the age-old "True Israelites" in order to justify possession of Israel's Scriptures, supposedly made for Christians and not for Jews. That not a semblance of Gentile Christian "True Israelite" believers in Jesus Christ appeared during the 1500-year interval between Abraham and St. Paul is simply ignored. (See also Notes #7, p. 60; #18, p. 212; #19, p. 220.)

The high contrast between these five Gentile Christian notions and common Jewish beliefs, whether ancient or modern, makes it quite difficult to see St. Paul or any of his followers as "a Jew at heart." Not one of these concepts can be called a simple variant of Judaism that an observant Jew of any time or place could accept. In his *Philippians* letter (3.2–9), St. Paul's posture of being Jewish (circumcised, a Pharisee, etc., see also *Galatians* 2.15) is overshadowed by his argument that he can discard his Jewish background with impunity because his faith "in Christ" has liberated him from the "flesh." *Whatever gains I had* [as a Jew]*, these I have come to regard as loss because of Christ*" (*Philippians* 3.7).

In his own words, St. Paul's claim to being a Jew was merely expedient: "*To those under the* [Jewish] *law I became as one under the law (though I myself am not under the law) so that I might win those under the law. To those outside the law I became as one outside the law (though I am not free from God's law but am under Christ's law) so that I might win those outside the law*" (*1 Corinthians* 9.20–21). To St. Paul, , not even Jews, let alone Gentiles, need to be or remain Jewish.

"Paul routinely subordinated his birth identity to his new racial identity in Christ" (Sechrest, p. 227). He made clear that Jewish food laws do not apply to himself or to any faithful Jesus-believer. *"I know and am persuaded that nothing is unclean in itself; but it is unclean for anyone* [Jews] *who thinks it unclean"* (*Romans* 14.14); and he expresses the same attitude toward Jewish Sabbath observances (*Romans* 24.5–6). Scriptural Law observance therefore has no redemptive value, and according to Moo's analysis of St. Paul's letter to the *Galatians* 2.15–21, *"Jews are 'sinners' just like the* [non-Christian] *Gentiles"* and *"only a total reliance on Christ, by faith"* can *"put them right with God"* (p. 157).

Also, St. Paul's efforts in collecting funds for Jerusalem's Jewish Christian "Saints" (e.g., *Romans* 15.25–26) may have been no more than claiming a figurative tie to Jesus' original disciples, such as James the Just, in order to gain standing as an apostle. He showed little trust in the religious fellowship of Jesus' Galilean-Jerusalem disciples, vehemently denouncing their emissaries as "Judaizers" (Note #17) and was quite disdainful of their worth as "Saints," calling them *"supposed"* leaders who *"contributed nothing to me"* (*Galatians* 2.6).

Although St. Luke makes no special point of St. Paul discarding his Jewish name "Saul" (Acts of the Apostles 13.9), this act could signify, according to L. T. Johnson (1992, p. 227), discarding a burdensome Jewish load: *"Perhaps we are to see Saul, at the moment he takes on his new and proper identity as Paul the Apostle, fighting the final battle with the 'Jewish false prophet' within him, blinding the hostile magician that is his former* [Jewish] *self at the moment he assumes his* [Christian] *role as 'light to the Gentiles.'"*

As to realization of Jewishness by Gentile followers of St. Paul's letters, there is no indication they would consider themselves Jewish, either in behavior or belief. Nor so would Gentile readers of the heritage that St. Paul passed on to St. Luke, St. John, Acts of the Apostles, and other New Testament documents. Thus, St. John's

Gospel *"was not written to foster conversation between Jew and Christian but to set boundaries between them"* (Burns 2012, p. 43, also Note #12). *"With regards to his* [St. Paul's] *converts, it is noteworthy that not a single one can be identified from the Pauline letters as being Jewish"* (E. P. Sanders 1986, p. 88). Again, as in Note #2, St. Paul and the leaders of his churches created an unbridgeable gap separating their churches from all synagogues, whether Jewish or Jewish-Christian. The boundaries were not blurred, but firm.

Note that Marcion, whose followers were probably the most numerous of all Christians in the mid-second century (Clabeaux, p. 515) — who insisted that Jewish Scriptures and its God Yahweh were irrelevant to Gentile Christianity and proclaimed that Jesus was not a Jew but appeared to the Jews as an adult directly from heaven (R. M. Grant, p. 517) — restricted his "Scriptures" to St. Paul's letters and to an edited version of St. Luke. De Wet (p. 305) observes that for St. John Chrysostom *"Christians could become more like Christ by becoming more like Paul."* Obviously, Marcion and St. John Chrysostom the Jew-hater saw nothing Jewish in St. Paul.

Perhaps a charitable view of St. Paul's Jewishness is that he fathered Gentile Christianity "unintentionally" (Galambush, p. 115). However, "fathering" a virulent anti-Jewish religion does not say much for St. Paul's "unintentions." Can the claim that St. Paul inserted a hidden "Jewish" goal in his message justify the opposition to Jewishness St. Paul's Gentile converts derived from his message? As questioned above, was the fervent anti-Jewishness of Christian leaders the result of a continuous two-thousand-year misreading of his letters?

Thus, although some scholars propose that New Testament Gospel writers may have been disgruntled Jewish Jesus-believers cast out from Jewish synagogues (Note #10.*1–2*), this hardly diminishes the protracted vilifying anti-Jewishness embedded in these fundamental "canonized" documents of Gentile Christianity, nor does it supplant Gentile Christianity's more basic antisemitic motivation to replace Jews by assuming for itself Jewish Scriptural antiquity.

It seems reasonable that however "Jewish" Jesus-followers may have comported themselves after his crucifixion, Jewish status changed radically a generation or so later. By then St. Paul had established Gentile Christian churches in which Torah-commanded observances were declared an abomination, sharply distinguishing them not only from ordinary Jewish synagogues but even from St. James' Jesus-believing synagogues. According to B. Wilson (p. 134): "...*the Jesus Movement in Israel and the Christ Movement in the Diaspora...were not the same religion: one came from Jesus; the other came from Paul. One was within Judaism; the other was not. One focused on the teachings of Jesus; the other focused on the figure of Christ. ... the two movements were not branch operations of one common enterprise.*" They were "*competing religions*" differing "*in terms of origins, beliefs and practices,*" as can be evidenced by St. Paul's vilifying vituperations against "Judaizing" Jewish Christians (Note #17).

The claim that Jesus' death by crucifixion was a symbol of power and not of its absence (*1 Corinthians* 1.17), was another theological theme that departed widely from Jewish beliefs. Again, as shown above (Note #12, p. 142; also Note #2, p. 13), it was St. Paul who changed Baptism from a Jewish rite used for purification and John the Baptist's "penitence," into the Christian initiation ceremony of mystical death and rebirth "*in the name of Christ*" (see also Tabor, pp. 133–141). Similarly, St. Paul transformed the Jewish Passover communal meal (Jesus' "Last Supper") into a mystical sacrament ("Eucharist") where Christians partake in the flesh and blood of Jesus Christ through ingesting bread and wine (Notes #2, p. 13; #7, p. 51); a concept that would be anathema to Jews (Note #11.*f*).

Again, it is clear that although Judaism and Gentile Christianity shared Jewish Scriptures, they each bore different social/ethnic identities and interpreted these Scriptures differently. Although

Jewish identity may vary in degree and importance from one Jew to another, historically the term "Jew" connoted not only a Semitic origin but also shared language, and customs derived from the Jewish Scriptures and Jewish history, such as monotheistic beliefs in an invisible God, male circumcision, dietary restrictions, Sabbath observances, and specific Holy day celebrations. Impelled by St. Paul's mystical epiphanies there are no such emblems of "Jewishness" in Gentile Christianity, marking a different religion made suitable for a different ethnicity.

As noted earlier (Note #2, page 12) St. Paul's Gentile Christianity —embodied in the New Testament and in sayings of the Christian Fathers — did not originate from any Christian passage in the Jewish Scriptures, but from St. Paul's imagined conversation with the dead Jesus. *"For I want you to know, brothers and sisters, that the Gospel that was proclaimed to me is not of human origin, for I did not receive it from a human source, nor was I taught it, but I received it through a revelation of Jesus Christ"* (*Galatians* 1.11–12). To this, St. Paul adds other exclusive visions that far surpass those of his Jewish Christian competitors: "[F]*ourteen years ago* [I] *was caught up in the third heaven — whether in the body or out of the body I do not know; God knows. ...* [I] *was caught up into Paradise and heard things that are not to be told, that no mortal is permitted to repeat"* (*2 Corinthians* 12.2–4).

In willingness to die for his "Gospel," St. Paul obviously meant that his beliefs must be true. *"For to me, living is Christ and dying is gain ... my desire is to depart and be with Christ"* (*Philippians* 1.21–23). Purposeful dying (martyrdom) to testify for the truth of a "belief" or "cause" was a legendary motif in all groups, Jews, Greeks, and Romans. In *2 Maccabees* (7.37), a Jewish youth facing the Greek despot Antiochus IV Epiphanes who sought to suppress Jewish customs, makes the plea: *"I, like my brothers, give up body and life for the laws of our ancestors, appealing to God to show mercy soon to our nation and by trials and plagues to make you*

170

confess that he alone is God." In asserting that "orthodox" Christianity must be the only "true religion," Christians applied this notion of martyrdom to many "Saints" (Moss 2013), as though willingness to die for a cause testifies to more than one's own persuasion. Ignored is the fact that "heretical" Christian sects, such as Donatists and others, produced even more martyrs than the "orthodox" (Ste. Croix 2006, p. 198). "[T]*here is evidence that all kinds of Christians could be unfavorably disposed towards martyrdom, if it was experienced by someone not belonging to their own group*" (Dunderberg 2013b, p. 422).

Aside from St. Paul's highly imagined visions, there is no evidence that Jesus the Galilean Jew ever conceived himself as "Jesus Christ/Christ Jesus" to be worshipped by posterity as the Divine Son of God, nor did any of Jesus' Jewish disciples act as though they also received, believed, or credited St. Paul's non-Jewish/anti-Jewish "Gospel." (See also Note #10.5.) Symbolic of theological hubris is that Christian Fathers and their successors never asked why St. Paul's anomalous revelations are more divinely authoritative than the opposed beliefs and practices of Jesus' original disciples, such as James the Just.

"Fleshly" Jesus and "spiritual" St. Paul had quite different objectives. To Jesus, the "world to come" is messianic justice on Earth (Note #15), albeit transformed by the New Testament into Jesus sitting on a throne of glory judging the nations (St. Matthew 25.31) and his followers judging the twelve tribes of Israel (Ibid. 19.28). St. Paul's aspiration for Jesus extended beyond Earth to a cosmic victory that covers all dimensions: "*so that at the name of Jesus, every knee shall bend, in heaven and on earth and under the earth*" (*Philippians* 2.10).

St. Paul's principal enemy is not oppressive Rome or its exploitative society, but a celestial Satan (*Romans* 16.20) "*who causes dissensions and offences in opposition to the teaching you have learned*" (*Romans* 16.17). Satan must be fought spiritually through faith in Jesus, for those who lose faith lose the heavenly battle. *"Do you not know that we are to judge angels — to say nothing of ordinary matters"* (*1 Corinthians* 6.3). However, to Jews, the repeated admonition *"Remember, you were slaves in the land of Egypt"* (Deuteronomy 5.15, 15.15, 24.18, 24.22) is to cherish redemption from oppression; not from Satan but from slavery.

What St. Paul saw in Jesus was obviously not what Jesus' Jewish audience saw in Jesus. Jesus' aim was to enjoin Jews to participate in a "Kingdom of God." St. Paul's aim was to enjoin Gentiles to place faith in the image of Jesus as their Savior from Satanic sin (*2 Thessalonians* 2.8–9) — "Christ crucified" (*1 Corinthians* 1.23) resurrected from the dead. *"He informs his hearers of a current cosmic contest that affects their lives and asserts that this battle goes back to the very beginning of time itself, into the apocalyptic drama begun at the dawn of creation. It is a battle between good and evil, between God and Satan (2 Corinthians 11.3, 14–15)"* (Bowers, p. 34).

Replacing Jesus' opposition to oppression with opposition to Satan was then carried forward in many ways. For example, St. Cyril of Jerusalem points to Christian baptism as *"the invocation of God and prayer give power to the exorcized oil not only to burn up and destroy the vestiges of past sins but also to drive away the invisible power of the evil one"* (Wiles and Santer, p. 182).

In sum, whatever St. Paul's personal feelings, his vision of Jesus Christ as the harbinger of a non-Jewish "New Covenant" is most trenchant. It seems obvious that readers of his letters could not have interpreted his unremitting opposition to Jewish religious rituals and Jewish Scriptural commandments as other than distancing his followers from the "Old Covenant" Jewish religion. This distancing is emblematic in the differences between St. Paul's Christian churches and Jewish synagogues, in which neither sought the other for affiliation or support. Goodman (2007b, p. 175) points out: *"If modern scholars find it hard to decide whether the author or intended reader*

172

of a particular text were Jews or Christians, it does not follow that those who produced the text in antiquity were similarly in doubt."

Clearly, St. Paul's opposition to Jewish customs/beliefs/practices established new Gentile Christianity with status as a unique religious entity, not a Jewish sect. "*Paul transformed the God-centered religion of Jesus* [the Jew] *into a* [Gentile] *Christ-centered Christianity*" (Vermes 2012, p. 237).

15

THE JEWISH MESSIAH AND
THE ROLE OF JESUS

To many Jews of Roman Israel, a Messiah (Hebrew "Mashiach"; Greek "Christ") was a divinely anointed leader who would deliver Israel from its oppressors into an imminent "Kingdom of God," establish world peace, reward the righteous, punish the wicked (Charlesworth 1983-1985 Vol. 1, pp. xxxi–xxxiii), and *restore the traditional ideals of a free and egalitarian society*" (Horsley and Hanson, p. 116). The messianic model was Biblical David who fought Philistine attacks, domination and injustice. *"Everyone who was in distress, and everyone who was in debt, and everyone who was discontented gathered to him*" (1 Samuel 22.2). *"[A]ll the tribes of Israel came to David at Hebron, and said, 'Look we are your bones and flesh ... The Lord said to you: It is you who shall be the shepherd of my people Israel, you who shall be ruler over Israel' ...and they anointed David king over Israel*" (2 Samuel 5.1–3). In time, the intended Messiah became *"the anointed son of David,"* with different Jewish groups offering different concepts of the believed God-sent redeemer as either human or divine.

However the term "Messiah" came into popular usage, this theme of appealing to a messianic figure — a present or future king offering rescue and liberation — reverberates through Israel's history; from Moses in the book of Exodus, to the Babylonian destruction of Jerusalem and beyond. *"The days are surely coming, says Yahweh, when I will raise up for David a righteous Branch, and he shall reign as king and deal wisely, and shall execute justice and righteousness in the land. In his days Judah will be saved and Israel will live in safety*" (Jeremiah 23. 5–6). More than a dozen allusions to a "Messiah" occur in Jewish Biblical and apocryphal documents extending into the Roman conquest of Israel (Bird 2009, p. 48).

The prophet Isaiah's paean to the coming "Kingdom of God" (60. 1–22, condensed) illustrates Jewish expectations: *"Arise, shine;*

for your light has come, and the glory of Yahweh has risen upon you. Nations shall come to your light, and kings to the brightness of your dawn. The descendants of those who oppressed you shall come bending low to you, and all who despised you shall bend down at your feet; they shall call you the city of Yahweh, the Zion of the Holy One of Israel. I will appoint Peace as your overseer and Righteousness as your taskmaster. Violence shall no more be heard in your land, devastation or destruction within your borders. Your people shall all be righteous; they shall possess the land forever. I am Yahweh; in its time I will accomplish it quickly."

Prayers to Yahweh's Messianic Davidic king are repeated in Psalm 72 (1–15, condensed): *"Give the King your justice O Yahweh. May he judge your people with righteousness. May he defend the cause of the poor of the people, give deliverance to the needy, and crush the oppressor. May he be like rain that falls on the mown grass, like showers that water the earth. May he have dominion from sea to sea, and from the River to the ends of the earth. May his foes bow down before him, and his enemies lick the dust. He has pity on the weak and the needy, and saves the lives of the needy. From oppression and violence he redeems their life, and precious is their blood in his sight. Blessed be Yahweh, the God of Israel."*

The coming, if not imminent, messianic "Kingdom of God" echoes Jewish prophecies in which religious beliefs are given political impact. Amos (9.11–15): *"On that day I will raise up the booth of David that is fallen, and repair its breaches, and raise up its ruins, and rebuild it as in the days of old. ... I will restore the fortunes of my people Israel ... I will plant them upon their land, and they shall never again be plucked up out of the land that I have given them, says Yahweh your God."* Psalms (37.9–11): *"For the wicked shall be cut off, but those who wait for Yahweh shall inherit the land. Yet a little while, and the wicked will be no more; though you look diligently for their place, they will not be there. But the meek shall inherit the land, and delight themselves in abundant prosperity."* Joel

(3.18–21): *In that day the mountains shall drip sweet wine, the hills shall flow with milk, and all the stream beds of Judah shall flow with water ... Judah shall be inhabited forever, and Jerusalem to all generations. I will avenge their blood, and I will not clear the guilty, for Yahweh dwells in Zion."* Daniel (12.1–3): *"At that time your people shall be delivered, everyone who is found written in the book. ... Those who are wise shall shine like the brightness of the sky, and those who lead many to righteousness, like the stars forever and ever."* 1 Enoch (91.8–9): *"In those days, injustice shall be cut off from its sources, and from its roots — likewise oppression with its deceit; they shall be destroyed from underneath heaven."*

Perhaps the most immediate Jewish prophetic reaction to Roman rule were *The Psalms of Solomon*, written around the time of Pompey's 63 B.C.E. conquest of Jerusalem. *Psalm 17* (condensed, Wright, pp. 639–670): *"Lord, raise up for them their king, the son of David, to rule over your servant Israel. Undergird him with the strength to destroy unrighteous rulers, to purge Jerusalem from gentiles who trample her to destruction. He will gather a holy people whom he will lead in righteousness; and any person who knows wickedness shall not live with them. He will purge Jerusalem and make it holy as it was from the beginning, for nations to come from the ends of the earth to see his glory. All shall be holy, and their king shall be the Lord Messiah. He shall be compassionate to all the nations who reverently stand before him. He will expose officials and drive out sinners by the strength of his word. He will lead them all in holiness and there will be no arrogance among them that any should be oppressed."*

Based for the most part on subsistence-level agriculture, dependent on capricious rainfall, and impacted by the Roman occupation, Israel's social-political-economic problems persisted throughout Jesus' time and beyond (Hanson and Oakman, pp. 123–147). It is not surprising that visions of messianic deliverance would have been common among Israel's farmers who numbered over 90 percent of the population (Fiensy 1991, p. 170), whose crops and labor were siphoned off in large measure for Roman tribute, royal aristocratic privilege, priestly tithes, and repayment of usurious loans. Whereas Israel's peasant farmers saw their land as owned by God and promised to them in their covenant with God (Leviticus 25.18, 25.23, Isaiah 5.7), Romans, native nobility, and priestly families saw the land as a commodity to be exploited for status and wealth through confiscations and taxes.

According to Oakman (2012, pp. 38–42), mainstays of the "Ruling Elites" were taxes, rents, tolls, religious tithes and obligations, loan payments, levies, labor duties, and commercialized farm products. Among taxes, Hanson and Oakman (p. 106) list soil taxes, poll taxes, port taxes, transit tolls, and special poll taxes that supported the priesthood. Except for the Jewish "Sabbatical" year, tribute to Rome, as decreed by Julius Caesar (Josephus, *Antiquities of the Jews*, XIV:X), may itself have extracted 12.5 to 20–25 percent annually from each household's produce (Adams p. 172).

Attributing Jesus' association with tax collectors ("publicans") to Jesus' tolerance and reform of even the most hated of exploiters, may also have had the more oblique purpose of tax evasion. According to Oakman (2008, Chapter 16), tax collectors were village scribes who could manipulate tax records and help peasants to reduce or evade taxation, a capital offence that St. Luke's Gospel (23.2) brought Jesus to the attention of Pontius Pilate. *"We found this man perverting our nation, forbidding us to pay taxes to the emperor, and saying that he himself is the Messiah, a king."*

"The ancient economy was agrarian and relatively static. It allowed for little growth or entrepreneurial initiative because the organization and use of resources was acquisitive rather than productive. Hence there was no unified market for the commercial exploitation of the empire or any middle class to undertake such activities. So most of the empire were born into poverty, and their only chance to escape it was the tomb" (Friesen 2004, pp. 338–339). Given good

terrain and rainfall, *"peasant plots were traditionally barely large enough* [as little as two hectares — four to five acres] *to provide a subsistence living for a family of five or six as well as meet the dues imposed from above.....Tithes* [to the priesthood and the temple], *and apparently tribute* [to the Roman empire], *and royal taxes* [to Jewish kings and aristocracy] *were taken right from the threshing floors. Conceivably over one-third of their crops may have been taken with the combination of the three different demands"* (Horsley 1995, p. 219). The New Testament letter of "James the Just," held to represent beliefs of Jesus' earliest Jewish disciples (Note #1), echoes these sentiments. *"You* [rich] *have dishonored the poor. Is it not the rich who oppress you? Is it not they who drag you into court? Is it not they who blaspheme the excellent name* [of God] *that we invoke over you?"* (2.6–7). *"Listen! The wages of the laborers who mowed your field, which you kept back by fraud, cry out, and the cries of the harvesters have reached the ears of the Lord of hosts"* (5.4).

J. H. Elliott. (pp. 20–21): *"In general terms this crisis was a product of the political domination, economic exploitation, and social destabilization of Palestine by Rome, on the one hand, coupled, on the other hand, with diversified strategies of domestic interest groups* [local rulers, landlords, money lenders] *to maintain and expand their bases of power and legitimacy. The situation in which earliest Christianity emerged was not simply rife with tension ... it was a situation created by conflict over power and the grossly imbalanced and alienating allocation of goods and resources (economic, social, and cultural), a situation strained by struggle over self-interests, values, ideologies and principles of freedom, equality and justice."*

Jewish prophets had long condemned many gross injustices perpetrated against Israel's peasants: *"They sell the righteous* [to slavery] *for silver and the needy for a pair of sandals — they who trample the head of the poor into the dust of the earth"* (Amos 2.6–7). *"Ah, you who join house to house, who add field to field, until there is no room for no one but you"* (Isaiah 5.8). *"Alas for those who devise wickedness and evil deeds ... they count fields and seize them; houses and take them away"* (Micah 2.1–2). *"Like the partridge hatching what it did not lay, so are all who amass wealth unjustly"* (Jeremiah 17.11). *"Here we are, slaves to this day — slaves to the land that you gave to our ancestors to enjoy its fruits and good gifts. Its rich yields go to the kings whom you have set over us because of our sins; they have power also over our bodies and over our livestock at their pleasure, and we are in great distress"* (Nehemiah 9.36–37).

To peasants, economic life was "zero-sum": for some to be rich, others became poor. *"The only way one could become wealthy in that (agrarian) society was by getting people in debt and charging high rates of interest. This is just what the high-priestly figures and Herodian rulers were doing under Roman imperial rule"* (Horsley 2012, p. 128).

To prophets, being rich rather than poor had little to do with virtue, and was plainly immoral. Financial impediments depriving the poor of their needs and comforts simply end in the new messianic era. *"Ho! Everyone who thirsts, come to the waters; and you who have no money, come, buy and eat! Come, buy wine and milk without money and without price"* (Isaiah 55.1). Prophetic faith aimed at timely remedial justice. *"The spirit of Yahweh is upon me, because Yahweh has anointed me; he has sent me to bring good news to the oppressed, to bind up the brokenhearted, to proclaim liberty to the captives, and release to the prisoners; ... to provide for those who mourn in Zion — to give them a garland instead of ashes, ... They shall build up the ancient ruins, they shall raise up the former devastations; they shall repair the ruined cities, the devastations of many generations. ... Because their shame was double, and dishonor was proclaimed as their lot, therefore they shall possess a double portion; everlasting joy shall be theirs. For I Yahweh love justice"* (Isaiah 61.1–8, condensed). *"I will rejoice in Jerusalem, and delight*

*in my people; no more shall the sound of weeping be heard in it, or
the cry of distress. No more shall there be in it an infant that lives
but a few days, and an old person who does not live out a lifetime"*
(Ibid. 65.19–20).

According to Crossley (2006, pp. 60–61), prophetic struggles
against economic injustice *"are tied up with the issues of covenant,
law observance, and, ultimately, salvation. Wealth is therefore po-
tentially dangerous and can make a person no better than a Gentile.
... 'The love of money is a sure path to idolatry, because, when led
astray by money, men call gods those that are no gods, and it drives
to distraction whoever is in its grip' (Testament of Judah 19.1–2)."*

More optimistic opinions about the peasant economy have
been offered (A.–J. Levine 2007, pp. 64–65), and some archaeolo-
gists also insist that Galilee and its environs showed some degree of
prosperity (see, for example, Aviam). Nevertheless, prosperous as
some Galileans may have been, it is hard to overlook the poverty and
dissatisfaction of many others who, from the time of Herod the Great,
joined and supported the brigandage and revolts that led to the major
Jewish-Roman war of 66-72 C.E. (Josephus, *Antiquities of the Jews*,
XIV: XV; XV; XVII:X, XX:VIII). Subsistence easily departed from
optimal because of diminished harvests, excessive taxes, and financial failures.

*"Confiscations and the oppressive tax burden narrowed the
possibility for self-sufficiency, and thus more and more small farmers lost their land. Therefore, the indebtedness of small farmers and
expropriation of their land are the hallmarks of this Roman epoch.
...one can indeed speak of a regular process of pauperization. The
decline of free small farmers to small leaseholders, then day laborers, and even beggars was nothing unusual"* (Stegemann and
Stegemann, p. 112). *"[I]n Galilee in the late Second Temple period
trade did not move goods but taxation and tribute moved them. Thus
the movement of goods was under control of the state. This economic
system kept the peasantry impoverished"* (Fiensy 2013, p. 173).

"[T]he major cause of landlessness in Palestine (which may have been especially pronounced in Galilee and Judea) was the movement everywhere in the Roman empire to concentrate more and more land into the hands of the few" (Fiensy 1991, p. 79). *"The distribution of what little income was available in the Mediterranean world was entirely dependent on political power: those devoid of political power, the non-elite ... could expect little more from life than abject poverty"* (Meggitt 1998, p. 50). Even Root (p. 167), who claims reduced banditry in Galilee, acknowledges that *"all ancient economies produced enough misery to inspire class-bound hostility in the right political climate."*

Blenkinsopp (p. 81): *"The drive toward centralization, the need to subsidize a royal court and an elaborate cult, heavy taxation ('you...take from them levies of grain' [Amos 5.11]), frequent confiscations of patrimonial domain following on insolvency, military service, and forced labor, were the main factors undermining the old order and leading to a kind of rent capitalism,"*

Given such ever-present exploitative conditions, it is hard to think that only few of Israel's farmers, Judean or Galilean, fell into debt, lost their property, and became wretchedly poor. To repeat: the downward course of unpaid debts and confiscations converted peasant farmers into short-term tenants and hired laborers. Tenancy and dispossession thus transferred crucial agrarian decisions to landlords cultivating profitable "cash crops," such as grapes, olives, and flax, instead of traditional plants peasants had used for family subsistence. Production for tribute and commerce rather than for peasant household consumption destabilized basic historic peasant values, forcing farmers, tenants, and hired hands to enter a cash market, relying on money and loans to supply family needs, pay taxes, and repay debts. What the land produced became a commodity to be sold and exchanged as was the land itself — often with disastrous family consequences. For those who worked the land, its productivity no longer belonged to them, but to others.

Oakman (2008, p. 138) defines the structure of the Roman Empire as a "political economy" where those in power enforced a "redistributive network" so that "*taxes and rents flowed relentlessly away from the rural producers to the storehouses of cities (especially Rome), private estates, and temples.* Adams, (p. 172): "*With a vast empire and a demanding infrastructure* [bureaucracy, roads, armies, etc.], *including a capital city of more than a million inhabitants, the revenue and supply needs of Rome were enormous in the first century BCE and first century CE.*"

Friesen (2005, pp. 241–243) estimates that the dominant "Elites" who comprised about one percent of the Empire's total population, possessed most of the Empire's land and wealth, "*earning rent and produce from the subsistence of farmers or slaves who actually worked the land.*" Perhaps only a further seven percent, composed of some relatively well-off merchants, artisans, and military, had a "*moderate surplus of resources.*" The remainder of the Empire's population lived in relative or wretched poverty, close to or below the level of subsistence. In Scheffler's estimate (2011a, p. 119): "*Only a small percentage (about 3%) of the population could be regarded as wealthy, 25% were starving with another 40% nearly starving.*"

Although exact population economic scale percentages can be disputed (e.g., B. W. Longenecker, pp. 30–59, 317–332), all agree that poverty ran large in the Roman Empire with crushing social effects. "*The slide from peasant owner to tenant farmer, to day laborer ... was inexorable for many and, thus, gave rise to social resentment, debt, banditry and in the case of woman, prostitution*" (Freyne 2006, pp. 44–45).

Not surprisingly, Israel's messianic beliefs often accompanied the common hope that an approaching radical/revolutionary event ("apocalypse") would change conditions, affording relief from political, economic, and social oppression, allowing "good" to triumph over "evil." Jesus' Galilean pleas embodied such hopes and demands: *"Give us this day our daily bread, and forgive us our debts as we forgive our debtors"* (St. Matthew 6.11–12).

As pointed out earlier (Note #4), John the Baptist's motif, *"The time is fulfilled, and the kingdom of God has come near"* (St. Mark 1.15) was echoed by Jesus. Allison (pp. 33–43) catalogs more than 30 New Testament Gospel accounts in which the person of Jesus prophecies an immediate apocalyptic age. (For Jesus' apocalyptic eschatology, see also E. P. Sanders 2002, pp. 43–44, Ehrman 2014, pp. 103–112, and Ehrman 1999. For the apocalyptic notions of St. Paul, see Meeks 1983, pp. 171–180, and the more recent extensive review by J. P. Davies).

To Jews, apocalypticism was no novelty. The *"prophetic books as well as Daniel, foretell the defeat of Israel's enemies, the influx of* [Jews from] *the Diaspora, the transformation of the land of promise into a paradise, and the realization of God's perfect will throughout the world"* (J. P. Davies, p. 78). In Isaiah's last chapter (66.10–15, condensed): *"Rejoice with Jerusalem, and be glad for her, all you who love her, for thus says Yahweh. I will extend prosperity to her like a river, and the wealth of nations like an overflowing stream. As a mother comforts a child, so I will comfort you. And it shall be known that the hand of Yahweh is with his servants, and his indignation is against his enemies. For Yahweh will come in fire, and his chariots like the whirlwind, to pay back his anger in fury and his rebuke in flames of fire."*

Such ancient messianic/apocalyptic messages continue through Jewish history to the present. Thus, the *Amidah* prayer celebrating the Jewish New Year, does not entreat justice in heaven, but restates apocalyptic hope: *"Bring to early fulfillment the hopes and prayers of the House of Israel for the coming of the Messianic era of thy servant David, ushering in days of justice and peace, humanity and holiness on earth. ... Speed the time when those who love righteousness will behold these days and rejoice; when the upright and the kind will be glad and break into song, when wickedness shall be silenced and every form of violence will vanish like vapor, because thou wilt cause the rule of arrogance to cease from the earth"* (M. D. Klein, p. 297).

Bad as conditions were under Israel's Hasmonean-Herodian aristocracy, messianic/apocalyptic hopes swelled even further under exploitative Roman rule after Herod the Great, worsened by avaricious Roman prefects and procurators. Various messianic figures were either killed in battle with the Romans or summarily executed. Among recorded failed Messiahs, prophets, or leaders with messianic followings, dating from Herod's death (4 B.C.E.) into the first century, were Judas son of Hezekiah (ca. 4 B.C.E.), Simon (ca. 4 B.C.E.), Athronges (ca. 3 B.C.E.), Judas of Gamla/Galilee (ca. 6 C.E.), John the Baptist (ca. 27 C.E.), the "Samaritan" (ca. 28 C.E.), Theudas (ca. 45 C.E.), Benjamin the Egyptian (ca. 56 C.E.), Jesus Bar Hananiah (ca. 65 C.E.), Menachem (ca. 66 C.E.), and Simon Bar Giora (ca. 69 C.E.).

All of these movements were clearly reminiscences or reenactments of earlier Israelite movements led by a prophet, such as the exodus from bondage, the wilderness march and the entry into the land (e.g., 'the battle of Jericho') led by Moses and Joshua, with echoes of Elijah and his protégé Elisha in the wilderness and crossing the Jordan as well. ... The similar form and purpose of all these movements, along with their differences in peculiarities, suggest a common pattern that was very much alive in Israelite culture at the time of Jesus, clearly rooted in the collective memory of the ancient formative prophetic movements" (Horsley 2012, p. 93).

Note that prophetic and messianic activities could lead to consequences that were not that far apart. Prophetic demands for social justice paved the way for messianic movements and actions where words lead to followers and followers to organizations challenging the status quo: not unlike executed John the Baptist's history and his executed follower, Jesus the Galilean of the New Testament.

Jesus' claims were both prophetic and messianic. *"The time is fulfilled, and the Kingdom of God is at hand"* (St. Mark 1.15) *"Truly I tell you, there are some standing here who will not taste death before they see that the Kingdom of God has come into power"* (Ibid. 9.1; also St. Matthew 16.28). In fortifying his followers, St. Mark (9.41) has Jesus say *"Whoever gives you a cup of water to drink because you bear the name of Christ* [Messiah] *will by no means lose the reward."* To Jesus, the ideal state of the "Kingdom of God" is already in sight, in which he promises to drink wine again with his followers (St. Mark 14.25):

- where the poor are blessed (St. Luke 6.20),
- where debts are forgiven (St. Matthew 6.12),
- where material possessions are shared (St. Mark 10.21),
- where all are welcome to communal meals (St. Mark 2.15),
- where Jesus' twelve disciples judge Israel's restored twelve tribes (St. Matthew 19.28),
- where Jesus will renew or rebuild the Holy Temple (St. Mark 14.58),
- where justice triumphs (St. Matthew 12.20).

Jesus' populist message requiring compassion and goodwill to enter his "Kingdom of God," would thus have ranked high among the poor and oppressed: give food to the hungry, drink to the thirsty, welcome the stranger, clothe the naked, care for the sick, and visit prisoners (St. Matthew 23.34–36). Even more radical is Jesus' opposition to economic inequality: the injustice of being rich while others are poor. To the wealthy petitioner who obeys all commandments and begs him *"Good teacher, what must I do to inherit eternal life"* (St. Mark 10.17), Jesus replies *"You lack one thing: go sell what you own, and give the money to the poor, and you will have treasure in heaven"* (Ibid. 10.21, also St. Luke 12.33, 18.22). *"You cannot serve God and wealth"* (St. Matthew 6.24, St. Luke 16.13). *"He has brought down the powerful from their thrones and lifted up the lowly; He has filled the hungry with good things, and sent the rich away empty.*" (St. Luke 1.52–53). "*But woe to you who are rich, for you have received your consolation. Woe to you who are full now, for you will be hungry. Woe to you who are laughing now, for you will mourn and weep*" (St. Luke 6.25). "*What is prized by human beings is an abomination in the sight of God*" (St. Luke 16.15). James the Just's letter also condemns the rich, and prophecies their doom: "Come now, *you rich people, weep and wail for the miseries that are coming to you. Your riches have rotted and your clothes are moth-eaten. Your gold and silver have rusted, and ... it will eat your flesh like fire*" (5.1).

Such declarations would certainly appear as messianism of high order to an oppressed people, and would have been sufficient for St. Peter to proclaim "*You are the Messiah*" when Jesus asks "*Who do you think I am?*" (St. Mark 8.29). Thus, despite charging his disciples not to broadcast his messianic title (St. Mark 8.30), the popular enthusiasm that the Gospels claim greeted Jesus on entering Jerusalem (St. Mark 11.8–10, St. Matthew 21.8–11, St. Luke 19.36–38, St. John 12.12–13) shows that his followers and perhaps many other Jews regarded him as a messianic figure foretold by the Jewish prophet Zachariah (9.9–10). "*Rejoice greatly, O daughter Zion! Lo, triumphant and victorious is he, humble and riding on a donkey ... he shall command peace to the nations; his dominion shall be from sea to sea, and from river to the ends of the earth.*"

In answer to theologians who questioned Jesus' messianic status, R. N. Longenecker (1970, pp. 70–71) made the following comment. "*One is bound to wonder how a man who made no explicit messianic claim for himself ... or who absolutely rejected the ascription and did so little that was out of the ordinary ... could have aroused the intense opposition ... that culminated in his death. ... That Jesus understood his ministry in terms of messiahship is the underlying presupposition in the narratives concerning the baptism, the temptation in the wilderness, the transfiguration, and the triumphal entry ... Jesus could ...hardly have claimed to be the fulfilment of Old Testament prophecy without at least implying that he was in some sense the Messiah of Israel's hope."*

Jesus' acclamation in Jerusalem as a royal "Son of David" (St. Matthew 21.9) and leader of an imminent new socio-economic "Kingdom of God" (St. Mark 1.15) would have made him a prime seditious suspect. That Jesus apparently not only spoke but **acted** in the Temple "in the name of God," cast him further into the role of a rebellious Jewish populist, sardonically crucified by Pontius Pilate under the title "King of the Jews" (St. Mark 15.26, also Note #21). Jesus' Jerusalem crime may well have been active opposition to the Temple priestly system in which *"ordinary people are deprived of their own offerings for the most part ... a system of exploitative re-distribution for the benefit of the few"* (Oakman 2008, p. 195).

Jewish response to the Romans and their collaborative priestly authorities would hence have been no different from earlier critiques and supplications for justice by Israel's prophets. *"Even though you offer me your burnt offerings and grain offerings, I will not accept them. ... But let justice roll down like waters, and righteousness like an ever-flowing stream"* (Amos 5.22–24). Perhaps the most impassioned appeals for justice and commitment to Yahweh came from Micah. *"Alas for those who devise wickedness ... They covet fields, and seize them; houses, and take them away; they oppress householder and house, people and their inheritance"* (2.2–3). *"Listen, you heads of Jacob and rulers of the house of Israel! Should you not know justice? — you who hate the good and love the evil, who tear the skin off my people, and the flesh off their bones"* (3.1–2). *"With what shall I come before the Lord ... with burnt offerings, with calves a year old? Will the Lord be pleased with thousands of rams and with ten thousand rivers of oil? ... What does the Lord require of you but to do justice, and to love kindness, and to walk humbly with your God?"* (6.6–8).

In *Psalms of Solomon* (17.21–24, 32, Charlesworth 1985 vol. 2, p. 667), written after Israel's 63 B.C.E. absorption into the Roman

Empire, the Jewish Messiah is expected "*to destroy the unrighteous rulers, to purge Jerusalem from Gentiles who trample her to destruction ... to destroy the unlawful nations with the word of his mouth. ... There will be no unrighteousness in his days, for all shall be holy and their king shall be the Lord Messiah.*" Horsley (1994, p. 154) proposes Jesus' movement followed this theme to replace long-condemned systematic injustice with "*an independent and revitalized social order. [It] proclaimed God's overcoming of the old unjust and unfree order and insisted on the possibility of free, just, even creative personal and social life.*"

To the list of purported Jewish Messiahs, Horsley and Hanson add the names of various "bandits" and "brigands" who met ignominious deaths; some, if not many, contesting Herodian and Roman domination. "*As to the number of robbers he* [Felix, Roman Procurator] *caused to be crucified, and of those* [common people] *who were caught among them, and whom he brought to punishment, they were a multitude not to be enumerated*" (Josephus, *Wars of the Jews* II:XIII). Crossan (1991, pp. 451–452) lists 33 cases titled *Peasant Unrest in Early Roman Palestine*, and Kearney and Zeitz claim as many as twenty-seven Messiah-like figures can be identified between 28 B.C.E. and 135 C.E.

None of the messianic movements relieved the Jews of their oppressors, and none could withstand the Roman army, used throughout the empire to enforce taxation, conscript labor, defeat rebels, conquer territory, and enslave captives. In fact, conditions worsened for most Jews in Israel because of increased Roman oppression, leading to repeated rebellions in which many Jews were enslaved, crucified, or burnt alive.

Jesus' Galilean homeland was not immune to revolts: bands of guerillas fought Herod with uprisings that continued even after his death (Josephus, *Wars of the Jews* I:XVI, XVII). In 4 B.C.E., a major Galilean revolt was suppressed by the Roman Governor, Quinctilius Varus, who crucified 2,000 Jewish "rebels," sacked the Galilean city of Sepphoris, sold most of its population into slavery, and turned the city into a royal principality. (Sepphoris was only 3 miles from Nazareth, Jesus' birthplace.) By 6 C.E., the offensive behavior of Herod's son, Archelaus, in governing Jerusalem and Judea (Southern Israel), led the Romans to declare Judea a Roman province administered by a series of Roman "Prefects" who appointed the Temple High Priests. Among Roman Governors was Pontius Pilate (26–36 C.E.), described by the Jewish historian Josephus as greedy and savage, eventually recalled to Rome on charges of excessive brutality. To enforce order during Jewish holidays, a garrison of Roman troops quartered in the Antonia Fortress adjoining the Jerusalem Temple, furnished the cohort that captured and executed Jesus.

Josephus' history shows that tensions and disputes in Israel between ordinary Jews and the privileged elite increased rapidly through Jesus' life in the early first century C.E. and for more than generation after. "Brigandage," nationalistic or in response to exploitation and poverty, became a notable feature of Israel's landscape, and as indicated above, was severely punished by Roman authorities but not eliminated. By the time the great Jewish revolt began in 66 C.E., Galilean peasants had attacked elite enclaves in Sepphoris and Tiberias. In Jerusalem, rebels *"carried the fire to the place where the [debt] archives were deposited, and made haste to burn the contracts belonging to their creditors, and thereby dissolve their obligations for paying their debts; and this was done in order to gain the multitude of those who had been debtors, and that they might persuade the poorer sort to join in their insurrection with safety against the more wealthy"* (Josephus, *Wars of the Jews*, II:XXVII).

The ensuing Jewish-Roman War (66–72 C.E.), involving both Israel's cities and countryside, was put down by a host of Roman legions who destroyed the Jewish Temple and most of Jerusalem. All Jews throughout the Empire, young or old, were then charged an ethnically targeted tax lasting for centuries, *Fiscus Judaicus*. Penalty though it was, *"from AD 96 it came to be valued by Jews as their public license to live by their own rules"* (Judge, p. 367). As pointed out earlier (Note #3, p. 28), although paying the tax would have protected St. Paul's Christians from persecution as an illegitimate superstition, they nevertheless sought exemption from any form of Jewish identity. To this one can add: *"Why would* [Gentile] *Christians not opt to distance themselves from a group now being deliberately humiliated and financially disadvantaged?"* (M. H. Williams, p. 159).

In the second century, the messianic Simon Bar Kochba led another large Jewish rebellion (132–135 C.E.) also overwhelmingly defeated, in which Israel's Jewish population may have been reduced by almost half (Lapin, p. 33). On pain of death, Jews were then forbidden to enter Jerusalem, renamed *Aelia Capitolina* in honor of the great Jupiter Temple on Rome's Capitoline hill. On only one day of the year ("Tisha B'Av") were Jews, after paying tribute to the city guardians, allowed to enter Jerusalem and mourn at the site of their destroyed Temple.

Christian sympathy, however, was not forthcoming. St. Jerome, whose translation of the Jewish Scriptures into Latin was dependent on Jewish teachers, had nothing good to say about Jewish grief: *"These hypocritical tenants* [Jews] *are forbidden to come to Jerusalem, because of the murder of the servants of God, and the last of them — the Son of God; unless to weep, for they are given permission to lament over the ruins of the city in exchange for a payment ... The children of this wretched nation* [Jews] *bemoan the destruction of their temple, but are not worthy of compassion"* (Hamblin and Seely, p. 68).

If we consider that Jews actively protesting against oppressive conditions were often unjustly condemned as "robbers," "outlaws," or "insurrectionists," Jesus' Roman execution, (ca. 30 C.E.) was not unexpected. *"Jesus was arrested like a robber, tried on charges similar to those that might be used against such a person, executed between two lêstai* ["outlaws"] *and another lêstês — Barabbas — is set free*" (Richardson and Edwards, p. 264).

Interestingly, the New Testament Barabbas, supposedly saved from crucifixion by a highly unbelievable practice of Romans releasing a single prisoner at Passover (Ehrman 2012a, p. 184; Marcus, p. 1035; Vermes 2005, p. 61), is also labeled an "insurrectionist" (St. Mark 15.7). As far as the Romans were concerned, neither Jesus' messianic movement, nor his execution, nor others of Jesus' time were of significance. The Roman historian Tacitus, writing of "troubles" in Judea during 14 – 37 C.E., declares that "*Under Tiberius, peace* [nothing happened]."

For Jews, Christianity's demand to recognize Jesus as the Messiah ("Christ") could only be answered by comparing Jesus' accomplishments to those of the expected Messiah. Was Israel free of foreign domination? Was the Jerusalem Temple free of corruption? Protected from destruction? Was economic and political oppression eradicated? Was the world at peace? In the words of Micah (4.3–4): "*He shall judge between many peoples, and shall arbitrate between nations far away: they shall beat their swords into plowshares, and their spears into pruning hooks; ...neither shall they learn war anymore; but they shall all sit under their own vines and under their own fig trees, and no one shall make them afraid.*" Or, as famously put by the prophet Isaiah (11.5), "*The wolf shall live with the lamb, the leopard shall lie down with the calf and the lion and the fatling together, and a little child shall lead them.*"

According to Donaldson (2010, p. 155), "*Jewish expectations about the promised age of salvation did not contain any notion of a Messiah who would suffer and die, who would do so as a means of bringing salvation, and who would be removed to heaven without having established the expected era of righteousness under the reign of God.*" Similarly, "*Messianic claims were not a question of doctrinal heresy, but a matter of empirical testing. If a person was indeed the Messiah, history would prove it by showing that he did what a messiah does: redeem Israel from oppression under the nations, overcome sin and evil, inaugurate the new age of blessedness. ... Messiahs win — they do not get crucified*" (Ruether 1979, pp. 236, 238). In Isaiah's words (42.4), the Messiah "*will not grow faint or be crushed until he has established justice on earth.* Moreover, a Messiah's "Kingdom of God" is not postponed to a "Second Coming" after his death. In the Biblical book of Deuteronomy (18.22): "*If a prophet speaks in the name of the Lord but the thing does not take place or prove true, it is a word that the Lord has not spoken.*"

Christian theologians completely ignored Jewish objections to Jesus as the Messiah, as though there were no Jewish expectations to gain freedom from oppression, nor any obstacle to accepting Christian theological claims of Jesus as a divine figure (Note #11.*b*), nor sound opposition to Christian radical misinterpretations of Jewish Scriptures (Notes #7, #18). "*We blame the Jews...because they neither refute the arguments which we lay before them to prove that He* [Jesus] *is the Messiah...nor yet...do they believe in Him who was the subject of prophecy*" (Origen, ca. 240, *Against Celsus*, ANF vol. 4, p. 446). Christians repeatedly condemned Jewish disbelief of Jesus as if it were a crime and Jews as if they were criminals for asserting Jesus' failure to achieve Israel's messianic goals of freedom, liberty, justice, and peace on Earth.

The inability of any professed Jewish Messiah to gain victory ended Israel's contentions with Rome. After messianic Bar Kochba's second century defeat, the Romans considered Israel as "tamed" (Lapin, p. 16). Jewish nationalist aspirations fell dormant, and leadership left to the Jews was a religious scholar/teacher movement ("Rabbis") who doubted that Israel had reached the level of religious purity deserving the Messiah. To the Rabbis, salvation awaits piety: *If all Israel will keep a single Sabbath in the proper (rabbinic) way the Messiah will come.*" (Neusner 2004b, p. 14). In the absence of Israel's religious renewal, messianic claimants, such as Bar Kochba, were labeled "false Messiahs" and one Rabbi exclaimed *"grass will grow on your cheeks and the Son of David will still not come"* (L. I. Levine 1992, p. 144). Nevertheless, Messiah believers were not considered heretical: *"there was no sin in making the error ... of believing someone to be the Messiah"* (Schiffman, p. 147). To the Rabbis, a failed Messiah was a dupe or fool, not a blasphemer.

Although Jesus' messianic message was strictly from one Jew to other Jews (see, for example, Vermes 2003, p. 417; and also Note #4), liberation of Israel from Roman oppressors made little sense to Gentiles and was obviously unfulfilled. In accord with St. Paul (*Romans* 16.20), Jesus' adversaries in the New Testament Gospels do not include earthly Rome. In its place, Jesus' prime enemy is Satan, a celestial villain (St. Mark 1.13; St. Matthew 4.1–11; St. Luke 22.3; St. John 13.27) even more toxic than Jesus' supposed Jewish antagonists. As noted earlier (Note #14), the term "Christ/Messiah" thus lost its meaning among Gentile Christians as title for an earthly "anointed" Jewish leader and savior (e.g., "Jesus, the Christ/Messiah"), and became instead Jesus' surname ("*Christ*"), a new binomial divinity — "Our Lord *Jesus Christ*" or "*Christ Jesus* our Lord." St. Paul's letters use the term "Christ" more than 400 times; either combined with "Jesus" as above, or simply "Christ." *"Once the communities became largely Gentile, any titular* [messianic] *significance to Christos* [anointed] *disappeared"* (Scroggs, p. 93).

To attract Gentiles, Jesus' messianic claim for a forthcoming divine Jewish Kingdom was elevated to a distance far beyond Israel's goal to correct economic and national afflictions. Instead, emphasis was placed on three dogmata: Jesus Christ was now the savior of all mankind; it was Jesus Christ rather than God who would return in the future to triumph over evil; Christian redemption (deliverance from guilt and harm) is to be attained, not by militant action, but by faith in Jesus Christ. In Acts of the Apostles, *"to follow* [St.] *Luke's narrative is to read Christianity not as a call for insurrection but as a testimony to the reality of* [Jesus'] *resurrection"* (Rowe, p. 88).

Emphasizing Jesus Christ as a peaceful divine Christian savior helped de-emphasize his role as a crucified Jewish rebel. "*[T]he author of Acts is trying to establish a modus vivendi with the political powers in the empire. Rome and the provinces are not evil beasts. ... The politics of Acts means accepting the Greco-Roman political structure*" (Scroggs, p. 166).

There is little question that this mythic Jesus Christ empowered Christianity for millennia (see also Note #22). "*The thing that has functioned throughout history as the source of consolation and hope for perplexed humanity is not the historical Jesus, but the literary character of Jesus that we have in the Gospels*" (Ellens, p. 254). As described by some writers, the Gospels became a form of "narrative theology" which incorporates St. Paul's mystical Jesus and minimizes Jesus' socio-economic political mission.

16

RELIGIOUS DIFFERENCES AMONG JEWS

In New Testament Gospels, Jesus is always at variance with groups that epitomize contrasting Jewish practices whatever their Scriptural origin: "Jewish Scribes," "Jewish Pharisees," "Jewish Sanhedrin." Almost every statement attributed to Jesus is contrasted with an opposing statement or attitude attributed to "Scribes" and "Pharisees" (or "Jews" in St. John), whether or not such "disputes" had any religious substance, or reflected anything more than existing differences among Jews themselves.

St. Mark's Gospel, which served as a major source for St. Matthew and St. Luke, initiated such confrontations. *"The evangelist portrays Jesus as condoning the breaking of the Sabbath (2.23ff; 3.1–6). Jewish lustration practice* [hand-washing] *is disparaged as are other Jewish practices (7.1–23)"* (Telford, pp. 125–126). According to many modern scholars, such disputes derive from Early Gentile Christianity's need to denigrate Jewish (and Jewish-Christian) authority and attribute denial of Jewish Scriptural commandments to the historical Jesus.

E. P. Sanders (1985, p. 265) points out, *"there was no substantial conflict between Jesus and the Pharisees with regard to Sabbath, food, and purity laws."* St. Matthew, in spite of many unsupported fulminations against Pharisees, has Jesus make remarkable statements: *"Do not think that I have come to abolish the Law or the prophets; I have come not to abolish but to fulfill. For truly I tell you, until heaven and earth pass away, not one letter, not one stroke of a letter, will pass from the Law until all is accomplished"* (5.17–18). *"The Scribes and the Pharisees sit on Moses' seat, therefore do whatever they teach you and follow it"* (Ibid. 23.2–3).

In an extensive analysis of New Testament claims that Jesus was condemned by the Pharisees for flouting Jewish laws by curing the sick on the Sabbath, Collins points out (her emphasis), ***"no Pharisees or any other Jewish official was ever present at any of these*** *cures....No Jewish official would therefore have criticized the historical Jesus for performing a cure at the time of each event. There is moreover, also no reliable evidence that Jesus was ever criticized by any Jewish official **after** these events"* (p. 202). *"These facts completely exonerate the Pharisees from the long-held accusation that they watched, opposed and criticized Jesus, and even planned for his death because of his performance of Sabbath cures ... neither the Pharisees nor any other Jewish official ever opposed any of the acts of healing and/or saving life that Jesus performed on the Sabbath day"* (Ibid. pp. 435–436). *"[F]rom the time of the edict of Mattathias the Maccabean and his colleagues in 167 B.C.E., the Jewish sages were always prepared to allow acts of healing and/or saving life which violate Jewish law"* (Ibid. p. 439). Jewish sages followed the practice that *"it is more important to heal and/or save life than it is to adhere to Jewish law itself"* (Ibid. p. 446).

Rather than disputing Pharisees, Jesus' attitude may well have echoed certain Pharisaic views that faith in God prevents illness. Nevertheless, neither Jesus' "limited hand-washing" nor "healing on the Sabbath" extended into violating basic Scriptural principles, such as circumcision and eating pork — commands shared by Jesus' disciples, as can be seen in St. Paul's castigating Jewish Christian "Judaizers" (Note #17) and St. Peter (*Galatians* 2.14) for proposing that St. Paul's "Gentiles live like Jews." Interestingly, despite Gospel attacks on the Pharisees, it was Pharisees who protested the stoning of Jesus' brother "James the Just," leader of the Jerusalem's Jesus believers, *"and some of his companions,"* resulting in replacement of the High Priest Ananus (Josephus, *Antiquities of the Jews* XX:IX).

In all noteworthy respects, *"analysis of the Synoptic tradition* [the three New Testament Gospels other than St. John] *shows Jesus was an observant Jew who did not directly oppose any significant aspect of the Torah. He was circumcised, he observed the Sabbath, he attended the synagogue, he taught from the Torah, he went on pilgrimage to Jerusalem and celebrated the Jewish festivals, and he accepted the sacrifice at the temple*" (Harlow, p. 259). "*The simple but stern historical truth [is] that Jesus never once betrays the Judaism in which he was reared and never once implies that his friends and compatriots require a new religion*" (Eckardt 1992, p. 40). "[N]*o act of Jesus is against the Law, nor can any teaching be described as against the Law. ... Opposition strictly on issues of the Law and its interpretation would have been no more serious than other debates of the time*" (Efroymson 1993, p. 91). "[I]*n all cases there is no serious evidence that Jesus' view went beyond the boundaries of disputes known in early Judaism*" (Crossley 2008, p. 9). In the words of J. Wellhausen, an acclaimed Biblical scholar: "*Jesus was a Jew and not a Christian*" (Vermes 2010, p. 21).

First century Jews, as today, argued over many religious rules and rituals, and Judaism accommodated many such differences. "*Indeed, the existence of all kinds of sects and religious leaders was the norm of the day in the Second Temple period as we know from many sources*" (Shiffman, p. 442). "*Within Judaism, especially within Second Temple Judaism, most Jews were impressively tolerant of concepts that deviated from so-called Pharisaism*" (Charlesworth 2013, p. 292). For example, we know that historic differences between Pharisaic and Sadducean interpretations of Jewish law extended from Hasmonean rule (150 B.C.E., Chilton et al., p. 20) to the destruction of the Jerusalem Temple (70 C.E.). The Essenes were another religiously partisan faction known for practicing a life style in which all property was held in common; and in requiring their members, not slaves, to perform the labor and menial tasks necessary for communal health and function. In general, Jews retained their Jewish identity as long as they followed Jewish Scriptural rules and principles. Burns (2016, p. 85) points out that despite professing unique ideologies and practices, the Pharisees did not "*deny the Jewish identities of those who declined to join their groups. The same seems to have been the case for Sadducees, the Essenes, and, at least initially, those Christians who chose to live as Jews.*"

With loss of the Temple, divergent concepts and beliefs persevered in century-long Rabbinical debates that replaced priestly authority. Varied views, arguments, and commentaries on *"laws, rituals, and theology"* (Chilton et al., p. 29) comprise the Rabbinical Talmud, which became a fundamental part of religious Judaism, reaching into the fifth and sixth centuries C.E. (S. J. D. Cohen 1992; Gafni).

"At any given moment Jews practiced their religion in manifold different ways…The Judaism of the land of Israel was striated not only by numerous sects but also by numerous teachers and holy men, each with his band of supporters" (S. J. D. Cohen 1987, pp. 24–25). As indicated above, different and contentious as these sects were, all claimed to be "Jews," and, in contrast to St. Paul's Gentile Christianity, none denounced observance of Jewish Scriptural laws and rituals, and none believed that Gentiles replaced Jews in God's favor. Nickelsburg and Stone observe (p. 12): *"There was a great variety of groups, tendencies, and points of view, held together by certain common practices and allegiances, The Temple and the Sabbath, monotheism and the rejection of images, and reverence for the torah of Moses and circumcision."* Ancient Judaism *"is a picture of variegated Judaism, a spectrum of many hues and blends"* (Nickelsburg, p. 3) — none of which included Gentile Christianity.

Thus, although Jewish attitudes towards Jewish Christians may have hardened in the fifth century, accounting for Jewish Christian disappearance, the two Jewish groups seemed to have existed peacefully until then in the trans-Jordan Golan Heights (Daphine and Gibson, p.22; see also Joan Taylor). By contrast, "parting of the ways" between Gentile Christian churches and Jewish groups of any kind must have occurred much earlier, perhaps even before end of the first century — distinguished by St. Paul's many fundamental innovations that far exceeded even the most liberal concepts of Jewish identity (Notes #2, #14).

198

S. J. D. Cohen (1987) points out: "*Judaism, by contrast* [to Christianity] *has never had either a pope or church councils, and without these there is no objective criterion for the determination of 'orthodoxy.' The temple was the central authority against which sects defined themselves, but the high priests lacked sufficient power to be able to state which forms of Judaism were 'orthodox' or to exclude from the temple those Jews whose practices they condemned*" (p. 136). "[N]*o Jew of antiquity gave a creedal definition of Judaism*" (Ibid. p. 103). In fact, the high priest, long ranked as a ceremonial functionary despite his authoritative religious title, had become no more than a political appointee, chosen with Roman collaboration to help maintain "public order." Not surprisingly, after a rapid succession of failed appointees, the high priest involved in Jesus' conviction and crucifixion, Caiaphas, was regarded sufficiently reliable by the Romans that he "*remained in office for close to twenty years*" (Baumgarten, p. 154).

Bound by common belief in the Torah (Note #7), Jewish accommodation to sectarians persisted under Rabbinical leadership even after the Temple's 70 C.E. destruction. "*Even as the sages of subsequent generations cultivated their halakhah* [religious rules], *the Jews on the whole possessed no formal regulatory agency whereby to measure one's sense of Jewish identity against another's. ... Yet even ... sectarians* [who] *disagreed with other Jews on points of practice and belief ... generally agreed with one another on the imperative to maintain the religious and ethnic commitments of their ancestors*" (Burns 2016, p. 91). The primary goal of criticizing other Jews, whether it occurred in the Jewish Scriptures or by Jewish Prophets, was to improve their countrymen's behavior. Although some Christian Fathers belabor the issue (see, for example, Note #19), Jewish Biblical self-criticism was obviously not conceived by Jewish Scriptural writers to grant (non-existent!) Gentile Christianity superiority over Jews, but to achieve righteousness in Jewish countrymen.

However expressed in the Gospels, separating Jesus the Jew from his countrymen became essential for Gentile Christianity in separating itself from Jewish religion and Jewish ethnicity. St. John's Gospel has his Jesus figure refer to the Torah as "*your Law*" (8.17, 10.34), or "*their Law*" (15.25), to the Jews who escaped from Egypt in the Exodus as "*your ancestors*" (6.49, 6.58, 8.56), and to others than Jesus' disciples as "*the Jews*" (13.33, 18.36). Jesus' welcoming countrymen who were following him into his new "Kingdom of God," are presumptuously transformed into his mortal enemy — "*the Jews*" — who demand that Pontius Pilate put him to death. It is therefore quite possible for Gospel readers to believe that Jesus and his disciples, all bearing New Testament non-Jewish "Christian" names (e.g., James for Yaacov, Jesus for Yeshua, John for Yonah or Yonassan, Mary for Miriam, Matthew for Matisyahu, Peter for Shimon), and living as a sequestered group supposedly persecuted by "the Jews," were not "Jews" or at most "temporary Jews." To St. John's readers, being "Christian" is not being "Jewish."

Predictably, factors such as Jesus' circumcision, a prime symbol of Jewishness to Romans, became an embarrassment to Christian theologians who tried to explain it away as "*…one more indignity that Christ suffered in order to redeem humanity*" (Jacobs, p. 301). There have even been proposals not to allow Jesus a Jewish name at all — "*Jesus' name was, in fact, Jesus'* —since "Jesus' is the only name given to him in the Greek New Testament (Arnal 2005, p. 29).

Hardly longer than a generation after Jesus' death, Yeshua the Mashiach son of Yusuff and Miriam, attempting to liberate Jews from oppressors, became Jesus Christ the Son of God, liberating Gentiles from sin.

17

CHRISTIAN RANTS AGAINST
JEWS AND JUDAIZERS (see also Note #6)

St. Paul, *Philippians* 3.2: "*Beware of the dogs, beware of the evil workers, beware of those who mutilate the flesh* [Judaistic Jews or "Judaizers" proselytizing for Jewish-Christian sects]." St. Paul, *Galatians* 1.6–9: "*I am astonished that you are so quickly deserting the one who called you in the grace of Christ and are turning to a different gospel — not that there is another gospel, but there are some* [Jews and Judaizers] *who are confusing you and want to pervert the gospel of Christ. But even if we or an angel from heaven should proclaim to you a gospel contrary to what we proclaimed to you, let that one be accursed! As we have said before, so now I repeat, if anyone proclaims to you a gospel contrary to what you received, let that one be accursed!*" St. Paul, *2 Corinthians* 11.3: "*I am afraid that as the serpent deceived Eve by its cunning, your thoughts will be led astray* [by Jews and Judaizers] *from a sincere and pure devotion to Christ.*"

St. Paul's letters thus furnished a foundation for Gentile Christians to view Jews as heretics engaged in heretical acts (Jewishness), a posture that easily led to open antisemitism. St. John 8.44: "*You* [Jews] *are from your father the devil, and you choose to do your father's desires.*" Letter to the Hebrews 6.4–6: "*it is impossible to restore again to repentance those who have once been enlightened, and have tasted the heavenly gift, and have shared in the Holy Spirit, and have tasted the goodness of the word of God and powers of the age to come, and then have fallen away, since on their own they* [Jews and Judaizers] *are crucifying again the Son of God and are holding him up to contempt.*"

St. Ignatius (ca. 100) *Letter to the Magnesians* X: "*It is absurd to speak of Jesus Christ with the tongue, and to cherish in the mind a Judaism which has now come to an end. For where there is Christianity there cannot be Judaism*" (ANF vol. 1, p. 63). St. Gregory of

Nyssa (ca. 380) *Homilies on the Resurrection*: "*Jews are slayers of the Lord, murderers of the prophets, enemies of God, haters of God, adversaries of grace, enemies of their fathers' faith, advocates of the devil, a nest of vipers, purveyors of slander, scoffers, men of darkened minds, leaven of the Pharisees, a gang of devils. They are sinners, wicked men, stoners, and haters of righteousness*" (Flannery, p. 50; also Simon, p. 216). St. John Chrysostom (ca. 386), *Against the Jews, Oration* 1: "*The Jews gather bands of effeminate men and a great mob of female prostitutes; they drag the whole theatre and the actors into the synagogue: there's no difference between theatre and synagogue. ... Where a prostitute has established herself, that place is a brothel. I should say that the synagogue isn't only a brothel and a theatre, but also a cave of robbers and a resting place for wild beasts. When God abandons a place, that place becomes the dwelling of demons*" (Mayer and Allen, pp. 153–154).

Such virulent anti-Jewish rhetoric added little value to the Christian creed, except to use prejudice to reinforce a religious border against Jews; a border which might otherwise appear porous to Christians presented with Jewish Scriptures as the only support for Christian antiquity. These maledictions indicate how unimaginable it was to allow Christians to believe that Jews reject Christianity for reasons other than sinful willfulness and intransigence.

That essential elements of Christianity are unacceptable to Jews on valid Scriptural and rational grounds, as discussed in Note #11 and elsewhere in this monograph, had no merit to Christian leaders. Nor was the knowledge that Jesus and his disciples followed Jewish religious practices (Notes #4, #16) allowed to diminish anti-Jewish hostility. Interestingly, fears that "Judaizers" would join the Gentile Christian Church and resurrect Jesus' and his followers' Jewish roots were revivified in 18th century writings of Schleiermacher, a Protestant theologian (Batnitzky, p. 26). Important as anti-Jewish calumnies were in preserving Gentile Christian religious identity, their impact extended far beyond religion. Presented to Christian parishioners by leaders and theologians with high social standing offering salvation, some or even many listening Christians would have extended such attitudes into their social lives.

Note that although Christian leaders used "Judaizer" as an anti-Jewish epithet (Note #10.5), not all Jewish Christians were "Judaizers." Namely, some of these Jewish "non-Judaizers" apparently joined Jesus-believing assemblies without intending to "Judaize" their Gentile associates. That St. Paul had to defend such Jewish Christians against Gentile prejudice (*Romans* 14.1–15.6) shows how decidedly anti-Jewish Gentile Christianity had become within a single generation after Jesus' death. N. Elliot (p. 188–189): "*Indeed, the whole of* [St. Paul's] *letter is directed against the danger of a smug self-satisfaction on the part of the Gentiles, rooted in the latent toxic anti-Judaic propaganda current in Rome.*"

Nevertheless, no matter how conciliatory St. Paul's occasional expressions of tolerance may sound, they were not to preserve Jewish ethnicity or distinctiveness, but to eventually enroll Jews into the Pauline fold of "anti-Law" Gentile Christianity (Note #18). At their most tolerant best, like St. Paul's *Romans*, Christian Fathers regarded Jews as defiant delinquents destined to be converted upon Jesus' *Parousia* ("Second Coming"). Already apparent in St. Paul's first century Gentile Christian churches — that one cannot be both a Gentile Christian of "faith" and a practicing Jew of "works" —Gentile Christianity's estrangement and hostility towards Jews did not await Christianity's fourth century adoption by Rome.

The violent rhetoric which St. Paul began against "Judaizers" effectively turned those who practiced Jewish rituals and observances — "Jews" — into "others," cursed and anathematized for their "Jewishness." "*One of the most striking kinds of Christian writing, although the least attractive to modern sensibilities, is the very large body of polemical works, or even casual asides, addressed in Late Antiquity towards heterodox Christians, or towards Jews, with whom the former are often conflated*" (Cameron, p. 110). Anti-

Jewish monomania thus became a sanctioned feature easily induced in Christian leaders claiming "orthodoxy," even in arguments against other Christian leaders.

For example, Christian Fathers in the second century accused their anti- Jewish Gentile Christian adversary, Marcion, of *"championing the cause of the Jews"* for interpreting the Jewish Bible literally rather than allegorically by showing that it prophecies Messiahs other than Jesus. To Tertullian (ca. 198) Marcion was a heretic guided by the Jews: "[Marcion] *must now cease to borrow poison from the Jew— "the asp," as the adage runs, "from the viper" — and henceforth vomit forth the virulence of his own disposition, as when he alleges Christ to be a phantom"* (ANF vol. 3. p. 327). Conversely, Marcion then accuses his "orthodox" Christian opponents of fostering "Jewish" ties and nurturing "Jewish" roots because they insist on using the Jewish Bible to prophecy Jesus as Messiah, whereas the God of the Jewish Bible was really evil and defective, having been replaced by a superior Christian non-Jewish deity, Jesus, who was sent to Earth, not as a Jew, but as a Gentile.

Note that although the Christian Fathers considered Marcion's abandonment of Jewish Scriptures as "heresy," he overcame the "orthodox" Gentile Christian inconsistency of employing Jewish Scriptures to justify a non-Jewish religion. Failure of Marcionites to supplant "orthodox" Gentile Christianity shows how essential it was for Christianity to use its unique "exegesis" of Jewish Scriptures to pretend it possessed an antique origin.

Sadly for Jews, opposition to Marcion by Christian Fathers such as St. Justin Martyr, Tertullian, St. Irenaeus, led to declarations that it was not Marcion's Jewish Scriptural God who was "inferior," but it was the Jews, replaced in God's favor by the worthier Gentile Christians. *"Thus, the God of the Hebrew Bible was salvaged for Christians precisely by means of the anti-Judaic myth"* (Efroymson 1979, p. 101).

It is ironic that Marcion, the Christian leader furthest from any Jewish influence (see also Note #14, p. 167), was condemned for emulating Jews. It is also ironic that had the Christian Fathers adopted Marcion's form of Christianity with its opposition to Jews and Jewish Scriptures, Christian antisemitism (had Christianity survived) would most probably have been much less virulent, since Jews would not have been considered Scriptural competitors; and Gentile Christianity's impelling need to supplant Jews as the "True Israelites" would not have arisen. (See also Note #20.)

Accusations of "Jewishness" were also raised by "orthodox" theologians against Arius and other Gentile Christian "heretics" who subordinated the Son (Jesus) below the Father (God) rather than endow Jesus and God the same divine status. *"Direct contemporaries [St.] Athanasius and [St.] Ephraem, in the process of defining and actively reifying 'Arian' as a cohesive (and heretical) group, both used sharp anti-Jewish and anti-Judaizing language in order more clearly to define and more easily to denigrate their subordinationist Christian opponents"* (Shepardson, p. 701). St. John Chrysostom condemns any such "Arian," whether Christian or Pagan, as suffering from the "Jewish" disease: *"The Anomoean's [Arian] impiety is akin to that of the Jews ...because the Jews and the Anomoeans make the same accusation. ... He [Jesus] called God His own Father and so made Himself equal to God"* (*Discourses Against Judaizing Christians* 1.6, Harkins, p. 4).

In the *Gospel of Philip*, a fourth or fifth century Gospel believed written to support the orthodox Nicene creed, *"anti-Judaism does not seem to be directed only, or even primarily against Jews, but is rather used as a weapon or branding device against other Christians whose theology and ritual practice it implicitly associates with Judaism. In this respect the Gospel of Philip is representative of its time, as associative anti-Judaism of this kind was indeed a popular device used by a broad selection of church fathers, not least in the fourth and fifth centuries"* (Lundhaug, p. 245).

St. Jerome (ca. 400) used the "Jewish" accusation against Christian rivals indiscriminately: "*Sabellians, Arians, Photinians, Nestorians, and others could all become Jewish with a few strokes of the pen*" (Newman 2001, p. 422). On the other hand, St. Jerome's anti-Jewish credentials were no protection against accusations of himself being pro-Jewish. Rufinus castigates St. Jerome for having been sympathetic to Jews in enlisting Jewish teachers to help translate the Hebrew Scriptures into Latin. St. Jerome then defends himself: "*There is nothing to blame in my getting the help of a Jew in translating from the Hebrew*" (Jerome's *Apology for Himself Against the Books of Rufinus* Book 1, 13), and reaffirms his anti-Jewish credentials. "*I have a strange dislike to those of the circumcision. For up to the present day they persecute our Lord Jesus Christ in the synagogues of Satan*" (Letter LXXXIV, NPNF Series 2, vol. 6, p. 176).

Marshall (pp. 12–13): "*In the history of Christianity the accusation that a person is too Jewish has been damning indictment. From Ignatius of Antioch's condemnation of those who 'talk of Jesus and practice Judaism,' through the twentieth century in which to be a Judenchristen was to be less than fully Christian, the accusation of association with Judaism that did not properly subordinate Judaism to Christianity was a peculiarly Christian form of slander.*" Even John Calvin (ca. 1530), as firm a Christian as one could expect, was accused of "Judaizing" because he failed to interpret "Christologically" some Jewish Scriptural Psalms (Pak).

18

CHRISTIAN OPPOSITION TO BIBLICAL "LAW"; DENOUNCING JEWS WHO OBSERVE IT

With its need to gain religious legitimacy among Romans, St. Paul's Gentile Christianity's conflict with Jewish Christian "Judaizers" on Jewish practices gave way to a much broader conflict with Jews on possession of the Jewish Scriptures. Reinterpreting the Jewish Bible to prophecy the coming of Jesus thus became an abiding Christian pursuit that endures even in modern times (see, for example, Childs 2004). Again, the aim was to lend authority and antiquity to Christianity yet capriciously insist Christians were absolved from explicit Scriptural laws such as circumcision, dietary observances, and so forth. Celsus (ca. 180), the Pagan critic of Christianity, has a Jew question Christians: *"Why take your start in the religion of the Jews? How can you despise the origins in which you yourselves claim to be rooted? Or can you name some other origin for your doctrine than our law?"* (Hoffmann 1987, pp. 60–61, also Denzey, p. 504).

St. Paul contended that Biblical "Law" was given by Moses to Jews because of their predilection for sin. *"The power of sin is the* [Jewish] *law"* (*1 Corinthians* 15. 56). *"They* [Jews] *have been continually filling up the measure of their sins"* (*1 Thessalonians* 2.16). Following the "Law" was therefore not meant to venerate righteousness, but to counteract Jewish depravity. Congruently, St. Paul remarkably argues that "sin" is not caused by intention or malice but by its prohibition. *"For 'no human being will be justified in his sight' by deeds prescribed by law, for through the law comes the knowledge of sin"* (*Romans* 3.20). *"If it had not been for the law, I would not have known sin. I would not have known what it is to covet if the law had not said 'You shall not covet.' ... Apart from the law sin lies dead"* (*Romans* 7.7–8). What is prohibited in Jewish law thus produces the sin that is prohibited: the strange logic of claiming that "sin" is condemned by God, yet its condemnation is its "cause."

When St. Paul appears to acknowledge Mosaic Law (e.g., *Romans* 3.31), it is *"only to support his point about the termination of the Mosaic Law for the New Covenant* [Gentile Christian] *participants"* (Adeyemi, p. 51). The *Epistle of Barnabas* oddly accuses the Jews of sinning against Mosaic Law, yet misunderstanding the "Law" they sinned against was not to be taken literally, since only *"We* [Christians] *"rightly understand his commandments, explain them as the Lord intended. For this purpose He circumcised our ears and hearts, that we might understand these things"* (Chapter 10, ANF vol. 1, p. 144).

Following a sort of similar logic, Christian theologians claimed the Jews broke the "Law" when it was given to them, but perversely insisted on obeying the "Law" when Gentile Christianity abrogated it. For the theologians, "righteous non-Jews" such as Father Abraham were absolved from following the "Law" because of their "faith," understood as "faith in Jesus Christ." Ignored is that Father Abraham followed the "Law" and was circumcised, as were all his male progeny, with none showing awareness of "Jesus Christ.". Thus, although St. John's Gospel has Jesus say (8.58): *"Very truly, I tell you, before Abraham was, I am,"* there are no known uncircumcised Christian "faithful" present in history either before or after Father Abraham, or Old Testament Scriptural or non-Scriptural records of anyone named Jesus Christ before the first century C.E.

Despite the absence of any supporting evidence, Christian leaders never ceased their claims for an ancient origin. St. Clement of Alexandria (ca. 195): "[B]*efore the foundation of the world were we* [Christians], *who became destined to be in Him* [Jesus Christ] … *we date from the beginning; for in the beginning was the Word* [Jesus Christ]" (*Exhortation to the Heathen*, ANF vol. 2, p.173). According to Eusebius' *Ecclesiastical History* (1.4, ca. 330), "righteous" ancients who lived before and after Noah's Biblical flood were all therefore Christian: *"All these whose righteousness won them*

208

commendation going back from Abraham himself to the first man [Adam], *might be described as Christians in fact if not in name, without departing far from the truth. ... It is obvious that they knew God's Christ Himself, since He appeared to Abraham, instructed Isaac, spoke to Israel* [Jacob], *and conversed freely with Moses and the prophets who came later ... Obviously we must regard the* [Gentile Christian] *religion proclaimed in recent years to all nations through Christ's teaching as none other than the first, most ancient, and most primitive of all religions, discovered by Abraham and his followers.*"

These gross distortions of Jewish Scriptures —their histories, and their meanings — parallel the "exegetical" allegorizing process begun by St. Paul (*Galatians* 4.21–5.1). According to Levenson (p. 229), St. Paul equates "*the Church with Isaac, and the Jews...with Ishmael, the son of the slave woman whom Paul associates with Sinai. This makes the* [Jewish] *community of the Torah into usurpers and* [Gentile Christian] *community of the Pauline Gospel into the rightful claimants to the Abrahamic legacy.*" Like Isaac, ancient Jewish Biblical figures are thus brazenly flipped into non-Jewish "Righteous Christians of Faith," supplanting Jews in God's favor as the "True Israel" (Note #19), sanctioning Gentile Christian termination of Jewish Biblical "Law."

St. Augustine (ca. 400), named by the Church as "The Supreme Authority of Christian Tradition," maintains an unbridled claim: "*The whole* [Biblical] *narrative ... in the minutest details, is a prophecy of Christ and the Church*" (*Reply to Faustus* XII.8, NPNF Series 1, vol. 4 p. 186). To St. Augustine, Jews served only as carriers of Jewish Scriptures meant to be read and interpreted for Christian purposes: "*A document the Jew carrieth, wherefrom a Christian may believe. Our librarians they have become, just as slaves are wont behind their masters to carry documents, so these* [Jews] *faint in carrying those* [Christians] *profit by reading*" (*On the Psalms* LVII.7, Ibid. vol. 8, p. 227). "*Like milestones along the route, the*

Jews inform the traveler, while they themselves remain senseless and immobile" (Nirenberg, pp. 130–131).

Some Christian Fathers claimed Jewish-observed Biblical Law was made to satisfy angels rather than God. St. Aristides (ca. 130, *Apology* XIV): "[I]*n their imaginations they* [Jews] *conceive it is God they serve; whereas by their mode of observance it is the angels and not to God that their service is rendered: — as when they celebrate sabbaths and the beginning of the months, and feasts of unleavened bread* [Passover], *and a great fast* [Day of Atonement]; *and fasting and circumcision and the purification of meats*" (ANF vol. 9, p. 276). Others argued that ritualistic practices were imposed on Jews because of God's disapproval, punishing them for crimes against Jesus yet to come! *"For we too would observe the fleshly circumcision, and the Sabbaths, and in short all the feasts, if we did not know for what reason they were enjoined on you, on account of your transgressions and the hardness of your hearts*" (St. Justin Martyr (ca. 150) *Dialogue with Trypho, a Jew* XVIII, ANF vol. 1, p. 203). Tertullian (ca. 198, *Adversus Judaeos*) claimed circumcision was given to Jews for their later misdeeds so they would be recognized as Jews and prevented by Romans from entering Jerusalem after the Jewish-Roman war.

For "Jewish Law*"* Christians substituted St. Paul's new "*Law of Christ*" (*Galatians* 6.2), allowing many new practices and directives to be accepted and sanctified through illusory Jewish Scriptural reinterpretations. St. Ignatius (ca. 100, *Letter to the Magnesians* 8): "*For if we still live according to Jewish law, and the circumcision of the flesh, we deny that we have received grace. For the divinest prophets lived according to Jesus Christ*" (ANF vol. 1, p. 62). St. Justin Martyr (*Dialogue with Trypho, a Jew*, XXIX): "[The Jewish Scriptures are] *your scriptures, or rather not yours, but ours. For we believe them; but you, though you read them, do not catch the spirit that is in them*" (ANF vol. 1, p. 209).

St. Melito of Sardis (ca. 170): *"When the Church arose and the Gospel took precedence, the model* [Jewish Law] *was made void, conceding its power to the* [Gentile Christian] *reality, and the law was fulfilled, conceding its power to the Gospel"* (Williamson and Allen, p. 11). Tertullian (*Latin Christianity* XIV): *"Going about to establish their own righteousness, they* [Jews] *have not submitted themselves unto the righteousness of God; for Christ is the end of the law for righteousness to everyone that believeth"* (ANF vol. 3. p. 460). St. Cyprian (ca. 250, *Three Books of Testimonies Against the Jews*; Heads 9, 10, 11, 15): *"That the former law which was given to Moses was to cease; that a new law was to be given; that another dispensation and a new covenant was to be given; that Christ should be the house and temple of God"* (ANF vol. 5, pp. 510–511). St. Augustine (*Against the Jews* 1.2): *"They* [Jews] *do not listen to what we* [Christians] *say, because they do not understand what they read"* (*The Fathers of the Church*, Patristic Series, vol. 27, p. 392).

Although opposition to Mosaic Law and Law-observant Jews was repeated endlessly, neither St. Paul or his successors ever offered satisfactory explanations why following Biblical rules generates "sin" (*Galatians* 3.22), why the Law is a "curse" (*Galatians* 3.10–13), and why the Law is "the ministry of death" (*2 Corinthians* 3.7). That is: how do Jews and Gentiles who follow Biblical Law impede their salvation? In view of the compelling Biblical commandments in Genesis to Deuteronomy to obey the Law, St. Paul's "justification" for stating *"No one will be justified by the works of the* [Jewish] *Law"* (*Galatians* 2.16) appears quite "unjustified." Nowhere in the Jewish Scriptures can one find statements that the advent of Jesus Christ ended the "Law," or that opposition to Jewish Law gained through "faith" in Jesus Christ, makes such faithful into *"children of God"* (*Galatians* 3.26).

For Christian theologians, the inconsistency of claiming possession of the Jewish Scriptures and ignoring its "Law" would probably have had little effect in diminishing recruitment, since gaining antique religious prestige and distance from Jewish identity may have been more important to Gentiles than Biblical inconsistency. There was certainly an advantage in enabling Gentiles to believe that the end of Jewish Law must have come from God (*Romans* 10.4, *Galatians* 3.13) rather than from St. Paul's more mundane need to evangelize Gentiles averse to Jewish customs and religious rituals.

For Jews, however, their Biblical Covenant and its derived teachings had more than a millennium of moral, cultural, and emotional significance, and were not so easily disdained. *Psalms* (19.7–8):

> *"The law of Yahweh is perfect, reviving the soul;*
> *the decrees of Yahweh are sure, making wise the simple;*
> *the precepts of Yahweh are right rejoicing the heart;*
> *the commandment of Yahweh is clear, enlightening the eyes."*

Although Christian theologians often disparaged Judaism for its legalistic Talmudic intricacies, Christian "Law" involved itself in as many, or even more, complex liturgies and sacramental dicta, replacing the Old Covenant/Jewish-Torah with pieties from a New Covenant/Christian-Torah. For example, St. Cyril of Jerusalem, "Doctor of the Church" (ca. 350 C.E.), demands minute exacting conduct in celebrating the Eucharist: "*So when you come forward, do not come with arm extended or fingers parted. Make your left hand a throne for your right, since your right hand is about to welcome a king. Cup your palm and receive in it Christ's body, saying in response 'Amen.' Then carefully bless your eyes with a touch of the holy body, and consume it ... After partaking of Christ's body, go to the chalice of his blood. ... Bow your head ... and sanctify yourself by partaking also of Christ's blood. While your lips are still moist with his blood, touch it with your hands and bless your eyes, forehead and other organs of sense*" (Bradshaw, p. 216).

Similarly, Tertullian (*On the Soldiers' Crown*) gives precise instructions to converts: "*At every forward step and movement, at every going in and out, when we put on our clothes and shoes, when*

212

we bathe, when we sit at table, when we light the lamps, on couch, on seat, in all ordinary actions of daily life, we trace upon the fore-head the sign of the cross" (Stevenson, p. 171). Christian prayer must also follow exact procedure: towards the East, three times per day, in the kneeling position (except on Sunday), with raised arms forming or pointing to the Cross, with eyes toward Heaven (Hvalvik 2014).

Note that searching the Jewish Bible for appropriate quotes that could be rendered in favor of Christian religious beliefs was also, then as now, to convince Gentile Christians of their religious legiti-macy, and had little to do with converting Jews from whom Church leaders most willingly distanced themselves, and for whom such contortions made little sense (Kraabel 1992a). *"The remarkable thing about this Christian view of the world is that its complex system of thought was created to support a single claim. The claim was that Christians were the legitimate heirs of the epic of Israel, that the Jews had never understood the intentions of their God, and that the story of Israel, if one reads it rightly, was 'really' about the coming of Christ"* (Mack 1995, p. 252).

Both denigration of Jews and elevation of Gentile Christians "to God's favor" thus became justified by the habitual Christian ex-egetical process of reinterpreting the Jewish Scriptures to suit Chris-tian needs (Note #7). *"The portrait of the Jew was built up by pasting together verses of the Bible. The complaints the inspired* [Jewish] *writers had made were torn from their contexts of time and place and, combined into a single portrait, provided all the evidence that could be wished for of the utter depravity of the people of God. Thus was created the picture of the eternal Jew, a conventional figure, a literary fiction"* (Simon, p. 215).

[O]*ur traditional (orthodox) christology is often interpreted and preached in such a way that (explicitly or implicitly) fidelity in the Jewish tradition appears as a special evil or problem or at best an incomprehensible anachronism. ... [N]o reputable contemporary theologian will deny that Christian usage changes the focus of the title* ["Christ"] *and gives it a meaning it did not previously have. All the Hebrew Scriptures and traditions are reinterpreted by Christians in the light of this* [new] *specific meaning content*" (Hellwig, pp. 121–122).

As noted often elsewhere in this monograph (e.g., pp. 60, 165, 220), if we accept the presumed ever-present ever-ancient "Christian Faith" as belief in Jesus Christ as divine Savior, belief in Father Abraham as faithful Christian ancestor, and other illusory Gentile Christian phenomena and concepts, a discomforting issue prevails. Why, until a generation or so after Jesus' death, neither the Jewish Scriptures, nor the histories of any other group before the Common Era, Egyptian, Greek, Persian, Roman, etc., recorded the appearance of (1) Jesus Christ; (2) Gentile Christian Jesus-worshippers; (3) Gentile Christian practices and doctrines; or (4) Gentile Christian assemblies or Churches? That is, where can we find evidence of Pauline Christianity in the 1,500-year interval between Abraham and St. Paul's "Ecclesia"? It seems that the assumption that Gentile Christians existed anywhere on earth prior to the time and preaching of St. Paul is no more than the attempt to employ Scriptural sophistry to disguise unrealistic historical incongruities.

Jewish opposition to worshipping Gentile Christianity's "Jesus Christ" as the Biblically-prophesied Messiah has thus been a perennial problem for Christian theologians since such opposition comes from a Jewish ethnicity that created and maintained those Biblical Scriptures long before "Jesus Christ" appeared on Earth. From St. Paul onward, Christian theologians therefore repeatedly claimed their allegorical interpretations were more reliable than Jewish readings of Jewish Scriptures, because the true "hidden" meanings of Jewish Scriptural precepts and history remain understandable only to Christians. For example, St. Justin Martyr (ca. 150) *Dialogue with Trypho, a Jew* LV: "*God has withheld from you* [Jews] *the ability to discern the wisdom of His Scriptures*" (ANF vol. 1, p. 222). St. Cyril

214

of Alexandria (ca. 430): *"The Jews are the most deranged of all men. They have carried impiety to its limit, and their mania exceeds even that of the Greeks. They read the Scriptures and do not understand what they read. Although they had heavenly light from above, they preferred to walk in darkness"* (Wilken, p. 1).

In the words of a modern Christian theologian (Childs 1970, p. 105), "[Jewish] *Scripture served not as 'interesting sources' of historical information ... but as testimony that the salvation and faith of the old covenant was one with that revealed in Jesus Christ."* Or as stated by Seitz (p. 103), there is a theological *"need to account for the Old Testament as Christian Scripture."* To Pelican (p. 101), proper interpretation shows that the Jewish "Old" Testament's purpose can only be fulfilled when combined with the Christian "New" Testament: "[T]*he Christian Bible is unlike the Jewish Tanakh in being permanently and unavoidably plural, consisting as it does of two quite separate though interlocking Testaments: The New is in the Old concealed, The Old is in the New revealed."*

The attitude of Christian critics thus remains simple: were Jews to overcome their "blindness" and reinterpret their Scriptures according to Christian "faith," they would have no recourse but to relinquish Judaism and become Christians. Perversely, such critics seem "blind" to the many rational reasons why Jews consider Jesus-worship as idolatry and oppose adopting Christian beliefs and practices (Note #11).

19
THE "HOLY," "UNHOLY," AND "TRUE ISRAELITES"

Proclamations claiming Christian superiority over Jews began early. St. Ignatius (ca. 100) *Letter to the Magnesians* (X): "*Christianity did not embrace Judaism, but Judaism Christianity, so that every tongue which believeth might be gathered together to God*" (ANF vol.1, p. 63; also, Wilde, p. 84). St. Melito of Sardis (ca. 170): "*The* [Jewish] *Temple was precious, but it is worthless now because of the Christ above*" (MacLennan, p. 115).

Christians also used Jewish self-criticism, such as Biblical pleadings against idolatry, as contrast to Gentile Christian "virtue." Thus, Tertullian's *Adversus Judaeos* (ca. 198) counters Jewish opposition to Christian worship of Jesus Christ by claiming it is Jews who are the unholy idolaters whereas Christians are idolatry's holy opponents: "*...it is proven that they [Jews] have ever been guilty of the crime of idolatry, whereas our lesser or posterior people [the Gentile Church] quit the idols...and converted to the same God from whom Israel, as we have shown, departed*" (Ruether 1974, p. 126). According to Origen (ca. 230), Jewish understanding of their Jewish Scriptures is grossly defective because Jews are "*more fleshly and sexually depraved than their Christian counterparts*" (S. Drake, p. 40).

St. Aphrahat (Demonstrations Against the Jews, ca. 330): "*Israel has played the whore, and Judah has committed adultery. And the people which is of [the Christian Church] is the holy and faithful people, which has gone down and adhered to the Lord*" (Ruether 1974, p. 136). St. John Chrysostom (Against the Jews, Oration 1, ca. 386): "*The point is that, if their [Jewish] rituals are venerable and great, ours are false. But if ours are true, as indeed they are true, theirs are full of deceit*" (Mayer and Allen, p. 161).

St. Augustine's *Epistles* (ca. 400) follows St. Paul (*Galatians* 4.22-31) in audaciously revising Scriptural Genesis' straightforward genealogy: *"This Apostolic and Catholic doctrine shows sufficiently plainly to us that according to the origin of the flesh, the Jews belong to Sarah and the Ishmaelites to Hagar, but according to the mystery of the spirit, the Christians belong to Sarah and the Jews to Hagar"* (Simon, pp. 148; translated from the Latin on p. 511). Gentile Christianity's birth is thus placed a millennium before the first C.E. century's appearance of Jesus Christ, and pinned to Abraham and Abraham's wife Sarah, *"who is our mother eternal in the heavens"* (St. Augustine, *Against the Pelagians* 3, 13; NPNF Series 1, vol. 5, p. 408. Through such unrestrained exegesis, Christians perversely affix novel unique beliefs and practices on any personage or saying in the Jewish Scriptures. For example: *"That saying, 'the elder shall serve the younger,' is understood by our writers, almost without exception, to mean that the elder people, the Jews, shall serve the younger people, the Christians"* (St. Augustine, *City of God and Christian Doctrine*, NPNF Series 1, vol. 2, p. 331). Schaff (p. xi), feels such "exegesis" is extreme, but not blameworthy: *"In the Old Testament he [St. Augustine] looks upon almost every character and event as symbolic of Christ and Christian institutions. But as Trench well says, 'it is indeed far better to find Christ everywhere in the Old Testament than to find Him nowhere'."*

Transforming Biblical passages into allegories that change or reverse their meaning became accepted exegetical practice allowing self-serving Christian fancies to assume the status of holy writ. Christian theologians thus "dejudaized" Jewish Scriptures (Barclay 1996, p. 180), claiming that only Christians can discern hidden Scriptural messages which Jews cannot see or comprehend. St. Paul (2 Corinthians 3.15–16): *"Indeed, to this very day whenever Moses is read, a veil lies over their [Jewish] minds; but when one turns to the Lord [Jesus Christ], the veil is removed."* Little respect for Jewish understanding and the Jewish religion thus became a hallmark of Christian theology. Even St. Jerome (ca. 400), dependent on Jewish help in translating the Jewish Scriptures into Latin, left abusive anti-semitic diatribes: "*Jews are 'serpents,' 'haters of all men,' 'Judases'*" (Flannery, p. 50). To St. Jerome, Jewish prayers are like "*the grunting of a pig and the crying of donkeys*" (Charlesworth 1988, p. 47).

St. Paul also set the stage for the Christians claim to replace Jews as "God's Chosen People," by denying that circumcision (Genesis 17.10) and fealty to the Torah (Deuteronomy 30.6, 9–10) validate the Jewish covenant with Israel's God Yahweh. "*[A] person is a Jew who is one inwardly, and real circumcision is a matter of the heart — it is spiritual and not literal*" (*Romans* 2.29). "*It is not the children of the flesh* [Jews] *who are the children of God, but the children of the promise* [Christians] *are counted as descendants*" (Ibid. 9.8). "*For it is we* [Christians] *who are the circumcision, who ... boast in Jesus and have no confidence in the flesh*" (*Philippians* 3.3; also Note #7, p. 59). "*Our competence is from God, who has made us competent to be ministers of a new covenant, not of letter but of spirit; for the letter kills, but the Spirit gives life*" (*2 Corinthians* 3.5–6). "*All who rely on the works of the law are under a curse*" (*Galatians* 3.10, also Notes #18, #10.5). This theme of Gentile Christian superiority and Jewish ignobility was then repeated by Christian theologians as though St. Paul's imagined "Christian Covenant" must incontestably be true.

Epistle of Barnabas (ca. 100, IV): "*Their* [Jewish] *covenant was broken in order that the covenant of the beloved Jesus might be sealed upon our heart*" (ANF vol. 1, p. 139). "*Moses, as a servant received it* [the Torah]*; but the Lord himself* [Jesus]*, having suffered on our behalf, hath given it to us, that we* [Christians] *should be the people of inheritance*" (Ibid. p. 146). St. Justin Martyr (*Dialogue with Trypho, a Jew* CXXXV, ca. 150): "*Christ is the Israel and ...we, who have been quarried out from the bowels of Christ, are the true Israelite race.*" (ANF vol. 1, p. 267, also Donaldson 2013). "*For the true spiritual Israel, and descendants of Judah, Jacob, Isaac, and*

Abraham ... are we [Christians]" (Ibid. XI, vol. 1, p. 200). *"The blood of that circumcision is obsolete, and we trust in the blood of salvation; there is now another covenant, and another law"* (Ibid. XXIV, vol. 1, p. 206).

St. Irenaeus (ca. 180): *"Inasmuch as* [the Jews] *have rejected the Son of God, and cast Him out of the vineyard when they slew Him, God has justly rejected them, and given to the Gentiles outside the vineyard the fruits of its cultivation"* (ANF vol.1, p. 515). St. Cyprian (ca. 250): *"In repudiation of these* [Jews], *we Christians, when we pray, say Our Father; because He has begun to be ours, and has ceased to be the Father of the Jews, who have forsaken him"* (ANF vol. 5, p. 450). *Didascalia Apostolorum,* (ca. 300): *"That the Jews were disinherited, because they rejected Christ, and that we, who are of the Gentiles, were adopted into their place, is proved by the Scriptures"* (XLVII, ANF vol 7, p. 242).

St. Augustine (ca. 400, *Reply to Faustus* XII.11): *"The Church admits and avows the Jewish people to be cursed, because after killing Christ they continue to till the ground of an earthly circumcision, an earthly Sabbath, an earthly Passover, while the hidden strength or virtue of making known Christ, which this tilling contains, is not yielded to the Jews while they continue in impiety and unbelief, for it is revealed in the New Testament. While they will not turn to God, the veil which is on their minds in reading the Old Testament is not taken away"* (NPNF Series 1, vol. 4, p. 187). *"*[T]*he unbelief of the Jews has been made of signal benefit to us; so that those who do not receive in their heart for their own good these truths, carry in their hands for our benefit the writings in which these truths are contained. ... They testify to the truth by not understanding it"* (Ibid. XVI.21, p. 227).

Jewish insistence on being Yahweh's favored "Israelites" was pronounced illusory because Jews rejected newly invented Christian Scriptural exegesis. To St. Paul, non-Judaized Christian recruits "of faith" are the "true Israelites" (*Galatians* 6.16, *Romans* 11.26), whereas "faithless" Jews, even Jewish Christians, who dispute Pauline Scriptural renderings, are not Israelites at all. *"Not all those from Israel are Israel" (Romans* 9.6). Disconnecting "Jew" from "Israelite," allowed Gentile Christianity to use the "Christ event" (*Galatians* 3.24) to oppose any ethnic identity with Jews tied to Scriptural covenantal "works," yet claim "Israelite ancestry" as *"Abraham's Children of the promise" (Galatians* 3.16, 3.29). "Israelites" was therefore an ancient identity that could only be assumed by St. Paul's Gentile converts. This "supersessionist" theme — assumption of an antique origin by replacing Jews with Gentiles as the Scripturally ancient "True Israel" — extends through Gentile Christianity's history even to modern times.

James Dunn, a prominent Christian theologian, declares (1998, p. 508): *"A Christianity which does not understand itself in some proper sense as 'Israel' forfeits the claim to the scriptures of Israel."* Christian claims to being the "True Israel" thus continue to serve the "supersessionist" basis for Christian antisemitism. Dunn, in fact, infers that dialogue between *"'Judaism' and 'Christianity' cannot really begin"* because of conflicting claims as to who are the true bearers of "Israel's" identity (Ibid.). Discounted by Dunn and others are that the Jewish Scriptures were based on the unique history, customs, rituals, and laws made by Jews for Jews and not by Gentiles for Gentiles.

Although some may view the term "True Israelites" as unity of Gentiles and Jews under a new Christian banner, there is little to commend it since the Christian Fathers obviously defined the term to appropriate for themselves Jewish covenantal "Israelite" identity. (See also Lieu 2011.) *"For Christian thinkers intent on establishing the legitimacy of the religion as ancient only one real option was available: to present the Christian faith as the 'true' form of Judaism, a religion that could be traced as far back as Moses ... and beyond him all the way to Abraham. In a world that respected antiquity and suspected novelty, Judaism was a religion with venerable roots, and Christians needed to claim them as their own*" (Ehrman 2013, p. 482). In a sense, St. Paul's Gentile Christian offshoot of the Jewish religious tree, proclaimed Gentile Christianity as the tree itself.

Omitted in these Christian "supersessionist" claims is a rational explanation of why and how St. Paul and Christian Fathers gained "divine authority" to blatantly controvert history and confer upon themselves, and their newly minted Gentile religion, exclusive ownership and interpretation of the Jewish Scriptures. Again: how can Gentile Christianity be the ancient "True Israel" when there is nary a hint of Gentile Christian theology, Gentile Christian practices, Gentile Christian liturgy, or Christ-worshipping Gentile Christians until first century C.E.? Where were such uncircumcised "True Israelite" Gentile Christians during the more than thousand-year period between circumcised Abraham and circumcised Jesus?

Ruether (1981, p. 32): "*Christian theology set out to demonstrate the rejected status of the Jewish people and the spiritual blindness of its exegesis and piety in order to vindicate the correctness of its own exegesis and its claim to be the rightful heir of Israel's election.*"

20

DO CHRISTIANS NEED TO DEMEAN JEWS? WHAT IF JESUS HAD NOT BEEN A JEW?

By simply existing as non-Christians opposing Christianity, Jews remained a bane to Christianity's contention that the Jewish Scriptures composed and sustained by Jews were written for Christians. According to M. S. Taylor (p. 139): "*We have here a* [Christian] *tradition which remains constant over centuries, and forms a coherent body of mutually reinforcing arguments. It functions according to internal logic in which the invalidation of Judaism emerges as a theoretical necessity in the appropriation of the Jewish God and the Jewish Bible for the Church.*" Tertullian (ca. 198, *Apologies* XX): "*We point to the majesty of 'our' scriptures if not their antiquity*" (my emphasis, ANF vol. 3, p. 33).

It was thus extremely unfortunate for Jews that Christianity needed to use Jesus' ties to Judaism to provide it with the façade of antiquity. Had Jesus, his followers, and his message not been Jewish, Christianity — had it survived (under whatever name) without Jewish connection— would have been forced to seek historic legitimacy elsewhere than from Jewish Scriptures. That is, had a non-Jewish messianic figure like charismatic Jesus arisen from a Gentile non-Jewish environment, such new savior-based religion would have faced finding other means than appropriating Jewish Scriptures to justify a historic divine origin. Its antisemitism would most likely then have been less virulent, scaling no differently from other Roman ethnic/religious/cultural prejudices. Moreover, had such a Gentile movement not been dependent on exploiting the Jewish Scriptures, it would have been obvious to that movement that Jesus the Jew was not a Messiah for either the Jews or the non-Jews (see Note #15, p. 190).

Meeks (1985, p. 114): "*If Marcion's movement* [Christian rejection of any ties to Jews, Judaism, and the Jewish Torah — Note #17] *had endured, Christianity would have become a different*

222

thing." Ehrman (2003, p. 111) points out that had Marcion's movement succeeded, it could "*have led simply to benign neglect* [of Jews] *as Jews and their religion would have been considered to be of no relevance and certainly no competition for Christians. The entire history of anti-Semitism might have been avoided, ironically, by an anti-Jewish religion.*"

Again, it is essential to recognize that **it was not direct conflict** with Jews that accounted for the intense antisemitism in Christianity's development. For Christian Fathers, such as Tertullian (ca. 198), to write polemical anti-Jewish (*Adversus Judaeos*) tracts, dialogue with Jews or intimate knowledge of Judaism was not necessary (Ruether 1974, p. 148). Efroymson (1976) notes: "*Tertullian's anti-Judaism is an inheritance from his Christian and Roman and African roots. But if he did not really know any Jews, if there were no personal confrontations and disputations with living Jews to keep this inheritance from wasting away, what kept it alive? Briefly, it can be argued that he grew to need anti-Judaism…. He uses it rhetorically to win arguments against his* [Christian] *opponents, and he uses it theologically, or symbolically, to construct a Christianity, a Christian social identity which is centrally, crucially, un-Jewish, anti-Jewish, and better-than-Jewish.*"

21

CURRYING FAVOR WITH THE ROMANS; ROMAN OPPRESSION, AND JESUS' CRUCIFIXION

There are many indications that Gentile Christians used overt praise of Roman rule to withstand Romans hostility, and to also distance themselves from repeatedly rebellious Jews (Note #15). St. John's Gospel (18.36) has Jesus claim the "Kingdom of God" is no threat to authority: "*My Kingdom is not from this world ... my Kingdom is not from here.*" St. Paul (*Romans* 13.1–2, 7): "*Let every person be subject to the governing* [Roman] *authorities; for there is no authority except from God, and those authorities that exist have been instituted by God. Therefore whoever resists authority resists what God has appointed, and those who resist will incur judgment ... Pay to all what is due them — taxes to whom taxes are due, revenue to whom revenue is due, respect to whom respect is due, honor to whom honor is due.*"

Similarly, accounts of St. Paul's travels in Acts of the Apostles show compliance with Roman authorities, if not cooperation. According to Diehl (p. 52): "*Paul speaks openly to Roman rulers Festus and Agrippa in Acts 25:1–26:32 about his gospel message, and he does not appear to be a major threat to the imperial system (Acts 26:30). We can note that in the book of Acts the Roman authorities actually aided and protected Paul in his conflict with the Jewish leadership in various cities: in Corinth (Acts 18:12–17), in Jerusalem (Acts 21:27–40; 22:22–30), in Caesarea (Acts chapters 23–25), and in Rome (Acts 28:17–20).*" In Scroggs' judgment (p. 147): "*The author of Acts ... wants to convince his readers that the Church has nothing to fear from civic and Roman government, that the Church and Rome are compatible.*" M. Grant (p,219): "*Acts is hostile to the Jews. Like the Gospels, it is very eager to show that the early Christians never shared disloyalty towards Rome. ... We are also assured that it was never the Romans who persecuted the Christians, but only the Jews.*"

Vaage (2006b, pp. 258–259): "*Christianity ... promised its practitioners a greater measure of individual well-being and contentment but always entirely within the bounds of the existing* [magisterial] *social order. If occasionally one might be obliged to 'serve God rather than man,' such service was ... as a martyr or witness to the truth in question. Luke's representation of Jesus and his disciples, including the figure of Paul, as men of (ascetic) valour is quite compatible with the evangelist's larger political vision of early Christian accommodation and submission to Roman rule.*"

Obedience to Roman authority became a common Christian ecclesiastical theme. "*For the Lord's sake accept the authority of every human institution, whether of the emperor as supreme, or of governors, as sent by him to punish those who do wrong and to praise those who do right*" (*1 Peter* 2.13). In *Titus* (3.1), a second century pseudonymous letter ascribed to St. Paul, Christians are admonished "*to be subject to rulers and authorities, to be obedient.*" In a fourth century treatise on Christian doctrine (*Constitutions of the Holy Apostles*, VII.1): "*Thou shalt fear the king, knowing that his appointment is of the Lord. His rulers thou shalt honor as the ministers of God, for they are revengers of all unrighteousness; to whom pay taxes, tribute and every obligation with a willing mind*" (ANF vol. 7, p. 468).

St. Irenaeus (ca. 180, *Against Heresies* V, Wiles and Santer, p. 226): "*It is by God's decree that men are born and it is by the same God's decree that rulers are set up — rulers appropriate to the people to be ruled over by them at that particular time. Thus some rulers are given by God with a view to the improvement and benefit of their subjects and the preservation of justice; others are given with a view to producing fear, punishment and reproof; yet others are given with a view to displaying mockery, insult and pride — in each case in accordance with the deserts of the subjects. Thus, as we have already said, God's just judgment falls equally on all men."*

Slavery is not to be challenged: *"Let all who are under the yoke of slavery regard their masters as worthy of all honor ... Those who have believing masters must not be disrespectful of them on the ground that they are members of the church; rather they must serve them all the more, since those who benefit by their service are believers and beloved"* (*1 Timothy* 6.1–2). *"Tell slaves to be submissive to their masters and to give satisfaction in every respect; they are not to talk back, not to pilfer, but show complete and perfect fidelity, so that in everything they may be an ornament to the doctrine of God our Savior"* (*Titus* 2.9–10). Briggs (p. 117): *"There is no Pauline or New Testament passage that addresses the vulnerability of slaves to sexual exploitation or physical torture. ... It is unlikely that Paul or the New Testament 'Haustafeln'* [household code] *intended to prevent owners from physically beating their slaves for what they perceived as disrespectful speech, laziness, tardiness, or lack of success in a task."*

St. Augustine (ca. 410) offers the notion (*City of God* XIX, 15) that slavery is somehow justified by war's victory over the vanquished, whose servitude in defeat *"could never have arisen save through sin ... a result of the first judgment of God, who humbles the vanquished either for the sake or of punishing their sins. ... This servitude is, however, penal, and is appointed by that law which enjoins the preservation of the natural order and forbids its disturbance"* (NPNF Series 1, vol. 2, p. 141). According to St. Ambrose (ca. 380), slaves can draw comfort that *"the lower the station in life, the more exalted the virtue"* (Ste. Croix 2006, p. 352).

St. Clement of Rome (ca. 95) beseeched the Corinthian Christians to subject themselves to priests and presbyters like soldiers in the Roman Imperium: *"Let us consider those who serve under our generals, with what order, obedience, and submissiveness they perform the things which are commanded them.... each one in his own rank performs the things commanded by the king and the generals. The great cannot subsist without the small, and the small without the great"* (ANF vol. 1, p. 15). To distinguish Christians (probably from rebellious Jews), St. Justin Martyr (ca. 150) proclaims to the Romans: *"more than all other men are we your helpers and allies in promoting peace"* (*Apology* 1.12, ANF vol. 1 p. 166). St. Irenaeus (ca. 180): *"Through their* [Roman] *instrumentality, the world is at peace"* (ANF vol. 1, p. 503). Tertullian (ca. 198): *"A Christian is enemy to none, least of all to the Emperor of Rome, whom he knows to be appointed by his God, and so cannot but love and honour; and who's well-being moreover, he must needs desire, with that of the empire over which he reigns so long as the world shall stand— for so long as that shall Rome continue"* (ANF vol. 3, p. 195).

Eusebius (ca. 330), *Ecclesiastical History*: *"The* [Roman] *Emperor directs his gaze above, and frames his earthly government according to the pattern of that divine original, feeling strength in its conformity to the monarchy of God"* (Davis, p. 73). In his book, *In Praise of Constantine* (III–IV), Eusebius exclaims: [T]*his is the law of royal authority, the law which decrees one rule over everybody. Monarchy excels all other kinds of constitution and government. For rather do anarchy and civil war result from the alternative, a polyarchy based on equality. ... Him the voices learned in God have acclaimed in prophecy as Supreme Commander and Chief High Priest, Prophet of the Father and Carrier of Great Counsel, Radiance of the Paternal Light and Sole-Begotten Son ...* [Jesus Christ] *has modeled the kingdom on earth into a likeness of the one in heaven, toward which He urges all mankind to strive, holding forth to them this fair hope"* (H. A. Drake, pp. 87–88).

Eusebius' *Ecclesiastical History* (5.5) also recounts Emperor Marcus Aurelius' letter (ca. 169) in which Rome's German legions *"parched with thirst"* were saved by Christian soldiers' prayers for rain and victory. *"The message was clear. Christians are no danger to Rome; they are instead the cause of its security"* (Attridge, p. 189).

"Generally Eusebius presented the empire as an institution that accorded the church the respect it deserved. ... and in spite of the persecutions, saw the Roman empire as an institution ordained by God as part of his scheme for the propagation of the Christian faith" (Humphries, pp. 38–39). *"The elimination or sublimination of local identities is the means to peace and unity for both church and empire. ... Eusebius unites Constantine's imperial aspirations and the church's proselytizing desires most powerfully when he describes the cross as symbolic of their dual victory"* (Schott, pp.157–158).

By contrast, Jewish Rabbis saw Rome as the Biblical Esau, long term enemy of Israel (Neusner 1987, p. 187), and made little attempt to curry favor with Rome. *"Of the thousands of Jewish inscriptions that have been discovered in the Land of Israel, whether Greek, Hebrew or Aramaic,* [this] *is the only one dedicated to the welfare of a reigning* [Roman] *monarch"* (S. J. D. Cohen 1992, p. 203). Gribetz (p. 60) points out that Rabbis equated Roman Emperor birthday celebrations with those of Egyptian Pharaohs, casting *"the contemporary Roman leader in the shadow of an ancient enemy of the Jews, a biblical character who epitomizes the enslavement of Israel and the denial of God."* Rabbinical opposition to Roman dominance extended from *"refusal to collaborate with, and contempt for their* [Roman] *rulers"* to cautioning Jews that *"attendance of sanguinary games"* is *"tantamount to murder unless they could save the human victims"* (Schwartz, p.114). Compared to Gentile Christianity's submissiveness to Roman rule, it is obvious that Jesus' call for an imminent "Kingdom of God" in Israel (Note #15, pp. 182, 184, 185) would have conflicted with Roman despotism, crucifying him as "King of the Jews."

Unfortunately for those Christians who sought freedom and justice in a "Kingdom of God," their leaders' demand for obedience to Roman authority meant preservation of Roman social and economic divisions. Oakman (2008, pp. 161–162): *"What was originally a radical social critique by Jesus and his followers of the violent and oppressive political-economic order in the countryside of the early Empire becomes in Luke's conception a rather innocuous sharing-ethic ambiguous in its import for rural dwellers. No dramatic social reconstruction ... is expected or is necessary."*

By substituting obedience and piety for Jesus' social justice, Christianity proposed reforming people to improve their subjection to the state, rather than restructuring the state to improve peoples' lives. *"Follow the rules, and only desire what is given."* Social hierarchies of rich and poor, politically powerful and politically weak, thus prevailed in both earthly Rome and earthly Christianity. Jesus Christ's delayed "Kingdom" and its rule of justice was hence transferred to the spiritual Heaven to which Jesus had ascended. Until Christ's second coming, Gentile Christians must await justice, not in an earthly "Kingdom of God" (Note #22, pp. 245*ff*) but in St. Paul's *"Our citizenship is in Heaven"* (*Philippians* 3.20). However, Heaven, like earth, also followed the Christian concept of imperial political power, so when Christ returns, it will be with celestial authority *"in the same way"* he went to Heaven (Acts of the Apostles 1.11), allowing Jesus to say imperiously *"All authority in Heaven and on Earth has been given to me"* (St. Matthew 28.18).

Sadly, throughout all these pronouncements, the New Testament bears no mention of the recurrent Jewish struggle, nor of any other struggle, against injustice and impoverishment caused by the avarice and tyranny of Rome's rulers, armies, procurators, and collaborators. As discussed in Note #15, exploitation was an impelling motive for Roman conquest, east to west. Agricultural Israel, like other conquered territories, was brought *"into the orbit of empire to siphon off its surplus product in the form of tribute, taxes, rents, interests and loans, and a variety of other devices"* (Arnal 2001, p. 101). "Pax Romana" was "Tax Romana" for many whom the Romans vanquished.

In a famous anti-Roman speech by Calgacus, a learned British leader (ca. 85 C.E.): *"Nature has willed that every man's children and kindred should be his dearest objects. Yet these are torn from us by conscriptions to be slaves elsewhere. Our wives and our sisters, even though they may escape violation from the enemy, are dishonored under the names of friendship and hospitality. Our goods and fortunes they collect for their tribute, our harvests for their granaries. Our very hands and bodies, under the lash and in the midst of insult, are worn down by the toil of clearing forests and morasses. Robbers of the world, having by their universal plunder exhausted the land, they rifle the deep. If the enemy be rich, they are rapacious; if he be poor, they lust for dominion; neither the east nor the west has been able to satisfy them. Alone among men they covet with equal eagerness poverty and riches. To robbery, slaughter, plunder, they give the lying name of empire; they make a desolation and call it peace.*"

Roman society was a slave society, characterized by Conzelmann (p. 40) as ruled by *"rapacity and injustice."* In an existence continually supplemented by fresh conquests and ruined peasants, Rome followed the tenet that military power primarily determines society's social and economic structure, furnishing an empire of which more than one third were slaves (Hubbard, p. 91). *"The Roman legions purposely terrorized subject peoples in the 'shock and awe' devastation of villages and their land, slaughter and enslavement of the people, and public crucifixion of any who dared lead resistance"* (Horsley 2012, p. 80). To Cicero, perhaps the most famous of Roman orators, Jews and Syrians were among the *"nations born to slavery"* (*De Provinciis Consularibus* 5.10).

In all of its literature and activity, Gentile Christianity never expressed opposition to Roman political, economic, and social exploitation. Not a single Christian saint was martyred for struggling against exploitative injustice in the Roman Empire. The "subversion" of which Christians were accused, was that of opposition to Roman civic religion, but never "subversion" of abusive Roman rule. Even after the failed Bar Kochba rebellion (135 C.E.), some Jewish

Rabbis, by contrast, began to predict the fall of Rome from the second century onward (Feldman 2006, pp. 791–799, Neusner 1987). A passage in the Babylonian Talmud (*Shabbat* 33b) condemning Roman "improvements," quotes Rabbi Simeon bar Yohai: "*Everything they* [Romans] *established they established for their own needs. They established markets to seat prostitutes in them; baths to pleasure themselves; bridges to extract taxes*" (Lapin, p. 127).

"*The underlying perception of many Palestinian sages, already evident in the Mishnah and later even more so in the Palestinian Talmud, is that Roman rule is not only evil but in fact illegitimate, at least within the boundary of Eretz Israel*" (Gafni, p. 254). According to some Sibylline oracles of Jewish origin, such sentiments go further: "*Alas city of the Latin land* [Rome]*, unclean in all things…You have a bloodthirsty heart and an impious mind…But now the eternal God will destroy you…Mingle with the flames of fire…Inhabit the lawless regions of Hades*" (Barclay 1996, p. 227). In one Talmudic story (*Yerushalmi Avodah Zorah* 1:2), Rome's origin came not from the mythic struggle of Romulus/Remus (twin sons of Mars, the god of war) against the king of Alba Longa, but from angel Michael's curse. "*It was Solomon's sin of marriage with a foreign princess and the subsequent introduction of idolatrous practices into Solomon's home that provoked the angel Michael to throw a reed into the sea, causing the geographical territory of Israel's archenemy, Rome to arise out of it*" (Gribetz, p. 67).

∙∙∙

Roman responsibility for Jesus' execution was also minimized, if not jettisoned, as an accommodation to Roman despotism. In the so-called Gospel of Peter, a popular second century document with fragments dating to the first century (Miller 1992, p. 394), it is Jews rather than the Romans who judge, torture, and crucify Jesus. This claim is repeated in various early Christian anti-Jewish polemics (Note #8), such as those of St. Melito of Sardis (ca. 170), who excludes any Roman involvement in Jesus' passion. St. Melito insisted that Jesus, like Israel's Passover lamb commemorating Jewish freedom from the Egyptians, was sacrificed to free Christians from the Jews. Baseless accusations that Jewish complaints caused Christian martyrdom (as that of St. Polycarp, ca. 155) also diverted attention from Roman oppression, using martyrdom as a virtuous Christian "*counterpart to Judaism*" (Moss 2012, p. 85), as though Jews did not have martyrs.

Among scholars commenting on the Gospel stories of Jesus and the Passion, Vermes (2005) recounts a glut of contradictions and inconsistencies. "*It is hard, indeed almost impossible, to imagine a nationalist Jewish crowd encouraging Romans to kill one of their countrymen*" (p. 61). Similarly, the declared innocence of the Roman procurator, Pontius Pilate, "*is best held to be fiction, devised by the evangelists with a view to currying favour with Rome, in whose empire the nascent Church was developing. Christianity being generally unpopular in Roman eyes — Tacitus calls it a 'pernicious superstition' (Annals 15.44) — it was in the interest of the Gospel writers to placate the authorities. Also, by the time of the recording of the Passion narratives the Jewish rebellion had been put down by the armies of Vespasian and Titus. It was therefore politically doubly correct to blame the Jews for the murder of Christ and to absolve the Roman Pontius Pilate*" (Ibid. p. 121).

Ehrman (2016, pp. 156–157): "*The attempts to show* [Pilate's] *innocence differ from one Gospel to the next, but as you line them up chronologically, Pilate becomes more and more exculpated in the decision that Jesus had to die. Historically, it would have been Pilate's own decision, pure and simple, probably on the basis of a very brief trial in which he decided that Jesus was a troublemaker. Later, some Christians began to claim that he washed his hands of the affair and declared Jesus not guilty* [St. Matthew 27.24]. *Somewhat later, he was explicitly said to have declared Jesus innocent three times* [St. Luke 23. 4–22]. *Yet later, he was recorded as handing Jesus over to Jewish chief priests themselves for execution* [St. John 19.16].

232

It is likely that these are not things that actually happened. They are distorted memories of what happened by later Christians in the throes of controversies with Jews over whether Jesus was really the messiah."

In Simon's words (p. 118): *"The theological need to show the Jewish people as rebels against the divine message* [Jesus Christ as universal savior] *chimes in with the political need to exculpate the Roman power."* (See also Brandon 1968.) *"It is, moreover, counter-intuitive to hold that Jews generally would consider compatriots executed by an oppressive occupying force to be anything other than victims, if not the heroes"* (Fredriksen 1986, p. 12).

It is also difficult to conceive that Jesus' trial and execution resulted from religious differences — that Jesus was *"a blasphemer of God"* (St. Matthew 26.65) — as though professing to be a prophet or Messiah contravened a sacred law (Note #15.6, p. 192). From all indications (Notes #4, #16), neither Jesus nor his disciples opposed Temple worship, purification rites, and Temple sacrifices. In St. Matthew (23.19), Jesus declares it is *"the altar* [Temple] *that makes the gift* [sacrifice] *sacred."* Had Jesus been a religious transgressor, the Jewish Sanhedrin had the right to order capital punishment by stoning (Brandon 1967, pp. 3–8, 246–249).

Occurring in Israel's most prominent edifice, a Temple disturbance would have been seen by Romans and their collaborators as a political act, a threat to the dominant "order." Since the Temple, in addition to its religious role, *"played an integral role in the organization, legitimation, and administration of the national community"* (Meyers, p. 1022), any proclamation or action in the Temple precincts to replace governing powers with a new "Kingdom of God" would have been sufficiently radical for the Romans to charge a Jewish preacher for "sedition" (Note #15, p. 185). Jesus' execution by crucifixion, a common Roman punishment for provincial opposition, was thus eminently political: caused by an action *"directed not only against the Roman oppressors, but also against the ruling authorities among the Jews, the elite priests and their followers*" (Ehrman 2014, p. 245). The titular heading on Jesus' cross was "King of the Jews" — a satirical tag given to a rebellious political upstart.

"[I]*t is clear from what we know of the Roman and high-priestly rule of Judea that a demonstration against the Temple would have been viewed as a challenge to the imperial order*" (Horsley 2012, p. 147). "[Jesus'] *act can be regarded as that of a political revolutionary, representing the protest of the Galilean underclass to its exploitation by the political and hierarchical elites of the cities*" (Brent, p. 28). "*The words of Jesus make sense when he contrasts what he sees as the ideal function of the Temple ('a house of prayer') with what he hyperbolically sees as its present state ('a den of robbers')*" (Crossley 2008, p. 10). Jesus' "*vision of the liberation coming with the reign of God directly attacked a principle element of the Roman order in Palestine and attracted a following of people victimized by debt*" (Oakman 2008, p. 32, also Note #15).

To the Romans, variant Jewish religious beliefs were probably no more disquieting than other variant religious beliefs throughout the empire. However, a messianic leader supplanting Rome's exploitative regime with a new "Kingdom" of any kind was seditious (Feldman 1992, p. 16), and sedition (*seditio*) equaled treason (*maistas*), a capital offence.

The ruling pattern of killing popular Jewish charismatics acclaiming "a new Kingdom of God" echoed what happened to other messianic figures such as John the Baptist. "*Now, when others came in crowds about him, for they were greatly moved by hearing his words, Herod, who feared lest the great influence John had over the people might put it into his power and inclination to raise a rebellion (for they seemed ready to do anything he should advise), thought it best, by putting him to death, to prevent any mischief he might cause*" (Josephus, *Antiquities of the Jews* XVII:V). "*In the footsteps of John, Jesus appeared as the envoy inaugurating the eagerly awaited onset of the reign of God over Israel and the world*" (Vermes 2012, p. 32).

Some Gospel statements obliquely reveal Jesus' threatening undercurrent of forceful change: promoting a new restorative Kingdom of God, and organizing followers and disciples to engage in action to attain a new King for this new "Kingdom." *"From the days of John the Baptist until now the kingdom of heaven has suffered violence and the violent take it by force"* (St. Matthew 11.12). *"[S]ince then the good news of the kingdom of God is proclaimed, and everyone tries to enter it by force"* (St. Luke 16.16). The crowds who followed Jesus hailed him as *"the prophet who is to come into the world"* and *"take him by force to make him king"* (St. John 16.14–15). *"Lord, is this the time when you will restore the kingdom to Israel?"* (Acts of the Apostles 1.6). As their kingly leader, Jesus preaches to his disciples *"I confer on you just as my Father has conferred on me, a kingdom "*(St. Luke 22.29). *"He said to them ... the one who has no sword must sell his cloak and buy one. For I tell you, this scripture must be fulfilled in me"* (St. Luke 22.36–37). Even after Jesus' death, St. Luke (24.21) has his disciples express disappointed hopes to the resurrected Jesus *"that he was the one to redeem the kingdom to Israel."*

"There can be no reasonable doubt why Pilate decided to crucify Jesus and his followers ... Pilate had incontrovertible proof that they were a subversive group. Their leader had been preaching a coming kingdom, made royal claims in Jerusalem during the sensitive period of Passover, opposed the payment of tribute, and was surrounded by a band of men who were armed with swords and were ready to use them. Perhaps he also organized some disturbance at the gates of Jerusalem and/or the Temple, in which case things would have been even worse. Having gathered together this consistent body of evidence, no ruler in his right mind would have regarded Jesus as a harmless preacher or a deluded lunatic, and no further investigation would have been necessary. There is every indication that, not only subjectively but objectively, Jesus and his followers constituted a threat to public order. Any Roman governor would have sought to remove such a (crucifiable) group, particularly its

*leader. This explains why Jesus was **crucified as an insurrectionist and self-style king**, why he was crucified **along with some of his followers or collaborators (or people ideologically related to him)**, and why he was crucified **in the middle**"* (Barmejo-Rubio, pp. 148–149, his emphases). *"A Roman prefect needed no more reason for crucifying a Galilean than discovering him surrounded by a band of armed men in Jerusalem at Passover"* (D. B. Martin, p. 9).

Analysis by 79 Biblical scholars concluded overwhelmingly that *"the assertion that the Romans were innocent of Jesus' death and the Jews responsible is pure Christian propaganda. ... It is not just the content of the trial but the fact of a trial that lacks historical foundation"* (Funk et al. 1998, p. 568). Unfortunately, some Christian apologists still support major anti-Jewish elements in the crucifixion story, claiming that Gospel accounts should not be disputed by *"too rigorous a quest for certitude*[!]" (Brown, p. 19). Or, as avowed in a more theologically Christianized mode: the significance of the historical Jesus *"is clearly secondary to the significance of the theological and mythical Jesus'* (Taussig, p. 193).

22

CHRISTIAN MISSIONARY SUCCESS AND ACCOMMODATION TO ROMAN SOCIETY

Among appealing features Gentile Christianity offered Romans:

1. Worship in an antique religion via Christianity's claimed origin as far back as Creation in the Jewish Book of Genesis. *"In the beginning was the Word [Jesus Christ], and Word was with God, and the Word was God. And the Word became flesh and lived among us, and we have seen his glory, the glory of a father's only son"* (St. John 1.1, 1.14).

2. Because all humans are sinners facing divine judgment, only faith in Jesus Christ offers redemption from censure and punishment. *"[A]ll of us must appear before the judgment seat of Christ, so that each may receive recompense for what had been done in the body, whether good or evil"* (St. Paul, *2 Corinthians* 5.10). *"The wages of sin is death, but* [for faithful Christians] *the free gift of God is eternal life in Christ our Lord"* (*Romans* 6.23).

3. An unexceptional identity compatible with indigenous Gentile life styles, in contrast to ethnically "alien" Jewish customs. *"[W]e know that a person is justified not by works of the* [Jewish] *law but through faith in Jesus Christ"* (St. Paul, *Galatians* 2.16).

4. A marked change from Pagan gods whose behaviors were often unseemly coarse and salacious, each demanding its own set of beliefs, rules, and rituals. *"I imply that what pagans sacrifice, they sacrifice to demons and not to God. I do not want you to be partners with demons"* (St. Paul, *1 Corinthians* 10.20).

5. Derived from Jewish sources: humanistic health and welfare benefits to needy members in a society that provided little, if any, such support. *"Religion that is pure and undefiled before*

God, the Father, is this: to care for orphans and widows in their distress" (Letter of James 1.27).

6. Full compliance with the Roman Empire's governing structures and acceptance of Roman social and economic divisions: masters/slaves, rich/poor, empowered/powerless. Such deferential submission enabled Romans to fear nothing from Christianity. *"Let every person be subject to the governing authorities, for there is no authority except from God, and those authorities that exist have been instituted by God"* (St. Paul, *Romans* 13,1).

At first, Gentile Christianity may have appeared almost invisible in the Roman Pantheon of multiple Gods and religions. "[N]*on-Christian authors of the first two centuries rarely refer to* [Christianity]*, and when they do, their accounts are relatively brief"* (Carleton Paget, p. 253). "[F]*or at least two centuries (until approximately 180 C.E.) and effectively well into the third, there is no extant material (apart from literary) evidence of Christianity as a distinct socio-religious phenomenon"* (Vaage 2006a, p. 6). By the middle or end of the third century, however, Gentile Christianity appears to have become a notable force, offering a vision of Jesus Christ, as a shepherd, hero, crucified symbol of humanity, as well as a seated civil authority, and even a toga-clad philosopher, (Ludlow, p. 224).

Compared to the remote and invisible Jewish God Yahweh, Christianity's Jesus Christ was a full-figured visible divinity on whom one imbued personable traits — a god whose persona was complexly human and humane (*"a God who looks and feels like us"*). Although accepting appeasing sacrifices, Pagan gods by comparison appeared one-dimensional, showing little interest in humans, offering their celebrants no heavenly comforts to alleviate earthly ordeals.

Contrary to all other divine figures, Jesus Christ exhibited the image of a blameless victim with whom one could identify, and whose divine power could suit almost any contemporary emotional need. The many personalities adduced to Jesus in the four Gospels made it easy to invest him with any desirable identity: from merciful judge and consoling confidant to loving advocate. Where else in the Pagan Pantheon can one envision a God-figure who exhorts his followers to moral and emotional heights?

"Be merciful, that you may obtain mercy. Forgive, that it may be forgiven to you. As you do, so shall it be done unto you. As you judge, so shall you be judged. As you are kind, so shall kindness be shown to you. With what measure you dole, with the same it shall be measured to you" (First Epistle of Clement to the Corinthians, XIII, ANF vol. 9, p. 233). *"Jesus, my Shepherd, Brother, Friend, My prophet, Priest, and King. My Lord, my Life, my Way, my End, Accept the praise I bring"* (Christian hymn: Hooker, p.49*).*

Facing parishioners at the apex of all churches, Jesus Christ epitomized an avatar embodying worldly and heavenly authority, whose image compelled reverence and worship. *"Jesus Christ, the Son of God who prays for us, and prays in us, and is prayed to by us"* (St. Augustine, *On the Psalms* LXXXVI.1, NPNF Series 1, vol. 8, p. 410). *"Only through Jesus Christ can one's sins be forgiven: God does not remit sins but to the baptized"* (Ibid. *On the Creed*.16, NPNF Series 1, vol. 3, p. 375).

Stories devised to show Jesus' miraculous power over nature championed a coming "Kingdom of God" to early Christian converts, and to those whom they converted. *"In the Kingdom of God there will be no natural disasters: Jesus controls nature even now. In the kingdom there will be no more demons: Jesus casts out demons now. In the kingdom there will be no more disease or bodily ailments or physical impairments: Jesus heals the sick now. In the kingdom there will be no more death: Jesus raises the dead now"* (Ehrman 2016, p. 224).

That this imminent "Kingdom of God," found also in St. Paul and Synoptic Gospels (St. Mark, St. Matthew, and St. Luke), had not yet materialized by the early second century, became a challenge that needed response. St. John's Gospel, written at that time, deemphasizes Jesus' looming Kingdom by changing its goal from earthly anticipation to Jesus Christ's claim for an other-worldly existence: *"No one can see the Kingdom of God without being born from above"* (3.3); *"My kingdom is not from this world"* (18.36).

"In light of the delay in the Parousia or expected end-time, the early church turned its attention less and less to the message of the coming Kingdom which Jesus had proclaimed and more and more to the person of the one who proclaimed it. ... Salvation came increasingly to be seen therefore as a present experience realized in union with him and not as in the Jewish-Christian tradition, a participation in the bliss of the [earthly] *age to come"* (Telford, p. 87).

One Christian solution for delayed earthly salvation for the poor was *"to shift the way from reversal of poverty to providing a way to live with it, by seeking joy and peace within oneself in the spiritual realm, or by sustained or regular spiritual experiences. This then marginalizes the importance of poverty or dismisses its relevance or makes it a virtue of necessity and even imposes it on others as a pathway to spirituality"* Loader (p. 28).

Nevertheless, concern for the eagerly anticipated rule of justice, when all wrongs are righted and all behaviors judged, remained crucial for many Christian believers. Its earthly absence was resolved by transferring rewards and punishments to a life after death. Jesus' original "Kingdom of God" was now envisaged as an unearthly world of the dead: a supernatural Christian Heaven and Hell in which every human faced a hypercritical future — *"The Lord's dread tribunal of judgment"* (St. John Chrysostom, *Against the Jews Oration* 8, Harkin, p. 222).

Christianity's solemn message to fearful humans was that sinners can only be redeemed from eternal damnation and unforgiving tortures after death by faith in Jesus Christ. *"[T]he unjust and intemperate shall be punished in eternal fire, but that the virtuous and those who lived like Christ shall dwell with God in a state that is free from suffering — we mean, those who have become Christian"* (St.

Justin Martyr, *Second Apology* I, ANF vol. 1, p. 188). *"We maintain that after life has passed away thou still remainest in existence, and lookest forward to a day of judgment, and according to thy deserts art assigned to misery or bliss, in either way of it forever"* (Tertullian, ANF vol. 3, p. 177).

Ekelund and Tollison (p. 56): *"the promise of a well-defined, promulgated afterlife in return for specified beliefs and behavior with mortal assurance of eternal salvation ... was the fundamental product change that led to* [Christianity's] *rapid adoption."* As Brox put it (p. 17), Christianity was *"a religion of redemption,"* and the need for redemption looms if one is to gain *"a life everlasting."* Although heaven may not ameliorate misery on earth, it was probably more distressing to await sins penalties in hell. St. John Chrysostom (Mayer and Allen, p. 155): *"Our* [churches] *... are truly frightening and filled with awe. For this place where God is present, possessing power over life and death, is a frightening place — where homilies are delivered on everlasting punishments, on rivers of fire, the poisonous worm, chains that can't be broken, external darkness."*

In *The Apocalypse of Peter*, commonly preached in Gentile churches from about 150 C.E. onward, a Christian hell is described in detail. *"The head is in the mud; hair is used to hang up women by it; eyes are burned; there is a burning flame in the mouth; people bite their tongues and are hanged up by them. Innards are eaten by worms; flames burn people waist–high; men are hanged up by their thighs — a euphemism for genitals. Legs are also involved when the rich ones dance on sharp pebbles. The whole body is roasted on flames, and often hanged upside down"* (Czachesz, p. 11; also ANF vol. 9, pp. 145–147). According to some modern theologians (Walls), the prospect of Heaven, Hell, and Purgatory is still real and should not be ignored by Christian believers. Stendahl (p. 211) relates a story of how a clergyman implemented hellish information: *"We all have heard about the person who preached about gnashing our teeth in hell. And one parishioner said, 'But what about those who have no teeth?' And the preacher answered, 'Teeth will be pro-vided.'"*

Somehow, "love" and "forgiveness," oft-promoted Christian virtues, do not apply to those who are not Christian or improper Christian. Thus, even more fearsome than having sinned against one's fellow man was to sin against Jesus Christ by rejecting Christianity. *"They who believe in Christ shall be led into a good place, and those to whom that delight is given are caressed; but to you who are of a double mind, against you is punishment without the body. …Thou shalt be taken where it grieveth thee to be: there the spiritual punishment, which is eternal, is undergone; there are always wailings; nor dost thou absolutely die therein"* (Commodianus, ca. 240, ANF vol. 4, pp. 207–208). *"Believe Him who will give to all that believe the reward of eternal life. Believe Him who will call down on them that believe not, eternal punishments in the fires of Gehenna"* (St. Cyprian, ca. 250, ANF vol. 5, p. 464). Without proper Christian faith, one suffers death *"everlastingly"* (Athanasian Creed, ca. 500 C.E.).

However effective it may be in subjecting humans to religious authority, insisting on Hell's "everlasting" existence creates the contradiction of *"reconciling belief in God with the fact that a major aspect of reality remains unredeemed and in rebellion against God"* (Spiegel, p. 247). It is striking that the often-condemned "exclusive" Jewish religion is hardly as exclusive as Christianity's claim to being the sole source for everlasting salvation.

Also instrumental in Christianity's success was opportune timing of its entry into the Roman world of religious flux. *"That Christians prayed to Christ as to a God is clear, and also undeniable is assimilation to the cultic language and imagery of the* [Pagan] *religious world around them"* (Young 2006, p. 13). J. T. Sanders (2000, p. 120) points out: *"The first decades of Christianity occurred during a time when it was not unusual for people to take up the worship of new* [imported] *international Gods"* such as Isis, Mithras,

Cybele, and others. *"Oriental beliefs, not discredited as was so much traditional Greek faith, and semi-oriental mysticism met a spiritual need of the times, a demand for something clear and dogmatic which explained the universe, and for an assured hope of immortality. The East conquered the West because it had something to give. In the widest sense the tide was turning from rationalism to faith ... even when there was not a definite turn to religious observances, there was an antiquarian interest in old cults"* (Nock, p. 16). Becoming a Christian also endowed one with *"combined belief in God's perfect justice with the conviction that he loved the sinner even in the sin and desired his salvation"* (Ibid. p. 103).

Conversion to Christianity came mainly from social networks: interpersonal ties between church members and their families, friends, dependents, and contacts in *"households, workplaces, marketplaces, neighborhoods, and so on"* (Crossley 2006, p. 158). *"Christianity attracted converts because it appeared on the scene at the right time and did all the right things — in its encounter with people in a situation of distress or who were seekers, in its interaction with these people, and in its promotion of commitment among and successful encapsulation of new members"* (J. T. Sanders 2000, p. 129). In contrast to Jews, whose special codes of civil law helped make them an autonomous community within the Roman Empire, early Christians relied exclusively on Roman law. *"For this reason, Christianity was able to integrate more easily into the various elements of the Roman public sector, such as the market, the army, and the public administration, and to a certain degree, gradually assimilated into it"* (Edrie and Mendels 2014, p. 217).

To Christian advantage, the Roman Empire provided a common culture of shared languages (Greek and Latin) as well as widespread transportation systems (roads, seaways) that bolstered religious and communal communication between urban centers, enabling missionary outreach to the extent it could be supported. Although no attempts were made to break down social and economic distinctions, Christian proselytization reached out to all social strata, from nobles to slaves and from the educated to the illiterate. Most importantly, Christianity claimed an antique origin by adopting the Jewish Scriptures as its own, which helped make it successfully competitive with prevailing religions.

Disparaging Jewish rules, practices, and life styles in attracting Gentiles, paralleled adopting religious attitudes and practices from Roman Pagan society. As shown in Note #11.*a*, Jesus Christ's supposed virgin birth matched Pagan legends. The Goddess Isis, probably the most popular of Hellenistic Gods, often compared to the Virgin Mary, was believed to have borne the God Horus without sexual intercourse. Transforming Jesus into a divine savior who died and was resurrected, emulated other god-like Pagan deities in human form. The Christian multiple godhead, a Binary (God/Son) or Trinity (God/Son/Holy Ghost), had Pagan polytheistic overtones, and may also have been influenced by later Roman governance of two "divine" Emperors, separated into east and west. Recapped in Christian baptism was also the notion common to Greco-Roman "mystery" religions that one gains salvation by performing a secret ritual reenacting death and reentry into life.

Maccoby (1991, p. 71): "*For the resurrection of a deity after a violent death, we must look again to the mystery religions. Dionysius, torn to pieces by the Titans, is brought to life again by Rhea. Adonis, killed by a boar, is raised on the third day. Attis, after dying of his wounds, comes back to life and dances. Osiris, after being dismembered by Set, is put together again and revived, after which he becomes a god. In Mithraism, the bull killed by Mithras was itself resurrected, but it provided life, through its body and blood, for the whole created universe.*" St. Paul (*Romans* 6.3–4): "*Do you not know that all of us who have been baptized into Christ Jesus were baptized into his death? Therefore we have been buried with him by baptism into death, so that just as Christ was raised from the dead by the glory of the Father, so we too might walk in newness of life."* (See also Note #11.*d.*)

Jesus' resurrection may well have suited different prevailing beliefs. To his Jewish followers, it probably echoed the Pharisaic notion that the dead will reappear in the coming earthly Kingdom of God to be rewarded or punished. To Gentiles, it would also have appealed for its parallel to living, dying, and rejuvenated Pagan gods.

"Christianity, probably more than any other religion of the time, adapted itself to a variety of cultural and religious currents and appropriated numerous foreign elements until it was ready to succeed as a world religion — thoroughly syncretistic in every way" (Koester 1995, p. 159). *"The language which men chose to describe the supreme God of both Pagans and Christians was sometimes undistinguishable"* (Mitchell, p. 48). *"That Christians prayed to a god is clear, and also undeniable is assimilation to the cultic language and imagery of the* [Pagan] *religious world around them"* (Young 2006, p. 13).

St. John Chrysostom's admonition against Christians participating in Jewish festivities (Note #6) also followed his admonition against Christians participating in civic festivities *"which were always associated with pagan religious occasions or ceremonies ... Here the acculturation of the inhabitants of the city evidently sets very clear limits of the Christianization of the whole metropolis: certainly at a very early stage Christianity moved into the cities, but there in antiquity it threatened at least partially to lose its identity"* (Markschies, p. 124).

Gentile Christian attempts to conform to Roman society seems far from the radical social restructuring expected by Jesus of Galilee. To Jesus, righteousness and riches are opposites. In all three "Synoptic" Gospels (St. Mark 10.25, St. Matthew 19.24, St. Luke 18.25) Jesus proclaims *"It is easier for a camel to go through the eye of a needle than for someone who is rich to enter the Kingdom of God"* (see also Note #15, p 184). Nevertheless, polarized class divisions remained in Gentile Christianity as indicated earlier: nobles, plebes; rich, poor; landowners, peasants; masters, slaves. For example, "*By incorporating slavery into the theological and pastoral framework of Christian life, church teaching actually reinforced the institution of slavery*" (Oriek, p. 286)

Among accommodations made to preserve class distinction was to allow wealthy parishioners divide what had earlier been the communal "Lord's Supper" into two components: their own private nutritious meal, followed by a public celebration of the more meager Eucharist ritual (a sip of wine and a wafer) that included the poor (J. Becker, p. 195). Thus, although St. Paul admonishes against the vices of the rich and their injustices to the poor, he does not proscribe them (Ibid. pp. 190–192). In contrast to Jesus (Note #15 p. 184) and the Jewish Prophets, St. Paul's emphasis on "faith" rather than "deeds/works" stifled issues of inequality and its base of social/political/military exploitation. "*Nowhere in Galatians do we find Paul presenting any clear resisting power against the hegemonic power of the Romans*" (Charles, p. 184).

Redistribution of wealth, a prominent feature of early Jewish Christians as expressed in *Teachings of the Twelve Apostles* (ca. 50–100, Milavec, p. 13) was abandoned: "*You will not turn away the one being in need; you will partner together, on the other hand, sharing all things with your brother/sister, and you will not say things are your own.*" In contrast, Gentile Christianity's lasting economic policy became "*individual charity and household hospitality ... The model that informs Acts* [of the Apostles] *is clear. There is no explanation of unequal distribution of goods, no critique of systematic causes of poverty, no denunciation of exploitation*" (Friesen 2005, pp. 253–255). St. Luke's Acts of the Apostle (2.42–45, 4.32–37) "*portrays economic sharing as a quaint artifact of an idealized past*" (Ibid. p. 25). "*People measured their worth in* [Roman] *society by the people over whom they could exercise social power*" (Reasoner, p. 48).

246

The Church made clear that Christian charity did not mean social change. To counter Jesus' barrier to the rich in entering the Kingdom of God, St. Clement of Alexandria (ca. 160–215) assures the rich that their wealth must be preserved to provide charity for the poor (ANF vol. 2, pp. 591ff). Wealthy Christians are consoled *"that the call by Jesus to give away all possessions was not to be followed literally, but in the spirit"* (Oriek, p. 291). *"Poverty? Give alms."*

In *The Shepherd of Hermas*, written in the middle second century and accepted for a while as part of the Christian Biblical canon, economic inequality is considered *"simply a fact"* (Friesen 2005. p. 255), and *"wealth as a divine gift"* that *"must be properly used"* (Ibid. p. 256). *"Hermas suggests that the poor need wealthy people in order to meet their daily needs for material survival and that the rich need the poor so they have objects for charity that will eventually get the rich into heaven. It is a codependent model that is individualistic and ultimately antithetical to the goal of ending economic inequality. ... For Hermas, wealth comes not from injustice but from God"* (Ibid. p. 258). That this attitude persists has caused some modern Christians to complain: *"In the majority of US Catholics, social charity belongs to the core of their Catholic identity, social justice to its periphery"* (Hughson, p. 27).

St. Paul's transformation of the "fleshly" Jesus into the "spiritual/mystic" Jesus Christ (*Romans* 1.3–4, *2 Corinthians* 5.16–17), *"shaped the contours of this new form of Christianity for the next nineteen hundred years, a Christianity wholly oriented to salvation in the heavenly world, in sharp contrast to the movement the Jewish Messiah had inspired with its emphasis on a kingdom of peace and justice on earth"* (Tabor, p. 133). In the words of Thiessen and Merz (p. 277): *"Jesus proclaimed an imminent Kingdom of God, but a Christianity came which was far removed from the Kingdom of God."* Jesus' *"Second Coming"* was an unearthly experience of *"the hope laid up for you in heaven"* (Colossians 1.5, 3.1–4).

As reported by Kaufman (p. 7), one view of this radical change is that, "*corruption of Christianity ... began already with Paul, who turned Jesus' simple gospel on its head. Jesus had preached the kingdom of God but Paul preached Jesus, accompanied by baptism, the Lord's Supper* [Eucharist], *and the doctrine of Jesus' substitutionary death and resurrection for the atonement of sins. And what Paul began, the Church continued.*" St. Paul had made clear "*the fact that the Christian community and civil authority can coexist as God-appointed social entities, authenticates that the kingdom of God does not usurp the Roman Empire*" (Hanc, p. 316).

To many modern theologians, the purpose of achieving the Christian "Kingdom of God" is still not to eliminate inequality between rich and poor, privileged and underprivileged, exploiters and exploited. "*The Kingdom is God's and he alone determines who may enter ... High as the priority for the poor is, there may be particular situations where even higher priorities prevail ... Jesus' call to and teaching on the poor are not reducible to some class-war dogma*" (Dunn 2003, pp. 522, 524). In Gentile Christianity it was therefore not Jesus the Jew but the Church which came to define the relationship between man and God, and man and man. To paraphrase Ste. Croix (2006, p. 369): *It was the exclusive concentration of Christian Fathers upon prescribing only 'orthodox' sanctioned relations to their flocks, and their complete indifference to oppressive institutions of the world in which they lived, that prevented Christianity from having much effect for good on the relations between man and man.* Attaining one's eventual reward in the Church's "Kingdom in Heaven" provided very cold comfort to an exploited workforce, subjugated women, and wretched poor. Paraphrasing the poet William Blake: "*the suffering oppressed deprived of bliss on earth gain their bliss in heaven,*" is the Church's message in an unjust society.

The transition of Gentile Christianity into a multi-ranked magisterial institution proceeded steadily during the first two centuries. "*Very gradually bishops* ["overseers" — "episcopos" — the "episcopacy"] *became the core of a conservatively structured society with lasting effect*" (Freeman, p. 270). Fairly independent Christian congregations, each designated as an "*ecclesia*" (assembly), were re-organized into a broad-based hierarchically-controlled authoritarian "*Ecclesia.*" St. Ignatius (ca. 100): "*I exhort you to do all things with a divine harmony, while your Bishop presides in the place of God, and your Presbyters in the place of the assembly of the Apostles*" (*Letter to the Magnesians* VI, ANF vol. 1, p. 61). "*See that you all follow the Bishop, even as Jesus Christ does the Father....He who honors the Bishop has been honored by God; he who does anything without the knowledge of the Bishop, does serve the devil*" (Ibid. *Letter to the Smyrnaeans* VIII, IX, pp. 89–90).

Within the episcopacy, this new hierarchical organization — "*The Church*" — was transformed into a novel entity never taught or envisaged by Jesus, either as a sacred holy body or theological foun-tainhead. "*The religion of Jesus was to regulate a short-term period, which would end after the angelic trumpets marking the inaugura-tion of the kingdom of God. It did not envisage the cross*" (Vermes 2013, p. 21).

By the second century, Bishops had begun to control the most reprised communal Christian sacrament — the Eucharist — deciding who performs the sacrifice of bread and wine and who receives it. "*It is not lawful without the Bishop either to baptize or to celebrate a love-feast* [Eucharist]; *but whatsoever he shall approve of, that is also pleasing to God*" (St. Ignatius, *Letter to the Smyrnaeans* VIII, ANF vol. 1, p. 90). This gave Bishops "*the right to administer or to excommunicate, to retain sins or remit them...the power of salvation or damnation*" (Guy, p. 96).

Through Bishops and their conferences, "the Church" facili-tated Christianity's success by providing a more cohesive structure than its more disjointed Pagan competitors. According to Rousseau (p. 128), "*The key to its success was not the quality of its doctrine — orthodoxy's triumph and the marginalization of heretics — but its efforts to establish continuity."* In appearance to converts, Christianity posed as a single world-wide ("Catholic") unchanging faith handed down from generation to generation in "apostolic succession" (Note #12).

With Christianity's legalization under Emperor Constantine and its rise to power, the Church metamorphosed Jesus' "Kingdom of God" into a "Holy Roman Empire of God," placing Jesus "Second Coming" into a very distant future. In the words of Dungan (2007, p. 76): *"Now that the Christian God in his providence had raised up a Christian emperor to be his champion on earth, and now that this 'rod of God's anger' was busily laying waste to the church's foes and simultaneously strengthening and enriching the Catholic church itself, it simply would not do to speak of Christ coming back to destroy the evil Roman empire along with all the other powers destined for wrath ... and setting up a physical Kingdom of God on earth which would necessarily supplant the newly triumphant Catholic church!"*

Not surprisingly, its increased authority led the Church itself to demand deference, admiration, and tribute. As indicated previously, this came to mean that faith in Jesus Christ was insufficient for salvation without submission to the Church personified by the Bishop. *"Whoever is separated from the Church...is separated from the promises of the Church; nor can he who forsakes the Church of Christ attain to the rewards of Christ. He is a stranger; he is profane; he is an enemy. He can no longer have God for his Father who has not the Church for his Mother"* (St. Cyprian, ca. 250, *On the Unity of the Church*, ANF vol. 5, p. 423). *"[F]rom the perspective of the prophet from Nazareth, it would seem that much was lost, as power and prestige replaced forgiveness and justice"* (Freyne, 2014, p. 355).

Religious membership numbers and distribution are hard to determine and highly conjectural. Out of a total population of about 60 million in the Roman Empire, estimates for Jews range from 4 to

8 million, and estimates for Christians go from as little as five to ten thousand in the first century to as high as six or seven million in the third century (Hopkins, p. 191). Better information is available of local Christian persecutions, most often of clergy. Yet in the more than 150-year interval, between the reigns of Emperors Domitian (81–96 C.E.) and Decius (249–251 C.E.), the Church was "at peace." Christian soldiers were spread throughout the Roman Army, and there was even a reported third century Christian Emperor, Philip "the Arab" (244–249 C.E., Attridge, pp. 189,191). "[I]*n addition the capacity of the Christian churches to own property was recognized, at least under some emperors*" (Ste. Croix 2006, p. 107). Sporadic persecutions nevertheless still occurred until the major general persecution by Diocletian in the last two years of his rule, just prior to Emperor Constantine's reign (305–337 C.E.) during which Christianity became legal (313 C.E.).

Lüdemann points out (2002a, p. 42): "*…no note is taken of the fact that Christianity could spread undisturbed in the first three centuries over wide areas. According to the most recent estimates, of a total of seven million Christians up to the beginning of the fourth century, fewer than a thousand suffered martyrs' deaths.*" According to Moss (2013, p. 91), the number of martyrs can be reduced even further: "*Once scholars had stripped away pious frauds, entertaining forgeries and well-intentioned legends, they were left with only a small handful of martyrdom stories from before* [the year] 250 *that they judged to be historically reliable.*" Nevertheless, the small number of Christians suffering persecution should not disguise their profound influence. "*Accounts of martyrdom served as powerful confirmation of the validity of Christian faith*" (Goodman 2007a, p. 512), each echoing the common illusion that choosing to "die for a cause" confirms the "truth" of the cause (Note #14, p. 169). "*The blood of martyrs is the seed of Christians*" (Tertullian, ca. 198). Although higher estimates of the Christian population have been offered (Stark), Finn (p. 296) points out that projection of Christian population size depends on variable factors such as city size and location, as well as "ominous" variables such as plagues, famines and wars; estimates that remain contentious.

We do know that through the third and fourth centuries, the authoritarian episcopal organization of Christianity led to preeminence of Rome's Bishops over all other bishoprics. Rome's Bishops' prerogatives were based not only on claims of Rome's civic importance, but on the supposition that Rome's first Christian church was founded by St. Peter (a presumption for which there is no reliable evidence, Demacopoulos), and Rome was believed the burial place of both St. Peter and St. Paul. St. Irenaeus (ca. 180): "[W]*ith this church, on account of her more powerful principality, it is necessary that every church should agree*" (Goodman 2007a, p. 518).

Vaage (2006b) suggests that although distancing itself from Pagan religions, Church hierarchical organization allowed Christianity to emulate the imperial structure of the Roman Empire, and gave Christianity "*a warrant for its right to exercise* [future] *imperial power*" (p. 259). That is, Christianity "*not only survived but soon proved to be ably suited to take over as imperial underwriter, once the Roman Empire ceased to function*" (p. 257).

Justifying Christianity's authoritative structure were prominent images of Jesus Christ, its' highest eminence. In St. Paul's letter to the Philippians (2.10), Jesus Christ warrants not only earthly but cosmic veneration and genuflection: "*At the name of Jesus every knee should bend, in heaven and on earth and under the earth.*" This echoes the prophet Isaiah's (45.22–23) missive from Israel's God: "*For I am Yahweh, and there is no other.... To me every knee shall bow, every tongue shall swear.*" In Tabor's words (p. 135), "*Christ as the newly exalted Lord of the cosmos is the functional equivalent of Yahweh.*"

St. Matthew (25.31–32) sees Jesus as a judge "*who will sit on the throne of his glory. All the nations will be gathered before him, and he will separate people from one another as a shepherd separates the sheep from the goats.*" Sinners then "*go away into eternal punishment but the righteous into eternal life*" (Ibid. 25.46). To justify all this, Jesus himself is made to proclaim "*All authority in heaven and earth has been given to me*" (Ibid. 28.18). The resurrected Jesus Christ "*is the one ordained by God as the judge of the living and the dead*" (Acts of the Apostles 10.42). To McKnight and Modica (p. 214), "*The New Testament conviction that Jesus is Lord, Caesar is not, is not a direct assault on the Roman Empire or even a veiled attempt to usurp it. Rather, to claim that Jesus is Lord is to place oneself in the servitude of an Emperor of a radically different kingdom — one which has no equal, now and forever.*"

Among the Eastern Orthodox Churches, Jesus is often portrayed as "Pantocrator" ("Ruler of All"), sitting on a gilded throne. "*The depiction of Jesus as emperor in the Gospels made it easy for [Christian] rulers like Constantine to cast themselves in the image of Christ as the ruler of the universe*" (Lössl, p. 212). In Eusebius' *Life of Constantine* (XXIV), the Emperor addresses a company of Bishops with the statement: "*You are Bishops whose jurisdiction is within the Church: I also am a Bishop, ordained by God to overlook whatever is external to the Church*" (NPNF Vol. 1, p. 546). In Mack's terms (2001, p. 172), "*Christianity was now the religion of the priesthood in charge of the purity of the people and their loyalty to the state ...the stage was set for the earthly king and the heavenly king to join forces in the control of a theocratic society.*"

Thus, when Christianity attained full recognition and state power in the fourth century, its hierarchy was assigned state functions. "*Bishops assumed the responsibilities and privileges of imperial civil servants ... bishops had to be greeted by kneeling down and kissing their hands and feet. An elaborate dress code was developed for bishops based on that of the imperial court. Bishops presided over the liturgy sitting on thrones*" (Lössl, pp. 141–142).

"*What had been the persecuted Church of the Martyrs underwent a period of rapid enculturation during which it shed its original antagonistic, otherworldly posture in favor of the values, concerns, and — if it is not putting the matter too strongly — the god of Mighty Rome. Catholic theology and church politics became thoroughly imbued with Roman imperial ideology.... In general, the Catholic church adopted the geographical divisions (dioceses) of Roman administration, and Catholic clergy took on the official titles of Roman government. They began to think and act like Roman officials, living in stately villas and conducting public worship services, not in the little house churches they were previously accustomed to, but in huge new temples or basilicas, packed with masses of half-converted parishioners. These new Christian temples were decorated by Roman craftsmen with glorious mosaics in the dome or apse at the front that depicted the Lord Jesus Christ in the posture and clothing of the Roman emperor — which made sense, since the Sunday morning service was now conducted as if everyone was in the presence of Christ the emperor"* (Dungan 2007, pp. 95–96). Opposition was not to be endured. In one of his edicts Constantine *"forbade heretics, the 'pests of society,' from ever meeting again, ordered their houses of worship to be confiscated, and their books to be destroyed"* (Ibid. p. 119).

When the Roman Empire fell in the fifth century, Rome's Bishop, Pope Leo I (440–461), assumed political control of the Empire's remains, leading to *"a Church office the holders of which were high above the people, just as the emperor had been beforehand"* (Brox, p. 91). The Emperor's title *Pontifex Maximus* ("High Priest") became also a title for the Pope, as did *Primus Inter Pares* ("First Among Equals"). *"And since the Bishop of Rome himself had acquired the same degree of dignity as the Emperor, like the Emperor he could claim the right to have his portrait hung in public buildings (i.e. in churches) to be greeted on his arrival at church by a choir of singers (whence the origins of the Introit in the eucharist today), to be waited on at the throne and the altar with covered hands and to have people genuflect to him and kiss his foot"* (Klauser, p. 34). Dungan (2007, p. 204) carries forth the story of a prominent Pagan reportedly joking that if he could be made a Roman Bishop, "*he would become Christian on the spot.*"

The advantages of achieving Papal status caused considerable rivalry. A contemporary commentator in the year 366 reports "*the [Papal] feud resulted in the death of 137 Christians in a single day;*" and those who attain victory "*will be so free from care that they are enriched from the offerings of matrons, ride seated in carriages, wearing clothing chosen with care, and serve banquets so lavish that their entertainments outdo the tables of kings*" (Barnes, p. 25).

Among these changes, the newly exalted Christian model of Jesus Christ not only encompassed the attractive attributes and powers of the Roman gods but supplanted them. "*Once Christ had taken the throne of Jupiter, the father of the gods had not so much as a stool on which to sit. ... Similarly, once Christ took the mild caring look of Asclepius and appeared everywhere working the miracles that the healing god had claimed, the shrines of Asclepius were abandoned. Taking the youthful beauty of a Dionysus or an Apollo, Christ charmed their coteries into his own shrines and churches. As androgyne he transcended the dichotomy of the sexes, he was a God of nurture as well as a God of victory. Assuming a divine halo and Olympian gold raiment, Christ replaced the entire pantheon of antiquity.... Emblazoned in countless Church apses, he was the omega, the end of the journey, the processional goal of all Christian life and worship. Simultaneously Child and Old Man, he was the Lord of all eternity*" (T. F. Matthews, pp. 179–180).

Again, it is important to note that this adoption of the Roman imperial model could hardly have come from the justice-seeking followers of Jesus the Jewish Messiah. "*Had Christians really lived up to the ideals and example of their first teacher, they would have 'perished like fools' and the movement would have come to grief as quickly as it arose. Christ did not lay the groundwork or structure for a workable religion, for what he espoused was not the stuff of an organized global movement. That task fell to his more worldly followers, who saw well enough that any chance of success lay in making a deal with this world. Betrayal was bred of the need for survival, even if that betrayal meant wars, empire and persecution of dissidents like Christ"* (Boer, p. 390). To Crossan (1991, p. 424) Christianity's "betrayal" of Jesus appears inevitable, *"else it might have died among the hills of lower Galilee."*

Gentile Christianity's successful material and communal history is well known: from house meetings to Churches to Basilicas and monumental Cathedrals; from artless decorations to ornate mosaics and stone carvings; from itinerant preachers to hierarchies of Deacons, Presbyters, Priests, Bishops, and Popes; from simple prayers to complex liturgies; from plainly dressed charismatics to elaborately costumed clerics; from female participation in leadership to patriarchal dominance (Eisen); from an officially despised religion to the official religion of the dominant society. In sum, Christianity arose from the Gentile sprout of a Jewish sect and became materially glorified into an Imperial Church. Throughout all this, its basic themes followed St. Paul's mythological innovations: that Jesus the Jew was Jesus the Divine Christ, Son of God, opposed to Jewish Law, rituals, and practices, who sacrificed himself to atone for the sins of mankind; and Christians are the self-ordained mystic beneficiaries of such sacrifice.

23

CHRISTIAN ANTI-JEWISHNESS, BEFORE AND AFTER GAINING POWER

Adversus Judaeos tracts by Tertullian (ca. 198, see also Note #20, p. 222) and other Christian Fathers (Notes #6, #8, #13, #17), cast "Jews," present or not, into enduring symbols of divine wickedness and treachery. *"The 'wrath upon the Jews,' poured out by Christianity, represents this ever-unsatisfied need of the Church to prove that it has the true content of the Jewish scriptures by finally making 'the Jews' (Jewish teaching authority) 'admit' that this is the true interpretation. Until Jewish religious tradition itself accepts this as the 'real meaning' of its own Scriptures, 'the Jews' must be kept in the status of the 'enemies of God,' in order to ward off that unthinkable alternative, suppressed at the very beginning, by the decision of faith upon which Christianity was founded"* (Ruether 1974, pp. 94–95). See also Notes #7, #18.

Failure to gain Jewish approval for Gentile Christianity's Scriptural presumptions made Jewish presence an uncomfortable contrast to Gentile Christianity's early social status. To many Romans, early Christianity was a disreputable sect, a rejected offshoot of disinterested Jewish parents. *"[T]he relationship between Jews and Christians may generally have been important for Christians as part of their self-definition, but it was much less crucial for Jews, who could ignore for much of Late Antiquity what Christians thought and did"* (Goodman 2007b, p. 175). According to Carleton Paget (p. 253) the Roman world did not recognize early Christianity as *"a movement of any significance."* Against such Christian ignominy, Jewish status in Roman society was quite the reverse. *"With their legal position secured by Roman law, a clearly defined sense of self, not least in theological terms, and a tangible presence throughout the communities that made up the urban infrastructure of the later Roman world, Jews possessed much of what* [early] *Christians could only dream of"* (Rutgers p. 5).

Unfortunately for Jews, disparaging Jews in Christianity's early century beginnings continued in various ways despite gaining Roman imperial power in the fourth century:

- As conscienceless murderers for the killing of Jesus (Notes #8, #21).

- As villainous misanthropes for their "exclusivity" and "peculiarities" (Notes #3, #22).

- As irreverent blasphemers for contesting Christian reinterpretations of the Jewish Scriptures (Notes #7, #18).

- As demonic sinners for refusing to become Christians (Note #11).

By the end of the fourth century, these abusive characterizations became standard in the Christian ethos. Anti-Jewish hostility now included governmental support for Christian bias that allowed forced conversion of Jewish synagogues into Christian churches (Rutgers). St. Justin Martyr's earlier plea that Christian forgiveness extends to all, even their Roman persecutors (*1 Apology* XIV, ANF p. 167), did not apply to Jews. Former Christian entreaties for tolerance and "love your enemies" was replaced by fierce contempt, followed by cruelty, and oppression that extended not only to Pagans and Jews but even to fellow Christians labeled as "heretics." Ordinary Christians were taught *"that life here and now is insignificant ... and that their real enemies were those enemies of God and his Church who, if they were not suppressed, would endanger men's immortal souls and bring them to perdition. 'Heretics' and 'schismatics', as well as 'unbelievers', were an entirely new kind of internal enemy, invented by Christianity, upon whom the wrath of 'right-thinking people' could be concentrated, for in paganism the phenomena of 'heresy' and 'schism', as of 'unbelief', were inconceivable"* (Ste. Croix 1981, p. 452).

"[U]nder most emperors from Constantine through Justinian and Zeno and others even later, it is not easy to separate ecclesiastical history from imperial, since to one degree or another emperors

regarded themselves and were accepted as having a most important voice, indeed very often a decisive voice, in church affairs. The two forces, ecclesiastical and imperial, have been seen working together, ... always in agreement about one essential, to rid God's world of nonbelievers" (MacMullen, pp. 29–30).

By the reign of Christian Emperor Theodosius II (408–450 C.E.), laws pertaining to Jews included the following, many fully enforced:

- Jews were excluded from public office.
- Jews were barred from any court rank or military position.
- Jews were forbidden to purchase Christian slaves.
- Jews who converted Christians to Judaism were sentenced to death, and the property of such converts was confiscated.
- Jews who married Christians were sentenced to death.
- Taxes collected by Jews for the Jewish Patriarch in Palestine were all to go to Christian charities.
- No new Jewish synagogues were to be built.
- It was a crime to repair Jewish synagogues.

In the *Codex Theodosianus* (429 C.E.), *"Jews are described as a 'dismal sect'; their meetings are 'sacrilegious gatherings'; to be a servant to a Jew is a 'shameful servitude'; Judaism is a 'moral turpitude'; the very name Jew is 'detestable' and 'offensive'"* (Abel, pp. 162–163). By the sixth century, Emperor Justinian's code declared that Jews were not to interpret the Jewish Bible any way other than to prophecy Jesus Christ, nor were Jews to deny Jesus Christ's resurrection and Last Judgment. Attempts at forced conversion of Jews to Christianity followed sporadically in later centuries (Michael, p. 38). *"The claim for equal toleration with others which was advanced by* [Christian] *apologists in the days of their suffering, the Church did not grant to others in the days of their triumph"* (Parkes, p. 157).

In the new triumphant Christian world, Jews who condemned or interfered with Christianizing other Jews were to be burnt alive.

"We want the Jews, their elders and their patriarchs informed that if anyone — once this law has been given — dare attack by stoning or other kind of fury one escaping from this deadly sect and raising his eyes to God's cult [that is, becoming Christian]*, when as we have learned is being done now, he shall be delivered immediately to the flames and burnt with all his associates"* (*Codex Theodosianus* 16.8; Fine, p. 246).

Although some scholars claim early Christian anti-Jewish statements and apologetics are irrelevant and long forgotten (Edwards et al., p. 10), their consequence is quite the reverse. Thus, Judas' ill repute, the assumed betrayer of Jesus, was repeatedly resuscitated to serve the Christian world for two millennia as a personification of Jewish malevolence. St. Jerome (ca. 400): "*In particular, this* [Jesus' passion] *is the story of Judas; in general it is that of the Jews….Judas, in particular, was torn asunder by demons — and the Jewish people as well….Judas is cursed, so that in Judas the Jews may be accursed….Whom do you suppose are the sons of Judas? The Jews. The Jews take their name…from the betrayer*" (Michael, p. 112).

For those Patristic Fathers like St. Ignatius of Antioch (ca. 100) and St. Polycarp of Smyrna (ca. 155), who chose their martyrdom in "Imitation of Christ," being anti-Jewish symbolized they were truly following the path of Jesus, the presumed anti-Jewish Christian, betrayed by Judas and killed by the Jews. Even some modern Christian theologians like Karl Barth preserve the notion of the "*essential equivalence of Judas and Jewry*" (J. Cohen, p. 259).

Although Christian Fathers often claimed "martyrdom" as testifying to the "truth" of Gentile Christianity (see p. 169), they never alluded to the many more thousands of martyred Jews killed, enslaved, and tortured by the Romans (Notes #9, #15). Empathy toward Jews and provincials who challenged Roman tyranny was not part of Christian doctrine. Christians objecting to Roman persecution never went beyond demanding they be considered as law-abiding as other Romans.

Judas' long service to Christianity as a Jewish fiend endures despite New Testament narrative inconsistencies. The earliest Christian writing about Jesus' death (St Paul, *1 Corinthians* 15.3–9) makes no mention of Judas at all, yet St. Paul's claim that the resurrected Christ *"appeared to Cephas* [St. Peter], *then to the twelve* [disciples]" (Ibid. 15.5) obviously includes Judas among the disciples. In St. Mark's Gospel (14.37–41), while Jesus prays at the Garden of Gethsemane, he repeatedly awakens his *twelve* disciples, who ignore him and continue sleeping. Yet suddenly Judas appears with an armed group to arrest him *"although no indication has been given that he ever left the company of Jesus'* (Maccoby 1992, p. 36). Embellished by later Gospels, *"the thirty pieces of silver"* presumably paid to Judas is an episode completely absent in St. Mark.

"The progression goes like this. The role of Judas is introduced at a later stage of the evolution of the story to account for Jesus' arrest on the same night as the Last Supper. Then in later Gospel versions his [Judas'] *character changes from misguided idealist (Mark), to disloyal friend (Matthew), to diabolical schemer (Luke), and finally to demonic antagonist (John). The play of each scene varies with the depiction to create the characterization and provide a fitting end"* (White, pp. 131–132).

Judas selling Jesus, God's "Beloved Son," to the Romans "for thirty pieces of silver" can also be questioned as a story made to gain Scriptural credibility by emulating Genesis' (37.26–28) account in which Judas' namesake, Judah, convinces his brothers to sell Joseph, Jacob's "beloved son," to Midianite slave-traders "for twenty pieces of silver." *"Here again one can reasonably suspect that the betrayal of Jesus by Judas is a midrashic play on the sale of Joseph by Judah, as his name suggests, perhaps typifying the Jews as the homicidal opponents of* [Jesus] *the beloved son of God"* (Levenson, p. 230).

The story of "Judas the traitorous Jew" is emblematic of how creatively dramatized New Testament spectacles were used for Christian antisemitic purposes.

24

THE PSYCHOLOGY OF ANTISEMITISM

Antisemitism offers a bastion of psychological/emotional comforts, however imaginary. For example: relieving anguish and anxiety by projecting one's own uncomfortable desires and feelings of avarice, lust, cheating, conspiracy, subversion, cowardice, heresy, onto Jews. Thus, whatever the conditions of Christian society, its embedded Jew-hatred always lies available to relieve personal as well as social angsts, blaming "the Jews" for social and economic failure; and even in prosperity, blaming "the Jews" for personal anguish or discomfort.

Tertullian's complaint (ca. 198 C.E.) that Romans persecuted Christians as scapegoats for any problem, can just as well pertain to later Jewish persecution by Christians (Note #23): *"They think the Christians the cause of every public disaster, of every affliction with which people are visited. If the Tiber rises as high as the city walls, if the Nile does not send its waters up over the fields, if the heavens give no rain, if there is an earthquake, if there is famine or pestilence, straightway the cry is 'Away with the Christians to the Lion!'"* (*Apology* XL, ANF vol. 3, p. 47). *"For Tertullian as for Justin* [Martyr] *and many 'church fathers,' anti-Judaism was a tool that could be applied to almost any problem, a weapon that could be deployed on almost any front"* (Nirenberg, p. 104).

In a sense, canonizing Jews in the New Testament as "Christ killers," sanctioned their role as resident ghouls of society in Christian paranoia. Jewish images could then be called up at any time and place to perform the role of blasphemy, treason, wickedness, betrayal, and deicide. In 1936 Nazi Germany, a leader of the German Christian Movement made the statement: *"Even if I know 'thou shalt not kill' is a commandment of God or 'thou shalt love the Jew' because he too is child of the Father, I am able to know as well that I have to kill him, I have to shoot him, and I can only do that if I am permitted to say 'Christ'"* (Heschel 2011, pp. 258–259). As Rubin and others have pointed out: to antisemites Jews are convenient internalized icons of uncomfortable, even indigestible self-contradictions that can be acted upon externally.

Among religious factors, antisemitism rooted itself in early Christian fears that basic Scriptural claims for Christian antiquity are open to challenge by the mere existence of non-believing Jews. Again, once instituted, hatred of Jews became so embedded in Christian culture that antisemitism could sprout even in the absence of Jews.

25
CHRISTIAN LITERATURE
AND PERPETUATION OF ANTISEMITISM

"This most virulent form of the teaching of contempt is firmly embedded within our specifically Christian Scriptures, the New Testament, the foundation documents of our Christian Church. If it remains within the texts used in our public and private worship and devotional life, all of our church statements in which we have repudiated the charge of deicide and the vicious denunciation of the Pharisees and of all the Jews will not eradicate this teaching of contempt. This teaching of contempt will continue to appear in our Christian educational materials, in our Christian liturgies and sermons, and in our Christian passion plays. We can try to sensitize all of our fellow-Christians, we can watchdog all of our educational materials and liturgies, and we can object to negative portrayals of Jews in our passion plays, but the source of this teaching of contempt for Jews in our Christian foundation documents will remain" (Beck 1994, p. 88).

A review of modern Catholic-Jewish relationships still shows the wide gap between statements some Catholic leaders make to comfort Jews for their World War II Holocaust misfortunes, and statements to each other to preserve the New Testament mythology that led to antisemitism and kept it alive (Pawlikowski 2006, pp. 102–103).

Although it may seem conciliatory for Christians to claim that "sharing" the Jewish Scriptures with Jews tokens a comradely or benign relationship, Christian adoption and reinterpretation of these Scriptures is a brash revision of history to Jews (Notes #7, #18). These Scriptures were all written by circumcised Jews (non-Gentile "Israelites") centuries before the appearance of Gentile Christianity. The people who transmitted these Scriptures — "Jews" —believed in the God Yahweh and in Scripturally proscribed practices and commandments, committing themselves to preserving these Scriptures by sharing language, rituals, culture, and a common history derived from these Scriptures. It seems hardly conciliatory for Gentile Christians with completely different theological notions, cultures, and traditions than those expressed in the Jewish Scriptures, to claim they are the "true Israelites," replacing Jews as inheritors of the Jewish Scriptures. Gentile Christians never identified with Jews, insisted on abrogating basic laws and commandments of these Scriptures, and showed no historical "Christian" presence prior to their first century C.E. appearance (see pp. 60, 165, 212 ,220).

Christian religious education still imposes the past onto the present, so that antisemitic issues remain. "[O]*ut of ignorance many pastors and religious educators strip Jesus from his Jewish context and depict that context in false and noxious stereotypes. ...The association of Theological Schools in the United States and Canada, the accrediting organization for these institutions* [Christian Seminaries and Divinity Schools] *does not as of 2011 recommend that candidates studying for the Christian ministry receive formal instruction in how to avoid anti-Jewish preaching and teaching*" (A.–J. Levine 2011, p. 501). The theological obsession to replace Jews as the "True Israel" persists in the claim that Christianity supersedes Jewish understanding of the Jewish Scriptures. "*Supersessionist views are still propounded — not only in homilies but even in documents from the* [Catholic] *hierarchy*" (Boys, p. 109). Even "*the reproaches of Israel as slayer of Christ ... were until recently part of the Catholic Good Friday liturgy*" (Moreschini and Norelli, p. 138).

Again, although the term antisemitism first appeared in nineteenth century Germany (Note #13), it should be obvious that one cannot restrict the origin of Jew-hatred to its nomenclature. From all shown in this monograph, Jew-hatred was embraced by Gentile Christianity from its earliest days. The claim by Malina (p. 6), "*To find anti-Semitism (nineteenth century coinage) in the New Testament is certainly and totally anachronistic*," is a bland exoneration of Gentile Christianity's long Jew-hatred history.

266

A. T. Davies (1979b, p. 203): [T]*he religion which watered the cultural soil of the West throughout the centuries with its negative myth of Jewish existence was no minor factor in the success of Nazi propaganda, because of its grip on the popular as well as the ecclesiastical mind right down to our own generation. ... To dismiss the Christian materials as irrelevant is to defy the immense weight of evidence as well as to support a Christian false consciousness that prevents any serious exploration of Christian responsibility.*"

Ruether (1979, p. 248): "*Without twenty centuries of Christian vilification of the Jews it would be impossible to understand why it was the Jews, rather than some other group, that became the particular sacrificial victim of Nazi nationalism.*" Sandmel (p. 173) "'*Nazism was not a Christian phenomenon*' [but] *the role of traditional Christian teaching about Jews and Judaism in creating the cultural climate in which Nazism could take hold and the participation of so many who considered themselves Christians in carrying out the Final Solution were a terrible shock to the world.*"

Could a twentieth century anti-Jewish Holocaust have occurred without Christianity?

26

CAN NEW TESTAMENT ANTISEMITISM
BE DELETED?

"Reason, science, enlightenment, progress, and all other bywords of modern civilization that we believe distinguish us from our medieval predecessors have not succeeded in overcoming a way of thinking about Jews that extends back to the first Christian centuries" (J. Cohen, p. 119). *"Preaching should be liberated from the inherited biases and ideologies of the tradition, including those that found their way into the Scriptures"* (Allen and Williamson, p. xxiii). Unfortunately, despite such cautions, Gospel stories, canonized as the "Word of God," till the ground for ideologues to maim and kill. *"There has never been an evil cause in the world that has not become more evil if it has been possible to argue it on biblical grounds"* (Stendahl, p. 205).

On the issue of curbing Gospel antisemitism, some Christian clerics insist that the "historical integrity" of the Gospels cannot be challenged, and Gospel antisemitism should only be corrected by *"explanation rather than by modification of the text"* (Van Wahlde, p. 83). That is, one must somehow present an unprejudiced view of Jews to Christians without questioning Gospel reliability. Among authors who discuss elements of this issue: Beck 1985; Crossan; A. T. Davies; Eckardt; Fisher; Fredriksen 2002; C. Klein; Nicholls; Parkes; Ruether; Swidler.

Because of the many differences in beliefs, customs, and practices (see, for example, Note #11), it seems illusory to search for common *religious* ground between Judaism and Christianity. That is, although conciliatory proposals have been offered (Littell 1990, p.18) that Gentile Christianity is only a spiritual form of Judaism, and Christians are only variants of Jews, such claims disguise essential difference. Must one be bearer of a shared religion and ethnicity to deserve respect? Since God is the symbol of an entity that (in the absence of other information) humans use to make sense of their particular realities (Hendriksen, p. 174), we can expect different divine attributes to be ascribed to God by different theologies. Must all God symbols be of only one kind? Must the adversities of the past continue to dominate the present? Gaston (p. 67): "*As long as Judaism is understood as a kind of Christian heresy to be combatted, there will never be an end to Christian antisemitism.*"

If Christians are serious in allowing Judaism to coexist with them as a Biblically based religion, dominant Christianity must allow Jews to deny "canonized" anti-Jewish mythology without rancor. The dilemma for Christian leaders and theologians then becomes "*A Christian Church with an antisemitic New Testament is abominable, but a Christian Church without a New Testament is inconceivable*" (Gaston, p. 48). Although overtly changing the New Testament may seem intolerable to religious Christians, can Christians conceive and teach a non-antisemitic Testament? Can its antisemitic stories be contradicted without questioning their authority?

The basic issue remains: Is there any way of maintaining religious and ethnic differences peacefully other than mutual tolerance? Since claimed "truth" for any theological notion cannot be tested (Note #11.*b*), there are no trustworthy grounds for any religious organization to impose its doctrines on others, nor is there any sign that such intolerance benefits human society. For those who believe in God, we can paraphrase Pawlikowski's message (1979, p. 165): "*Communion with God should involve peaceful communion with the rest of the human family.*"

CITED REFERENCES

Abel, E. L., 1975. *The Root of Anti-Semitism.* Fairleigh Dickinson Univ. Press, Rutherford NJ.

Abrabanel, I., 1991. *Abrabanel on PirkeAvot.* (Compiled and translated by A. Chill.) Sether-Hermon Press, New York.

Adamczewski, B., 2010. *Q or Not Q? The So-called Triple, Double, and Single Traditions in the Synoptic Gospels.* Peter Lang, Frankfurt, Germany.

Adams, S. L., 2014. *Social and Economic Life in Second Temple Judea.* Westminster/John Knox Press, Louisville KY.

Adeyemi, F., 2007. Paul's "positive" statements about the Mosaic Law. *Bibliotheca Sacra,* **164**:49–58.

Allen, R. J., and C. M. Williamson, 2004. *Preaching the Gospels without Blaming the Jews: A Lectionary Commentary.* Westminster/John Knox Press, Louisville KY.

Allen,W. S., 1990. Objective and subjective inhabitants in German resistance to Hitler. In *The German Church Struggle and the Holocaust*, F. H. Littell and H. G. Locke (Eds.). Mellen Research Univ. Press, San Francisco CA, 114–123.

Allison, D. C., Jr., 2010. *Constructing Jesus: Memory, Imagination, and History.* Baker Academic, Grand Rapids MI.

ANF *Ante-Nicene Fathers.* Roberts, A., and J. Donaldson (Eds.), 1885–1886 (Reprinted 1994). Hendrickson, Peabody MA.

Arnal, W. E., 2001. *Jesus and the Village Scribes: Galilean Conflicts and the Settings of Q.* Fortress Press, Minneapolis MN.

Arnal, W. E., 2005. The cipher "Judaism" in contemporary historical Jesus scholarship. In *Apocalyticism, Antisemitism and the Historical Jesus: Subtexts in Criticism,* J. S. Kloppenborg and J. Marshall (Eds.). T & T Clark, London UK, 24–54.

Attridge, H. W., 1992. Christianity from the destruction of Jerusalem to Constantine's adoption of the new religion: 70–312 C.E. In *Christianity and Rabbinic Judaism: A Parallel History of Their Origins and Early Development*, H. Shanks (Ed.). Biblical Archaeology Society, Washington, D.C., 151–194.

Aviam, M., 2013. People, land, economy, and belief in first century Galilee and its origins: a comprehensive archaeological synthesis. In *The Galilean Economy in the Time of Jesus*, D. A. Fiensy and R. K. Hawkins (Eds). Society of Biblical Literature, Atlanta GA, 5–48.

Ayres, L., 2015. Irenaeus vs. the Valentinians: towards rethinking of Patristic exegetical origins. *Journal of Early Christian Studies,* **238**:153–187.

270

Barclay, J. M. G., 1996. *Jews in the Mediterranean Diaspora: From Alexander to Trajan (323 BCE – 117 CE)*. T & T Clark, Edinburgh UK.

Barclay, J. M. G., 2010. Paul, the gift and the battle over Gentile circumcision: revisiting the logic of *Galatians*. *Australian Biblical Review*, **58**, 36–56.

Barnes, A., 2014. Female patronage and episcopal authority in late antiquity. In *Envisioning the Bishop: Images and the Episcopacy in the Middle Ages*, S. Danielson and E. A. Gatti (Eds.). Brepols, Turnhout, Belgium, 13–40.

Barth, K., 1975. *Church Dogmatics: The Doctrine of the Word of God*. T & T Clark, Edinburgh UK.

Barton, S. C., 2015. Why do things move people? *Journal for the Study of the New Testament,* **37**:351–380.

Baumgarten, A. I., 2009. How experiments end. In *Jewish Identities in Antiquity: Studies in Memory of Menahem Stern*, L. I. Levine, and D. R. Schwartz (Eds.). Mohr Siebeck, Tübingen, Germany, 147–161.

Beale, G. W., 2012. *Handbook on the New Testament Use of the Old Testament: Exegesis and Interpretation*. Baker, Grand Rapids MI.

Beck, N. A., 1985. *Mature Christianity: The Recognition and Repudiation of the Anti-Jewish Polemic of the New Testament*. Susquehanna Univ. Press, Selinsgrove PA.

Beck, N. A., 1994. The New Testament and the teaching of contempt: reconsiderations. In *Jewish-Christian Encounters over the Centuries: Symbiosis, Prejudice, Holocaust, Dialogue*, M. Perry and F. M. Schweitzer (Eds.). Peter Lang, New York, 83–99.

Becker, A. H., 2002. Anti-Judaism and care for the poor in Aphrahat's *Demonstration 20*. *Journal of Early Christian Studies*, **10**(3):305–327.

Becker, A. H. and A. Y. Reed (Eds.), 2003. *The Ways That Never Parted: Jews and Christians in Late Antiquity and the Early Middle Ages*. Mohr Siebeck, Tübingen, Germany.

Becker, J., 1993, Paul and his Churches. In *Christian Beginnings:Word and Community From Jesus to Post-Apostolic Times*, J. Becker (Ed.). Westminster/John Knox Press, Louisville KY, 132–210.

Bermejo-Rubio, F., 2013. (Why) was the Galilean crucified alone? Solving a false conundrum. *Journal for the Study of the New Testament*, **36**(2):127–154.

Bird, M. F., 2008. The historical Jesus. In *How Did Christianity Begin? A Believer and Non-Believer Examine the Evidence*, M. F. Bird and J. G. Crossley. Hendrickson, Peabody MA, 17–33.

Bird, M. F., 2009. *Are You the One Who Is to Come: The Historical Jesus and the Messianic Question*. Baker, Grand Rapids MI.

Blank, S. H., 1982. The Hebrew Scriptures as a source for moral guidance. In *Scriptures in the Jewish and Christian Traditions: Authority, Interpretation, Relevance*, F. E. Greenspahn (Ed.). Abingdon, Nashville TN, 169–214.

Blenkinsopp, J., 1996. *A History of Prophecy in Israel. (Revised edition)*. Westminster John Knox Press, Louisville KY.

Boccaccini, G., 1991. *Middle Judaism: Jewish Thought 300 B.C.E. to 200 C.E.* Fortress Press, Minneapolis MN.

Boer, R., 2011. Nurturing the indwelling protest: Max Herkheimer and the dialectic of religious resistance and betrayal. *Religion and Theology,* **18**:380–387.

Bowers, L. M., 2017. *An Apostle in Battle*. Mohr Siebeck, Tübingen, Germany.

Boyarin, D., 2004. *Border Lines: The Partition of Judaeo-Christianity*. Univ. of Pennsylvania Press, Philadelphia PA.

Boyarin, D., 2012. *The Jewish Gospels: The Story of the Jewish Christ.* New Press, New York.

Boys, M. C., 2014. Doing justice to Judaism: the challenge to Christianity. *Journal of Ecumenical Studies,* **49**(1):107–110.

Bradshaw, P. F., 2002. *The Search for the Origins of Christian Worship: Sources and Methods for the Study of Early Liturgy.* SPCK, London UK.

Brandon, S. G. F., 1967. *Jesus and the Zealots: A Study of the Political Factor in Early Christianity.* Manchester Univ. Press, Manchester UK.

Brandon, S. G. F., 1968. *The Trial of Jesus of Nazareth.* Stein and Day, New York.

Brent, A., 2009. *A Political History of Early Christianity*. T & T Clark, London UK.

Briggs, S., 2000. Paul on bondage and freedom in imperial Roman society. In *Paul and Politics: Ekklesia, Israel, Imperium, Interpretation*, R. A. Horsley (Ed.). Trinity Press, Harrisburg PA, 110–123.

Brown, R. E., 1994. *The Death of the Messiah: From Gethsemane to the Grave.* Doubleday, New York.

Brox, N., 1995. *A Concise History of the Early Church.* Continuum, New York.

Bultmann, R., 1933. *Glauben und Verstehen, Vol. 1.* Mohr, Tübingen, Germany.

Burke, T., 2010. Heresy hunting in the new millennium. *Studies in Religion,* **39**(3):405–420.

Burns, J. E., 2012. Like Father like Son. In *Portraits of Jesus: Studies in Christology*, S. E. Myers (Ed.). Mohr Siebeck, Tübingen, Germany, 27–43.

Burns, J. E., 2016. *The Christian Schism in Jewish History and Jewish Memory*. Cambridge Univ. Press, New York, NY.

272

Byrskog, S., 2012. From memory to memoirs: tracing the background of a literary genre. In *The Making of Christianity: Conflicts, Contacts, and Constructions. Essays in Honor of Bengt Holmberg*, M. Zetterholm and S. Byrskog (Eds.). Eisenbrauns, Winona Lake IN, 1–21.

Cameron, A., 2008. The violence of orthodoxy. In *Heresy and Identity in Late Antiquity*. E. Iricinschi and H. M. Zellentin (Eds.). Mohr Siebeck, Tübingen Germany, 102–114.

Cameron, A., and S. G. Hall, 1999. *Eusebius, Life of Constantine*. Oxford Univ. Press, Oxford UK.

Carleton Paget, J., 2010. *Jews, Christians, and Jewish Christians in Antiquity*. Mohr Siebeck, Tübingen, Germany.

Casey, M., 1991. *From Jewish Prophet to Gentile God: The Origins and Development of New Testament Christology*. James Clark, Cambridge UK.

Casey, M., 1996. *Is John's Gospel True?* Routledge, London UK.

Casey, M., 2010. *Jesus of Nazareth: An Independent Historian's Account of His Life and Teaching*. T & T Clark, London UK.

Catchpole, D. R., 2006. *Jesus People. The Historical Jesus and the Beginnings of Community*. Baker Academic, Grand Rapids MI.

Chancey, M. A., 2005. *Greco-Roman Culture and the Galilee of Jesus*. Cambridge Univ. Press, Cambridge UK.

Chapman, S. B., 2006. Reclaiming inspiration for the Bible. In *Canon and Biblical Interpretation*, C. G. Bartholomew, et al. (Eds.). Zondervan, Grand Rapids MI, 167–206.

Charles, R., 2014. *Paul and the Politics of Diaspora*. Fortress Press, Minneapolis MN.

Charlesworth, J. H. (Ed.), 1983–1985. *The Old Testament Pseudepigrapha, Vols. 1, 2*. Doubleday, New York.

Charlesworth, J. H., 1988. *Jesus Within Judaism: New Light from Existing Archaeological Discoveries*. Doubleday, New York.

Charlesworth, J. H., 2013. Did they ever part? In *Partings: How Judaism and Christianity Became Two*, H. Shanks (Ed.). Biblical Archaeological Society, Washington DC, 281–300.

Childs, B. S., 1970. *Biblical Theology in Crisis*. Westminster Press, Philadelphia PA.

Childs, B. S., 1997. Does the Old Testament witness Jesus Christ? In J. Adna, et al., *Evangelium Schriftauslegung Kirche: Festschrift für Peter Stuhlmacher zum 65. Geburtstag*. Vandenhoech and Ruprecht, Göttingen, Germany.

Childs, B. S., 2004. *The Struggle to Understand Isaiah as Christian Scripture*. Eerdmans, Grand Rapids MI.

Chilton, B., et al., 2010. *A Comparative Handbook to the Gospel of Mark: Comparisons with Pseudepigrapha, the Qumran Scrolls, and Rabbinic Literature*. Brill, Leiden, Netherlands.

Clabeaux, J. J., 1992. Marcion. *The Anchor Bible Dictionary*, **4**:514–516.

Cohen, J., 2007. *Christ Killers: The Jews and the Passion, From the Bible to the Big Screen*. Oxford Univ. Press, New York.

Cohen, S. J. D., 1987. *From the Maccabees to the Mishnah*. Westminster Press, Philadelphia PA.

Cohen, S. J. D., 1992. Judaism to the Mishnah: 135–220 C.E. In *Christianity and Rabbinic Judaism: A Parallel History of Their Origins and Early Development*, H. Shanks (Ed.). Biblical Archaeology Society, Washington, D.C., 195–223.

Cohen, S. J. D., 2013. In between: Jews and Christians and the curse of the heretics. In *Partings: How Judaism and Christianity Became Two*, H. Shanks (Ed.). Biblical Archaeological Society, Washington DC, 207–236.

Collins, N. L., 2014. *Jesus, the Sabbath and the Jewish Debate: Healing in the Sabbath in the 1st and 2nd Centuries*. T & T Clark, London UK.

Connelly, J., 2012. *From Enemy to Brother: The Revolution in Catholic Teaching on the Jews, 1933–1965*. Harvard Univ. Press, Cambridge MA.

Conway, J. S., 1968. *The Nazi Persecution of the Churches 1933–45*. Weidenfeld and Nicloson, London UK.

Conzelmann, H., 1992. *Gentiles, Jews, Christians: Polemics and Apologetics in the Greco-Roman Era*. (English translation by M. E. Boring). Fortress Press, Minneapolis MN.

Cook, M. J., 2000. Jewish reflections on Jesus: some abiding trends. In *The Historical Jesus Through Catholic and Jewish Eyes*, B. F. LeBeau, L. Greenspoon, and D. Hamm, S.J. (Eds.). Trinity Press International, Harrisburg PA, 95–111.

Cresswell, P. 2013. *The Invention of Jesus: How the Church Rewrote the New Testament*. Watkins Publishing, London UK.

Crossan, J. D., 1991. *The Historical Jesus: The Life of a Mediterranean Jewish Peasant*. HarperCollins, San Francisco CA.

Crossan, J. D., 1995. *Who Killed Jesus? Exposing the Roots of Anti-Semitism in the Gospel Story of the Death of Jesus*. HarperCollins, San Francisco CA.

Crossley, J. G., 2006. *Why Christianity Happened: A Sociohistorical Account of Christian Origins (26–50 C.E.)*. Westminster John Knox Press, Louisville KY.

Crossley, J. G., 2008. The historical Jesus. In *How Did Christianity Begin? A Believer and Non-Believer Examine the Evidence*, M. F. Bird and J. G. Crossley. Hendrickson, Peabody MA, 1–17.

274

Crowe, J., 1997. *From Jerusalem to Antioch: The Gospel Across Cultures*. Liturgical Press, Collegeville MN.

Curry, P. J., 2016. The number of variants in the Greek New Testament: a proposed estimate. *New Testament Studies*, **62**:97–121.

Czachesz, I., 2012. *The Grotesque Body in Early Christian Discourse: Hell, Scatology, and Metamorphosis*. Equinox, Sheffield UK.

Dauphine, C., and S. Gibson, 1992. Ancient settlements in their landscapes: the results of ten years of survey in the Golan Heights. *Bulletin of the Anglo-Israel Archaeological Society* **12**:7–31.

Davies, A. T., 1969. *Anti-Semitism and the Christian Mind: The Crisis of Conscience after Auschwitz*. Herder and Herder, New York.

Davies, A. T. (Ed.), 1979a. Introduction. In *Anti-Semitism and the Foundations of Christianity*, A. T. Davies (Ed.) Paulist Press, New York, XIII–XVII.

Davies, A. T. (Ed.), 1979b. On religious myths and the secular translation. In *Anti-Semitism and the Foundations of Christianity*, A. T. Davies (Ed.). Paulist Press, New York, 188–207.

Davies J.. P., 2016. *Paul Among the Apocalypses? An Evaluation of the 'Apocalyptic Paul' in the Context of Jewish and Christian Apocalyptic Literature*. T and T Clark, London UK.

Davis, L. D., 1990. *The First Seven Ecumenical Councils (325–787)*. Liturgical Press, Collegeville MN.

Demacopoulos, G. E., 2013. *The Invention of Peter: Apostolic Discourse and Papal Authority in Late Antiquity*. Univ. of Pennsylvania Press, Philadelphia PA.

Denzey, N., 2002. The limits of ethnic categories. In *Handbook of Early Christianity: Social Science Approaches*, A. J. Blasi, J. Duhaime, and P.-A. Turcotte (Eds.). Altamira Press, Walnut Creek CA, 489–507.

De Wet, C. L., 2013. John Chrysostom on Paul founder of churches. *Religion and Theology*, **20**:303–315.

Diehl, J. A., 2013. Anti-imperial rhetoric in the New Testament. In *Jesus Is Lord: Caesar Is Not: Evaluating Empire in New Testament Studies*, S. McKnight and J. B. Modica (Eds.). Intervarsity Press, Downers Grove IL, 38–81.

Donaldson, T. L., 2006. The field God has assigned: geography and mission in Paul. In *Religious Rivalries in the Early Roman Empire and the Rise of Christianity*, L. E. Vaage (Ed.). Wilfrid Laurier Univ. Press, Waterloo, Ontario, Canada, 109–137.

Donaldson, T. L., 2010. *Jews and Anti-Judaism in the New Testament: Decision Points and Divergent Interpretations*. SPCK, London UK.

Donaldson, T. L., 2013. "We Gentiles": ethnicity and identity in Justin Martyr. *Early Christianity,* **4**:216–241.

Donfried, K., 2002. *Paul, Thessalonica, and Early Christianity.* Eerdmans, Grand Rapids MI.

Drake, H. A., 1976. *In Praise of Constantine: A Historical Study and New Translation of Eusebius' Tricennial Orations.* Univ. of California Press, Berkeley CA.

Drake, S., 2013. *Slandering the Jew: Sexuality and Difference in Early Christian Texts.* Univ. of Pennsylvania Press, Philadelphia PA.

Dunderberg, I., 2013a. How far can you go? Jesus, John, the Synoptics and other texts. In *Beyond the Gnostic Gospels: Studies Building on the Work of Elaine Pagels*, E. Iricinschi, et al. (Eds.). Mohr Siebeck, Tübingen Germany, 347–366.

Dunderberg, I., 2013b. Early Christian critics of martyrdom. In *The Rise and Expansion of Christianity in the First Three Centuries of the Common Era*, C. K. Rothschild and J. Schröter (Eds.). Mohr Siebeck, Tübingen Germany, 419–440.

Dungan, D. L., 1999. *A History of the Synoptic Problem.* Doubleday, New York.

Dungan, D. L., 2007. *Constantine's Bible: Politics and the Making of the New Testament.* Fortress Press, Minneapolis MN.

Dunn, J. D. G., 1998. *The Theology of Paul the Apostle.* Eerdmans, Grand Rapids MI.

Dunn, J. D. G., 2003. *Jesus Remembered.* Eerdmans, Grand Rapids MI.

Dunn, J. D. G., 2008. *The New Perspective on Paul: Collected Essays* (Revised Edition). Eerdmans, Grand Rapids MI.

Dunn, J. D. G., 2012. Epilogue. In *Paul and Judaism: Crosscurrents In Pauline Exegesis And The Study Of Jewish-Christian Relations*, R. Beiringer and D. Pollefeyt (Eds.). T & T Clark, London UK, 208–220.

Dunn, J. D. G., 2016. The Christian life from the perspective of Paul's letter to the Galatians. In *The Apostle Paul and the Christian Life: Ethical and Missional Implications of the New Perspective*, S. McKnight and J. B. Modica (Eds.). Baker Academic, Grand Rapids MI, 1–18.

Eckardt, A. R., 1967. *Elder and Younger Brothers: The Encounter of Jews and Christians.* Scribner's, New York.

Eckardt, A. R., 1992. *Reclaiming the Jesus of History: Christology Today.* Fortress Press, Minneapolis MN.

Edrei, A., and D. Mendels, 2013. Social organization and parting in East and West. In *Partings: How Judaism and Christianity Became Two*, H. Shanks (Ed.). Biblical Archaeological Society, Washington DC, 269–279.

276

Edrie, A. and D. Mendels, 2014. Preliminary thoughts on structures of 'sover-eignty' and the deepening gap between Judaism and Christianity in the first centuries C.E. *Journal for the Study of the Pseudepigrapha, 23*(3):215–238.

Edwards, M., et al., 1999. Introduction. In *Apologetics in the Roman Empire, Pagans, Jews, and Christians*, Edwards, M., et al. (Eds.). Oxford Univ. Press, Oxford UK, 1–13.

Edwards, M., 2009. *Catholicity and Heresy in the Early Church*. Ashgate Publishing, Farnham, Surrey UK.

Efroymson, D. P., 1976. *Tertullian's Anti-Judaism and Its Role in His Theology* (Ph.D. Thesis), p. 63. From R. S. MacLennan, 1990. *Early Christian Texts on Jews and Judaism*. Scholars Press, Atlanta, GA, p. 42, footnote #110.

Efroymson D. P., 1979. The patristic connection. In *Antisemitism and the Foundations of Christianity,* A. T. Davies (Ed.). Paulist Press, New York, 98–117.

Efroymson D. P., 1993. Jesus: opposition and opponents. In *Within Context: Essays on Jews and Judaism in the New Testament*, D. P. Efroymson, E. J. Fisher, and L. Klenicki (Eds.). Liturgical Press, Collegeville MN, 85–103.

Efroymson, D. P., E. J. Fisher, and L. Klenicki (Eds.). 1993. *Within Context: Essays on Judaism in the New Testament*. Liturgical Press, Collegeville MN.

Ehrman, B. D., 1999. Jesus: *Apocalyptic Prophet of the New Millennium*. Oxford Univ. Press, Oxford UK.

Ehrman, B. D., 2003. *Lost Christianities: The Battle for Scripture and Faiths We Never Knew*. Oxford Univ. Press, New York.

Ehrman, B. D., 2011a. *The Orthodox Corruption of Scripture: The Effect of Early Christological Controversies on the Text of the New Testament*. Oxford Univ. Press, New York.

Ehrman, B. D., 2011b. *Forged: Writing in the Name of God — Why the Bible's Authors Are Not Who We Think They Are*. HarperOne, New York.

Ehrman, B. D., 2011c. The textual reliability of the New Testament: A dialogue. In *The Reliability of the New Testament*, R. B. Stewart (Ed.). Fortress Press, Minneapolis MN, 13–27.

Ehrman, B. D., 2012a. *Did Jesus Exist? The Historical Argument for Jesus of Nazareth*. HarperOne, San Francisco CA.

Ehrman, B. D., 2012b. *The New Testament: A Historical Introduction to the Early Christian Writings*. Oxford Univ. Press, New York.

Ehrman, B. D., 2013. *Forgery and Counterforgery: The Use of Literary Deceit in Early Christian Polemics*. Oxford Univ. Press, New York.

Ehrman, B. D., 2014. *How Jesus Became God: the Exaltation of a Jewish Preacher From Galilee*. HarperOne (Harper Collins), New York.

Ehrman, B. D., 2016. *Jesus Before the Gospels: How the Earliest Christians Remembered, Changed, and Invented Their Stories of the Savior.* HarperOne, New York.

Ehrman, B. D., and Z. Pleŝe, 2011. *The Apocryphal Gospels: Texts and Translations.* Oxford Univ. Press, New York.

Eisen, U. E., 2000. *Women Officeholders in Early Christianity.* Liturgical Press, Collegeville PA.

Eisenbaum, P., 2009. *Paul Was Not A Christian: The Original Message of A Misunderstood Apostle.* HarperCollins, New York.

Ekelund, R. B., and R. D. Tollison, 2011. *Economic Origins of Roman Christianity.* Univ. of Chicago Press, Chicago IL.

Ellens, J. H., 2010. Jesus' apocalyptic vision and the psychodynamics of delusion. In *Sources of the Jesus Tradition: Separating History from Myth*, R. J. Hoffman (Ed.). Prometheus Books, Amherst NY, 213–215.

Elliott, J. H., 1986. Social scientific criticism of the New Testament: more on methods and models. *Semeia,* **35**:1–33.

Elliot, J. K., 2005. *The Apocryphal New Testament: A Collection of Apocryphal Christian Literature in English Translation.* Oxford Univ. Press, New York.

Elliot, N., 2005. Disciplining the hope of the poor in ancient Rome. In *Christian Origins: A People's History of Christianity, Vol. 1*, R. A. Horsley (Ed.). Fortress Press, Minneapolis MN, 177–197.

Ellis, E. E., 1989. *Pauline Theology: Ministry and Society.* Eerdmans, Grand Rapids MI.

Endrei, A., and D. Mendels, 2013. Social organization and parting in East and West. In *Partings: How Judaism and Christianity Became Two.* H. Shanks (Ed.). Biblical Archaeological Society, Washington DC, 269–279.

Endres, J. C., 2003. Theology of worship in Chronicles. In *The Chronicler as Theologian: Essays in Honor of Ralph W. Klein,* M. P. Graham, et al. (Eds.). T & T Clark, London UK, 165–188.

Ericksen, R. P., 2012. *Complicity in the Holocaust: Churches and Universities in Nazi Germany.* Cambridge Univ. Press, New York.

Erickson, M. J., 2009. *Who's Tampering with the Trinity? An Assessment of the Subordination Debate.* Kregel Publications, Grand Rapids MI.

Esler, P. F. (Ed.), 2000. *The Early Christian World, Vols. I, II.* Routledge, London UK.

Esler, P. F., 2015. Intergroup conflict and Matthew 23: towards responsible historical interpretation of a challenging text. *Biblical Theology Bulletin,* **45**:38–59.

Eusebius. *Ecclesiastical History: The History of the Church from Christ to Constantine*. (Translated with an Introduction by G. A. Williamson, 1965.) Dorset Press, New York.

Eusebius. *The Church History*, (Translated by P. L. Maier, 1999). Kregel Publications, Grand Rapids MI.

Evans, C. A., 1992. *Noncanonical Writings and New Testament Interpretation*. Hendrickson, Peabody MA.

Evans, C. A., 2016. *'He Laid Him in a Tomb' (Mark 15.46): Roman Law and the Burial of Jesus*. In *Matthew and Mark Across Perspectives: Essays in Honour of Stephen C. Barton and William R Telford*, K. A. Bendoraitis and N. K. Gupta (Eds.). Bloomsbury T & T Clark, London UK, 52–66.

Evans, C. A., and D. A. Hagner (Eds.), 1993. *Anti-Semitism and Early Christian Issues of Polemic and Faith*. Fortress Press, Minneapolis MN.

Evans, C. S., 2006. Canonicity, apostolicity, and biblical authority. In *Canonical and Biblical Interpretation*, C. G. Bartholomew, et al. (Eds.). Zondervan, Grand Rapids MI, 146–166.

Falque, E., 2016. *Crossing the Rubicon: The Borderlands of Philosophy and Theology*. (Translated by R. Shank.) Fordham Univ. Press, New York.

Faulkner Rossi, L., 2015. Wehrmacht Priests: *Catholicism and the Nazi War of Annihilation*. Harvard Univ. Press, Cambridge MA.

Feldman, L. H., 1992. Palestinian and diaspora Judaism in the first century. In *Christianity and Rabbinic Judaism: A Parallel History of Their Origins and Early Development*, H. Shanks (Ed.). Biblical Archaeology Society, Washington, D.C., 1–39.

Feldman, L. H., 2001. Financing the Colosseum. *Biblical Archaeological Review* **27**(4):20–31, 60–61.

Feldman, L. H., 2006. *Judaism and Hellenism Reconsidered*. Brill, London UK.

Ferguson, E., 1993. *Backgrounds of Early Christianity*. Eerdmans, Grand Rapids MI.

Fiensy, D. A., 1991. *The Social History of Palestine in the Herodian Period: The Land is Mine*. Edwin Mellen Press, Lewiston NY.

Fiensy, D. A., 2013. Assessing the economy of Galilee in the late Second Temple period: five considerations. In *The Galilean Economy in the Time of Jesus*, D. A. Fiensy and R. K. Hawkins (Eds.). Society of Biblical Literature, Atlanta GA, 165–186.

Fine, S., 2013. The complexities of rejection and attraction: herein of love and hate. In *Partings: How Judaism and Christianity Became Two*, H. Shanks (Ed.). Biblical Archaeological Society, Washington DC, 237–252.

Finn, T. M., 2000. Mission and expansion. In *The Early Christian World, Vol. 1*, P. F. Esler (Ed.). Routledge, London UK, 295–315.

Fisher, E. J., 1977. *Faith Without Prejudice*. Paulist Press, New York.

Fisher, E. J., 1993. The passion and death of Jesus of Nazareth: catechtical approaches. In *Within Context: Essays on Jews and Judaism in the New Testament*, D. P. Efroymson, E. J. Fisher, and L. Klenicki (Eds.). Liturgical Press, Collegeville MN, 104–122.

Fitzmyer, J. A., 1991. *A Christological Catechism: New Testament Answers*. Paulist Press, New York.

Flannery, E. H., 1985. *The Anguish of the Jews: Twenty-three Centuries of Anti-Semitism*. Paulist Press, Mahwah NJ.

Foster, P., 2015. Echoes without resonance: critiquing certain aspects of recent scholarly trends in the study of the Jewish scriptures in the New Testament. *Journal for the Study of the New Testament,* **38**:96–111.

Fraade, S. D., 2009. The Temple as a marker of Jewish identity before and after 70 C.E.: the role of the holy vessels in rabbinic memory and imagination. In *Jewish Identities in Antiquity: Studies in Memory of Menahem Stern*, L. I. Levine, and D. R. Schwartz (Eds.). Mohr Siebeck, Tübingen, Germany, 237–265.

Fredriksen, P., 1986. Paul and Augustine: conversion narratives, orthodox tradition, and the retrospective self. *Journal of Theological Studies, New Series,* **37**:3–34.

Fredriksen, P., 1995. Excaecati Occulta Justitia Dei: Augustine on Jews and Judaism. *Journal of Early Christian Studies,* **3**(3):299–324.

Fredriksen, P., 1999. *Jesus of Nazareth, King of the Jews: A Jewish Life and the Emergence of Christianity*. A. A. Knopf, New York.

Fredriksen, P., 2002. The birth of Christianity and the origins of Christian anti-Judaism. In *Jesus, Judaism, and Christian Anti-Judaism*, P. Fredriksen and A. Reinhartz (Eds.). Westminster/John Knox Press, Louisville KY, 8–30.

Fredriksen, P., 2003. What "Parting of the Ways"? Jews, Gentiles, and the ancient Mediterranean city. In *The Ways That Never Parted: Jews and Christians in Late Antiquity and the Early Middle Ages*, A. H. Becker, and A. Y. Reed (Eds.). Mohr Siebeck, Tübingen, Germany, 35–63

Freeman, C., 2009. *A New History of Early Christianity*. Yale Univ. Press, New Haven CT.

Freke, T., and P. Gandy, 1999. *The Jesus Mysteries: Was the "Original Jesus' a Pagan God*. Harmony Books, New York.

Freyne, S., 2006. Galilee and Judaea in the first century. In *The Cambridge History of Christianity, Vol. 1, Origin to Constantine*, M. M. Mitchell, and F. M. Young (Eds.). Cambridge Univ. Press, Cambridge UK, 37–51.

Freyne, S., 2014. *The Jesus Movement and Its Expansion: Meaning and Mission*. Eerdmans, Grand Rapids MI.

Friesen, S. J., 2004. Poverty in Pauline studies: beyond the so-called new consensus. *Journal for the Study of the New Testament,* **26**(3):323–361.

Friesen, S. J., 2005. Injustice or God's will: explanations of poverty in proto-Christian communities. In *Christian Origins: A People's History of Christianity, Vol. 1*, R. A. Horsley (Ed.). Fortress Press, Minneapolis MN, 240–260.

Funk, R. W., R. W. Hoover, and the Jesus Seminar, 1993. *The Five Gospels: The Search for the Authentic Words of Jesus*. Polebridge Press, Macmillan, New York

Funk, R. W., and the Jesus Seminar, 1998. *The Acts of Jesus: The Search for the Authentic Deeds of Jesus*. Polebridge Press, HarperSanFrancisco, San Francisco CA.

Gafni, I. M., 1992. The world of the Talmud: from the Mishnah to the Arab conquest. In *Christianity and Rabbinic Judaism: A Parallel History of Their Origins and Early Development*, H. Shanks (Ed.). Biblical Archaeology Society, Washington, D.C., 225–265.

Gager, J. G., 1985. *The Origins of Anti-Semitism: Attitudes Toward Judaism in Pagan and Christian Antiquity*, Oxford Univ. Press, New York.

Gager, J. G., 2000. *Reinventing Paul*. Oxford Univ. Press, New York.

Galambush, J., 2005. *The Reluctant Parting. How the New Testament Jewish Writers Created A Christian Book*. HarperSanFrancisco., San Francisco CA.

Gamble, H. Y., 1985. *The New Testament Canon: Its Making and Meaning*. Fortress Press, Minneapolis MN.

Garroway, J. D., 2014. The Pharisee heresy: circumcision for Gentiles in The Acts of the Apostles. *New Testament Studies,* **60**(1):20–36.

Gaston, L., 1979. Paul and the Torah. In *Antisemitism and the Foundations of Christianity,* A. T. Davies (Ed.). Paulist Press, New York, 48–71.

Geraty, L. T., 2013. From Sabbath to Sunday: why, how and when? In *Partings: How Judaism and Christianity Became Two*, H. Shanks (Ed.). Biblical Archaeological Society, Washington DC, 255–268.

Goodman, M., 1987. *The Ruling Class of Judaea: The Origins of the Jewish Revolt against Rome A.D. 66–70*. Cambridge University Press, Cambridge UK.

Goodman, M., 1992. Jewish proselytization in the First Century. In *The Jews Among Pagans and Christians in the Roman Empire*, J. Lieu, J. North, and T. Rajak (Eds.). Routledge, London UK, 53–78.

Goodman, M., 2007a. *Rome and Jerusalem: The Clash of Ancient Civilizations*. A. A. Knopf, New York.

Goodman, M., 2007b. *Judaism in the Roman World: Collected Essays*. Brill, Leiden, Netherlands.

Gowler, D. B., 2007. *What Are They Saying About The Historical Jesus?* Paulist Press, Mahwah NJ.

Grant, M., 1973. *The Jews in the Roman World*. Charles Scribner's Sons, New York.

Grant, R. M., 1992. Marcion, Gospel of. *The Anchor Bible Dictionary*, **4**:516–520.

Gray, P., 1994. Jesus was a Jew. In *Jewish-Christian Encounters over the Centuries: Symbiosis, Prejudice, Holocaust, Dialogue*, M. Perry and F. M. Schweitzer (Eds.). Peter Lang, New York, 1–25.

Gregg, B. H., 2006. *The Historical Jesus and the Final Judgment Sayings in Q*. Mohr Siebeck, Tübingen, Germany.

Gribetz, S. K., 2016. A matter of time: writing Jewish history into Roman history. *Association for Jewish Studies Review*, **40**(1):57–86.

Gruen, E. S., 2002. *Diaspora: Jews Amidst Greeks and Romans*. Harvard Univ. Press, Cambridge MA.

Guy, L., 2004. *Introducing Early Christianity*. Intervarsity Press, Downers Grove IL.

Hagner, D. A., 2016. The newness of the Gospel in Mark and Matthew: continuity and discontinuity. In *Matthew and Mark Across Perspectives: Essays in Honor of Stephen C. Barton and William R. Telford*, K. Bendoraitis and N. K. Gupta (Eds.). T and T Clark, London UK, 67–82.

Hakola, R., 2005. *Identity Matters: John, the Jews, and Jewishness*. Brill, Leiden, Netherlands.

Hakola, R., 2007. The Johannine community as Jewish Christians? Some problems in current scholarly consensus. In *Jewish Christianity Reconsidered: Re-thinking Ancient Groups and Texts*, M. Jackson-McCabe (Ed.). Fortress Press, Minneapolis MN, 181–201.

Hamblin, W. J., and D. R. Seely (Eds.), 2007. *Solomon's Temple: Myth and History*. Thames and Hudson, London UK.

Hanc, O., 2014. Paul and empire: a reframing of *Romans* 13.1-7 in the context of the new exodus. *Tyndale Bulletin* 65(2):313–316.

Hanson, K. C., and D. E. Oakman, 2008. *Palestine in the Time of Jesus: Social Structures and Social Conflicts (Second Edition)*. Fortress Press, Minneapolis MN.

Hare, D. R. A., 1967. The relationship between Jewish and Gentile persecution of Christians. *Journal of Ecumenical Studies*, **IV**:446–456.

Harkins, P. W., 1977. *Saint John Chrysostom: Discourses Against Judaizing Christians*. The Catholic Univ. of America Press, Washington, D. C.

Harlow, D. C., 2010. Early Judaism and early Christianity. In *The Eerdmans Dictionary of Early Judaism*, J. J. Collins and D. C. Harlow (Eds.). Eerdmans, Grand Rapids MI, 257–278.

Hayman, A. P., 1985. The image of the Jew in the Syriac anti-Jewish polemical literature. In *"To See Ourselves As Others See Us": Christians, Jews, "Others" in Late Antiquity*, J. Neusner and E. S. Frerichs (Eds.). Scholars Press, Chico CA, 423–441.

Heemstra, M., 2010. *The Fiscus Judaicus and the Parting of the Ways*. Mohr Siebeck, Tübingen, Germany.

Hellwig, M. K., 1979. From the Jesus of story to the Christ of dogma. In *Antisemitism and the Foundations of Christianity*, A. T. Davies (Ed.). Paulist Press, New York, 118–136.

Hendriksen, O-J., 2013. Distinct, unique, or separate?. Challenges to theological anthropology and soteriology in light of human evolution. *Studia Theologica,* **67**(2):166–183.

Herr, M. D., 2009. The identity of the Jewish people before and after the destruction of the Second Temple: continuity or change? In *Jewish Identities in Antiquity: Studies in Memory of Menaham Stern*, L. I. Levine, and D. R. Schwartz (Eds.). Mohr Siebeck, Tübingen, Germany, 211–236.

Heschel, S., 2008. *The Aryan Jesus: Christian Theologians and the Bible in Nazi Germany.* Princeton Univ. Press, Princeton NJ.

Heschel, S., 2009. Race as incarnational theology: affinities between German Prostestantism and racial theory. In *Prejudice and Christian Beginnings: Investigating Race, Gender, and Ethnicity in Early Christian Studies*, L. Nasrallah and E. Schüsler Fiorenza (Eds.). Fortress Press, Minneapolis MN, 211–232.

Heschel, S., 2011. Historiography of antisemitism versus anti-Judaism: a response to Robert Morgan. *Journal for the Study of the New Testament,* **33**(3):257–279.

Hezser, C., 2001. *Jewish Literacy in Roman Palestine.* Mohr Siebeck, Tübingen Germany.

Hoffmann, R. J., 1987. *Celsus on the True Doctrine: A Discourse Against the Christians.* Oxford Univ. Press, New York.

Hoffman, R. J., 2010. On not finding the historical Jesus. In *Sources of the Jesus Tradition: Separating History from Myth*, R. J. Hoffman (Ed.). Prometheus Books, Amherst NY, 171–184.

Hooker, M. D., 1986. *Continuity and Discontinuity: Early Christianity in its Jewish Setting.* Epworth Press, London UK.

Hopkins, K., 1998. Christian numbers and its implications. *Journal of Early Christian Studies,* **6**:185–226.

Horbury, W., 1998. *Jews and Christians in Context and Controversy.* T & T Clark, Edinburgh.

Horner, T., 2004. Jewish aspects of the Protoevangelium of James. *Journal of Early Christian Studies,* **12**: 313–335.

Horrell, D. G., 2000. Early Jewish Christianity. In *The Early Christian World, Vol. 1*, P. F. Esler (Ed.). Routledge, London UK, 136–167.

Horrell, D. G., 2002. "Becoming Christian": solidifying Christian identity and content. In *Handbook of Early Christianity: Social Science Approaches*, A. J. Blasi, J. Duhaime, and P.-A. Turcotte (Eds.). Altamira Press, Walnut Creek CA, 309–335.

Horsley, R. A., 1994. *Sociology and the Jesus Movement.* Continuum, New York.

Horsley, R. A., 1995. *Galilee History, Politics, People.* Trinity Press International, Valley Forge PA.

Horsley, R. A., 1997. I Corinthians: a case study of Paul's assembly as an alternative society. In *Paul and Empire: Religion and Power in Roman Imperial Society*, R. A. Horsley (Ed.). Trinity Press International, Harrisburg PA, 242–251.

Horsley, R. A., 2005. Introduction: Unearthing a people's history. In *Christian Origins: A People's History of Christianity, Vol. 1*, R. A. Horsley (Ed.). Fortress Press, Minneapolis MN, 1–20.

Horsley, R., 2012. *The Prophet Jesus and the Renewal of Israel: Moving Beyond a Diversionary Debate.* Eerdmans, Grand Rapids MI.

Horsley, R. A., and J. S. Hanson, 1985. *Bandits, Prophets, and Messiahs: Popular Movements at the Time of Jesus.* HarperSanFrancisco, San Francisco CA.

Horsley, R. A., and N. A. Silberman, 1997. *The Message and the Kingdom: How Jesus and Paul Ignited a Revolution and Transformed the Ancient World.* Grosset/Putnam, New York.

Hubbard, M. V., 2010. *Christianity in the The Greco-Roman World.* Hendrickson, Peabody MA.

Hughson, T., 2013. *Connecting Jesus to Social Justice: Classical Christology and Public Theology.* Rowman and Littlefield, Lanham MD.

Humphries, M., 2006. *Early Christianity.* Routledge, London UK.

Hvalvik, R., 2007. Jewish believers and Jewish influence in the Roman Church until the early second century. In *Jewish believers in Jesus: The Early Centuries*, O. Skarsaune and R. Hvalvik (Eds.). Hendrickson, Peabody MA, 179–216.

Hvalvik, R., 2014. Praying with outstretched hands: nonverbal aspects of early Christian prayer and the question of identity. In *Early Christian Prayer and Identity Formation*, R. Hvalvik and K. O. Sandnes (Eds.). Mohr Siebeck, Tübingen Germany.

Irshai, O., 2009. Jewish violence in the fourth century CE — fantasy and reality: behind the scenes under the Emperors Gallus and Julian. In *Jewish Identities in Antiquity: Studies in Memory of Menahem Stern*, L. I. Levine, and D. R. Schwartz (Eds.). Mohr Siebeck, Tübingen, Germany, 391–416.

Isaac, B., 2004. *The Invention of Racism in Classical Antiquity*. Princeton Univ. Press, Princeton NJ.

Jackson-McCabe, M. A., 2013. Ebionites and Nazoraeans: Christians or Jews? In *Partings: How Judaism and Christianity Became Two*, H. Shanks (Ed.). Biblical Archaeological Society, Washington DC, 187–205.

Jacobs, A. S., 2007. Dialogical differences: (De-) Judaizing Jesus' circumcision. *Journal of Early Christian Studies*, 15(3):291–335.

Japhet, S., 1989. *The Ideology of the Book of Chronicles and Its Place in Biblical Thought*. Peter Lang, Frankfurt Germany.

Jenkins, P., 2010. *Jesus Wars: How Four Patriarchs, Three Queens, and Two Emperors Decided What Christians Would Believe for the Next 1,500 Years*. SPCK, London UK.

Johnson, K., 2015. Penal substitution as an undivided work of the triune God. *Trinity Journal*, 36(1):51–67.

Johnson, L. T., 1992. *The Acts of the Apostles*. Liturgical Press, Collegeville MN.

Johnson, L. T., 2007. The Bible's authority for and in the Church. In *Engaging Biblical Authority: Perspectives on the Bible as Scripture*, W. P. Brown (Ed.). Westminster/John Knox Press, Louisville KY, 62–72.

Judge, E. A., 1994. Judaism and the rise of Christianity: a Roman perspective. *Tyndale Bulletin*, 45(2):355–368.

Katz, J., 1980. *From Prejudice to Destruction: Anti-Semitism, 1700–1933*. Harvard Univ. Press, Cambridge MA.

Kaufman, J., 2016. Historical relativism and the essence of Christianity. *Nordic Journal of Theology*, 70(1):4–21.

Kaylor, R. D., 1994. *Jesus the Prophet: His Vision of the Kingdom on Earth*. Westminster/John Knox Press, Louisville KY.

Kearney, M. and J. Zeitz, 2009. *World Saviors and Messiahs of the Roman Empire, 28 BCE–135 CE. The Soterial Age*. Edwin Mellen Press, Lewiston NY.

Kee, P. V., 2013a. Sources in Acts. In *Acts and Christian Beginnings: The Acts Seminar Report*, D. E. Smith and J. B. Tyson (Eds.). Polebridge Press, Salem OR, 10–15.

Kee, P. V., 2013b. Hellenists and Hebrews. In *Acts and Christian Beginnings: The Acts Seminar Report*, D. E. Smith and J. B. Tyson (Eds.). Polebridge Press, Salem OR, 79–80.

Keith, C., 2014. *Jesus Against the Scribal Elite: The Origins of the Conflict.* Baker, Grand Rapids MI.

Kelly, H. A. 2014. Adam citings before the intrusion of Satan: recontextualizing Paul's theology of sin and death. *Biblical Theological Bulletin,* **44**(1):13–28.

Kelsey, D. H., 1982. Protestant attitudes regarding methods of Biblical interpretation. In *Scriptures in the Jewish and Christian Traditions: Authority, Interpretation, Relevance*, F. E. Greenspahn (Ed.). Abingdon, Nashville TN, 134–161.

Kent, H. A. Jr., 1978. Philippians. In *The Expositor's Bible Commentary, Vol. 11,* F. E. Gaebelein (Ed.). Zondervan, Grand Rapids MI, 102–159.

Kim, S., 2008. *Christ and Caesar: The Gospel and the Roman Empire in the Writings of Paul and Luke.* Eerdmans, Grand Rapids MI.

Kimber Buell, D., 2009. God's own people: specter of race, ethnicity, and gender in early Christian studies. In *Prejudice and Christian Beginnings: Investigating Race, Gender, and Ethnicity in Early Christian Studies,* L. Nasrallah and E. Schüsler Fiorenza (Eds.). Fortress Press, Minneapolis MN, 159–190.

Kimelman, R., 1981. *Birkat Ha-minim* and the lack of evidence for an anti-Christian Jewish prayer in Late Antiquity. In *Jewish and Christian Self-Definition. Vol. 2: Aspects of Judaism in the Graeco-Roman Period*, E. P. Sanders, A. I. Baumgarten, and A. Mendelson (Eds.). Fortress Press, Philadelphia PA, 226–244.

Klassen, W., 1986. Anti-Judaism in early Christianity: the state of the question. In *Anti-Judaism in Early Christianity*, P. Richardson and D. Granskou (Eds.). Wilfrid Laurier Univ. Press, Waterloo, Ontario, Canada. 1–19.

Klauck, H-J., 2003. *Magic and Paganism in Early Christianity: The World of the Acts of the Apostles.* Fortress Press, Minneapolis MN.

Klauser, T., 1979. *A Short History of the Western Liturgy: An Account and Some Reflections (Second Edition).* Oxford Univ. Press, Oxford UK.

Klein, C., 1978. *Anti-Judaism in Christian Theology.* (English translation of 1975 German edition.). Fortress Press, Philadelphia PA.

Klein, M. D., 2004. *Seder Avodah*: *Mahzor for Rosh Hashanah and Yom Kippur.* Elkins Park PA.

Klijn, A. F. J., 2003. *The Acts of Thomas: Introduction, Text, and Commentary (Second Revised Edition).* Brill, Leiden, Netherlands.

Kloppenborg, J. S., 1987. *The Formation of Q: Trajectories in Ancient Wisdom Collections.* Trinity Press International, Harrisburg PA.

Knowles, M. D., et al. (Eds.), 2009. *Contesting Texts: Jews and Christians in Conversation about the Bible.* Fortress Press, Minneapolis MN.

Koester, H., 1995. *Introduction to the New Testament, Vol. 1. History, Culture, and Religion of the Hellenistic Age (Second Edition).* Walter de Gruyter, New York.

Koester, H., 2005. Gospels and gospel traditions in the second Century. In *Trajectories through the New Testament and the Apostolic Fathers,* A. F. Gregory and C. M. Tuckett (Eds.). Oxford Univ. Press, Oxford UK, 27–44.

Koester, H., 2007. *From Jesus to the Gospels: Interpreting the New Testament in Its Context.* Fortress Press, Minneapolis MN.

Kraabel, A. 1992a. The Roman Diaspora: six questionable assumptions. In *Diaspora Jews and Judaism,* J. A. Overman and R. S. MacLennan (Eds.). Scholars Press, Atlanta GA, 1–20.

Kraabel, A. 1992b. Unity and diversity among Diaspora synagogues. In *Diaspora Jews and Judaism,* J. A. Overman and R. S. MacLennan (Eds.). Scholars Press, Atlanta GA, 21–31.

Kruger, M. J., 2012. *Canon Revisited: Establishing the Origins and Authority of the New Testament Books.* Crossway, Wheaton IL.

Lamb, D. T., 2011. *God Behaving Badly: Is the God of the Old Testament Angry, Sexist, and Racist?* Intervarsity Press, Downers Grove IL.

Langmuir, G. I., 1990. *Toward A Definition of Antisemitism.* Univ. of California Press, Berkeley CA.

Lapin, H., 2012. *Rabbis as Romans: the Rabbinic Movement in Palestine, 100–400 C.E.* Oxford Univ. Press, New York.

Lasker, D. J., 2007. Introduction. In R. Travers Hereford's *Christianity in Talmud and Midrash.* KTAV Publishing House, Newark NJ, xvii–xxv.

Levenson, J. D., 1993. *The Death and Resurrection of the Beloved Son: The Transformation of Child Sacrifice in Judaism and Christianity.* Yale Univ. Press, New Haven CT.

Levin, Y., 2007. Jesus, "Son of God" and "Son of David": the "adoption" of Jesus into the Davidic line. *Journal for the Study of the New Testament,* **28**:415–442.

Levine, A. I., 1992. Judaism from the destruction of Jerusalem to the end of the second Jewish revolt: 70–135 C.E. In *Christianity and Rabbinic Judaism: A Parallel History of their Origins and Early Development*, H. Shanks (Ed.). Biblical Archaeology Society, Washington DC, 125–149.

Levine, A.-J., 2007. Theory, apologetic history: reviewing Jesus' Jewish history. *Australian Biblical Review,* **55**:57–78.

Levine, A.-J., 2011. Bearing false witness: common errors made about Judaism. In *The Jewish Annotated New Testament*, A.-J. Levine and M. Z. Brettler (Eds.). Oxford Univ. Press, New York, 501–504.

Levine, L. I., 2009. Jewish identities in antiquity: an introductory essay. In *Jewish Identities in Antiquity: Studies in Memory of Menahem Stern*, L. I. Levine, and D. R. Schwartz (Eds.). Mohr Siebeck, Tübingen, Germany, 12–40.

Levinskaya, I., 1996. *The Book of Acts in Its Diaspora Setting*. Eerdmans, Grand Rapids MI.

Lienhard, J. T., 1995. *The Bible, the Church, and Authority*. Liturgical Press, Collegeville MN.

Lieu, J. M., 1996. *Image and Reality: The Jews in the World of the Christians in the Second Century*. T & T Clark, Edinburgh UK.

Lieu, J. M., 2002. *Neither Jew Nor Greek? Constructing Early Christianity*. T &T Clark, London UK.

Lieu, J. M., 2004. *Christian Identity in the Jewish and Graeco-Roman World*. Oxford Univ. Press, Oxford UK.

Lieu, J. M., 2011. The forging of Christian identity and the *Letter of Diognetus*. In *The Religious History of the Roman Empire: Pagans, Jews, and Christians*, J. A. North and S. R. F. Price (Eds.). Oxford Univ. Press, Oxford, 435–459.

Lightstone, J. N., 2006. My rival, my fellow. In *Religious Rivalries in the Early Roman Empire and the Rise of Christianity*, L. E. Vaage (Ed.). Wilfrid Laurier Univ. Press, Waterloo, Ontario, Canada, 85–105.

Littell, F. H., 1990. Church struggle and the Holocaust. In *The German Church Struggle and the Holocaust*, F. H. Littell and H. G. Locke (Eds.). Mellen Research Univ. Press, San Francisco CA, 11–30.

Littell, F. H., 1996. *The Crucifixion of the Jews*. HarperCollins, San Francisco CA.

Litwa, M. D., 2012. *We Are Being Transformed: Deification in Paul's Soteriology*. DeGruyter, Berlin, Germany.

Loader, W., 2009. "Good news for the poor" and spirituality in the New Testament: a question of survival. In *Prayer and Spirituality in the Early Church, Vol. 5*, G.D. Dunn, D. Luckensmeyer, and L. Cross (Eds.). St. Paul's Publications, Strathfield, Australia, 3–35.

Lohse, B., 1985. *A Short History of Christian Doctrine. (Revised American Edition.)* Fortress Press, Philadelphia PA.

Longenecker, B. W., 2010. *Remember the Poor: Paul, Poverty, and the Roman World*. Eerdmans, Grand Rapids MI.

Longenecker, R. N., 1970. *The Christology of Early Jewish Christianity*. Eerdmans, Regent College Publishing, Vancouver, Canada.

Longenecker, R. N., 1999. *Biblical Exegesis in the Apostolic Period*. Eerdmans, Grand Rapids MI.

Löning, K., 1998. The circle of Stephen and its mission. In *Christian Beginnings : Word and Community From Jesus to Post-Apostolic Times*, J. Becker (Ed.). Westminster/John Knox Press, Louisville KY, 103–131.

Lössl, J., 2010. *The Early Church: History and Memory*. T & T Clark, London UK.

Lucass, S., 2011. *The Concept of the Messiah in the Scriptures of Judaism and Christianity*. T & T Clark, New York.

Lüdemann, G., 1998. *Virgin Birth? The Real Story of Mary and Her Jesus*. Trinity Press International, Harrisburg PA.

Lüdemann, G., 2002a. *Primitive Christianity: A Survey of Recent Studies and Some New Predictions*. T & T Clark, London UK.

Lüdemann, G., 2002b. *Paul, the Founder of Christianity*. Prometheus Books, Amherst, New York.

Lüdemann, G., 2010. Paul as a witness to the historical Jesus. In *Sources of the Jesus Tradition: Separating History from Myth*, R. J. Hoffman (Ed.). Prometheus Books, Amherst NY, 196–212.

Ludlow, M., 2009. *The Early Church*. I. B. Taurus, London UK.

Lundhaug, H., 2013. Begotten and not made, to arise in this flesh: the post-Nicene soteriology of the *Gospel of Philip*. In *Beyond the Gnostic Gospels: Studies Building on the Work of Elaine Pagels*, E. Iricinschi, et al. (Eds.). Mohr Siebeck, Tübingen Germany, 235–271.

Luomanen, P., 2007. Ebionites and Nazarenes. In *Jewish Christianity Reconsidered: Rethinking Ancient Groups and Texts*, M. Jackson-McCabe (Ed.). Fortress Press, Minneapolis MN, 81–118.

Luz, U., 2005. *Studies in Matthew*. (Translated by R. Selle.) Eerdmans, Grand Rapids MI.

Lynch, J. H., 2010. *Early Christianity: A Brief History*. Oxford Univ, Press, New York.

MacArthur, J., 2001. Open theism's attack on the Atonement. *Master's Seminary Journal*, **12**(1) 3–13.

Maccoby, H., 1991. *Paul and Hellenism*. SCM Press, London UK.

Maccoby, H., 1992. *Judas Iscariot and the Myth of Jewish Evil*. The Free Press/Macmillan, New York.

Mack, B. L., 1995. *Who Wrote the New Testament? The Making of the Christian Myth*. HarperSanFrancisco, San Francisco CA.

Mack, B. L., 1999. Many movements, many myths: redescribing the attractions of Early Christianities. Toward a conversation with Rodney Stark. *Religious Studies Review,* **25**:132–136.

Mack, B. L., 2001. *The Christian Myth: Origin, Logic, and Legacy.* Continuum, New York.

MacLennan, R. S., 1990. *Early Christian Texts on Jews and Judaism.* Scholars Press, Atlanta, GA.

MacMullen, 1997. *Christianity and Paganism in the Fourth to Eighth Centuries.* Yale Univ. Press, New Haven CT.

Maier, P. L., 1999. *Eusebius, The Church History: A New Translation With Commentary.* Kregel, Grand Rapids MI.

Malina, B. J., 2002. Social-scientific methods in historical Jesus research. In *The Social Setting of Jesus and the Gospels*, S. W. Stegemann, B. J. Malina, and G. Thiessen (Eds.). Fortress Press, Minneapolis MN, 1–26.

Marcus, J., 2009. *Mark 8–16. A New Translation with Introduction and Commentary. The Anchor Yale Bible.* Yale Univ. Press, New Haven CT.

Markschies, C., 1999. *Between Two Worlds: Structures of Early Christianity.* SCM Press, London UK.

Marshall, J. W., 2012. Misunderstanding the new Paul: Marcion's transformation of the sonderzeit Paul. *Journal of Early Christian Studies*, **20**:1–29.

Martin, D. B., 2014. Jesus in Jerusalem: armed and not dangerous. *Journal for the Study of the New Testament,* **37**:3–24.

Martin, T. W., 1992. Hellenists. *The Anchor Bible Dictionary*, **3**:135–136.

Mason, S., 2006. The *Contra Apionem* in social and literary context, an invitation to Judean philosophy. In *Religious Rivalries in the Early Roman Empire and the Rise of Christianity*, L. E. Vaage (Ed.). Wilfrid Laurier Univ. Press, Waterloo, Ontario, Canada, 139–173.

Matera, F. J., 2012. *God's Saving Grace: A Pauline Theology.* Eerdmans, Grand Rapids MI.

Matthews, S., 2010. *Perfect Martyr: The Stoning of Stephen and the Construction of Christian Identity.* Oxford Univ. Press, New York.

Matthews, T. F., 1993. *Clash of Gods: A Reinterpretation of Early Christian Art.* Princeton Univ. Press, Princeton NJ.

Mayer, W., and P. Allen, 2000. *John Chrysostom.* Routledge, London UK.

McKnight, S., 1991. *A Light Among Gentiles: Jewish Missionary Activity in the Second Temple Period.* Fortress Press, Minneapolis MN.

McKnight, S., and J. B. Modica (Eds.), 2013. *Jesus Is Lord: Caesar Is Not: Evaluating Empire in New Testament Studies.* Intervarsity Press, Downers Grove IL.

Meagher, J. C., 1979. As the twig was bent: antisemitism in Greco-Roman and earliest Christian times. In *Antisemitism and the Foundations of Christianity*, A. T. Davies (Ed.). Paulist Press, New York, 1–26.

Meeks, W. A., 1983. *The First Urban Christians: The Social World of the Apostle Paul*. Yale Univ. Press, New Haven CT.

Meeks W. A., 1985. Breaking away, three New Testament pictures of Christianity's separation from the Jewish communities. In *"To See Ourselves As Others See Us": Christians, Jews, "Others" in Late Antiquity*, J. Neusner and E. S. Frerichs (Eds.). Scholars Press, Chico CA, 93–115.

Meggitt, J., 1998. *Paul, Poverty, and Survival*. T & T Clark, Edinburgh UK.

Meggitt, J., 2010. Popular mythology in the early Empire and the multiplicity of Jesus traditions. In *Sources of the Jesus Tradition: Separating History from Myth*, R. J. Hoffman (Ed.). Prometheus Books, Amherst NY, 55–80.

Meier, J. P., 1991–2009. *A Marginal Jew: Rethinking the Historical Jesus (4 Volumes)*. HarperSanFrancisco, San Francisco CA.

Meissner, W. W., 2000. *The Cultic Origins of Christianity: The Dynamics of Religious Development*. Liturgical Press, Collegeville MN.

Mendelssohn, M., 1783. *Jerusalem: or On Religious Power and Judaism*. (1983 English translation by A. Arkush.) Brandeis Univ. Press, University Press of New England, Hanover NH.

Metzger, B. M., 1987. *The Canon of the New Testament: Its Origin, Development, and Significance*. Clarendon Press, Oxford UK.

Meyers, C. L., 1985. The Temple. *Harpers Bible Dictionary*. HarperSanFrancisco, San Francisco CA, 1021–1029.

Michael, R., 2006. *Holy Hatred: Christianity, Antisemitism, and the Holocaust*. Palgrave Macmillan, New York.

Milavec, A., 2003. *The Didache: Text, Translation, Analysis, and Commentary*. Liturgical Press, Collegeville MN.

Miller, R. J. (Ed.), 1992. *The Complete Gospels*. Polebridge Press, Sonoma CA.

Miller, R. J., 1999. *The Jesus Seminar and Its Critics*. Polebridge Press, Santa Rosa CA.

Mitchell, S., 1994. *Anatolia: Land, Man, and Gods in Asia Minor, Vol. 2*. Oxford Univ. Press, Oxford UK.

Moberly, R. W. L., 2013. *Old Testament Theology: Reading the Hebrew Bible as Christian Scripture*. Baker Academic, Grand Rapids MI.

Moo, D. J., 2013. *Galatians* . Baker Academic, Grand Rapids, MI.

Moreschini, C., and E. Norelli, 2005. *Early Christian Greek and Latin Literature: A Literary History, vol. 1*. (Translated by M. J. O'Connell.) Hendrickson, Peabody MA.

Moss, C. R., 2012. *Ancient Christian Martyrdom: Diverse Practices, Theologies, and Traditions.* Yale Univ. Press, New Haven CT.

Moss, C. R., 2013. *The Myth of Persecution: How Early Christians Invented a Story of Martyrdom.* HarperCollins, New York.

Moyise, S., 2010. *Jesus and Scripture: Studying the New Testament Use of the Old Testament.* Baker, Grand Rapids MI.

Müller, M., 2014. The New Testament gospels as Biblical rewritings: on the question of referentialtiy. *Studia Theologica,* **68**(1):21–40.

Murray, M., 2004. *Playing a Jewish Game: Gentile Christian Judaizing in the First and Second Centuries C.E.* Wilfrid Laurier Univ. Press, Waterloo, Ontario, Canada.

Neusner, J., 1986. *Judaism in the Matrix of Christianity.* Fortress Press, Philadelphia, PA.

Neusner, J., 1987. *Judaism and Christianity in the Age of Constantine: History, Messiah, Israel, and the Initial Confrontation.* Chicago Univ. Press, Chicago IL.

Neusner, J., 2001. *Jews and Christians: The Myth of a Common Tradition.* Binghamton University, Binghamton NY.

Neusner, J., 2004. *Neusner on Judaism, Volume 1.* Ashgate, Burlington VT.

Newman, H. I., 1999. The death of Jesus in the *Toledoth Yeshu* literature. *Journal of Theological Studies,* **50**(1):59–79.

Newman, H. I., 2001. Jerome's Judaizers. *Journal of Early Christian Studies,* **9**:421–453.

Nicholls, W., 1993. *Christian Antisemitism: A History of Hate.* Aronson, Northvale NJ.

Nickelsburg, G. W. E., 2003. *Ancient Judaism and Christian Origins: Diversity, Continuity, and Transformation.* Fortress Press, Minneapolis MN.

Nickelsburg, G. W. E., and M. E. Stone, 1983. *Faith and Piety in Early Judaism: Texts and Documents.* Fortress Press, Philadelphia PA.

Niehoff, M. R., 2005. *Creatio ex Nihilo* theology in *Genesis Rabbah* in light of Christian exegesis. *Harvard Theological Review,* **99**(1):37–64.

Nirenberg, D., 2013. *Anti-Judaism: The Western Tradition.* Norton, New York.

Nock, A. D., 1964. *Early Gentile Christianity and Its Hellenistic Background.* Harper and Row, New York.

Norton, J. D. H., 2011. *Contours in the Text: Textual Variation in the Writings of Paul, Josephus and the Yahad.* T & T Clark, London UK.

Novak, D., 2005. *Talking With Christians: Musings of a Jewish Theologian.* Eerdmans, Grand Rapids MI.

NPNF *Nicene and Post-Nicene Fathers* (Series 1 and 2). Schaff, P., and H. Wace (Eds.), 1994. Hendrickson, Peabody MA.

Oakman, D. E., 2008. *Jesus and the Peasants.* Cascade Books, Eugene OR.

Oakman, D. E., 2012. *The Political Aims of Jesus.* Fortress Press, Minneapolis MN.

O'Brien, K. S., 2006. The curse of the Law (*Galatians* 3.13): Crucifixion, persecution, and *Deuteronomy* 21. 22–23. *Journal for the Study of the New Testament,* **29**(1):55–76.

O'Collins, G., 1997. The resurrection: the state of the question. In *The Resurrection: An Interdisciplinary Symposium on the Resurrection of Jesus*, S. T. Davis, D. Kendall, and G. O'Collins (Eds.). Oxford Univ. Press, Oxford UK, 5–28.

Oriek, C., 2006. The self-defining praxis of the developing ecclēsia. In *The Cambridge History of Christianity*, Vol. 1, Mitchell, M. M., and F. M. Young (Eds.). Cambridge Univ. Press, Cambridge UK, 274–292.

Pagels, E., 2012. *Revelations: Visions, Prophecy, and Politics in the Book of Revelation.* Viking Penguin, New York.

Pak, G. S., 2009. *The Judaizing Calvin: Nineteenth Century Debates over the Messianic Psalms.* Oxford Univ. Press, New York.

Parkes, J., 1969. *The Conflict of the Church and the Synagogue: A Study in the Origin of Antisemitism.* Atheneum, New York.

Pawlikowski, J. T., 1979. The historicizing of the eschatological: the spiritualizing of the eschatological: some reflections. In *Antisemitism and the Foundations of Christianity,* A. T. Davies (Ed.). Paulist Press, New York, 151–166.

Pawlikowski, J. T., 2006. Developments in Catholic-Jewish relationships: 1990 and beyond. *Judaism,* **55**:97–109.

Payton Jr., J. R., J., 2012. *Irenaeus on the Christian Faith.* James Clark, Cambridge UK.

Pelican, J., 2005. *Whose Bible Is It? A History of the Scriptures Through the Ages.* Viking Penguin, New York.

Pervo, R. I., 1987. *Profit with Delight.* Fortress Press, Minneapolis MN.

Pervo, R. I., 2010. *The Making of Paul: Constructions of the Apostle in Early Christianity.* Fortress Press, Minneapolis MN.

Petersen, W. L., 1992. Nazoreans. *The Anchor Bible Dictionary,* **4**:1051–1052.

Petersen, W. L., 2004. The Diatessaron and the fourfold Gospel. In *The Earliest Gospels:The Origins and Transmission of the Earliest Christian Gospels; the Contribution of the Chester Beatty Gospel Codex P45*, C. Horton (Ed.). Continuum International Publishing, London and New York, 50–68.

Philo. *Works of Philo,* translated by C. D. Yonge. (1993 Edition). Hendrickson, Peabody MA.

Porter, S. E., and B. W. R. Pearson, 2000. Why the split? Christians and Jews by the fourth century. *Journal of Greco-Roman Christianity and Judaism,* **1**:82–119.

Price, R. M., 2000. *Deconstructing Jesus.* Prometheus Books, Amherst NY.

Pritz, R. A., 1992. *Nazarene Jewish Christianity.* Magnes Press, Jerusalem, Israel.

Radnitzky, L., 2011. *How Judaism Became a Religion: An Introduction to Modern Jewish Thought.* Princeton Univ. Press, Princeton NJ.

Rajak,T., 2012. Theological polemic and textual revision in Justin Martyr's Dialogue with Trypho the Jew. In *Greek Scripture and the Rabbis,* T. M. Law and A. Salvesen (Eds.). Peeters, Leuven, Belgium, 127–140.

Rauser, R. D., 2009. *Theology in Search of Foundations.* Oxford Univ. Press, New York.

Reasoner, M., 1999. *The Strong and the Weak: Romans 14.1–15.13.* Cambridge Univ. Press, Cambridge UK,

Reed, A. Y., and L. Vuong, 2013. Christianity in Antioch: Partings in Roman Syria. In *Partings: How Judaism and Christianity Became Two*, H. Shanks (Ed.). Biblical Archaeological Society, Washington DC, 105–132.

Reinhartz, A., 2001. 'Jews' and Jews in the Fourth Gospel. In *Anti-Judaism in the Fourth Gospel: Papers of the Leuven Colloquium, 2000*, R. Bieringer, D. Pollefeyt, and F. Vandecasteele-Vanneuville (Eds.). Royal Van Gorcum, Assen, Netherlands, 341–356.

Richardson, P., and D. Edwards, 2002. Jesus and Palestinian social protest: archaeological and literary perspectives. In *Handbook of Early Christianity: Social Science Approaches*, A. J. Blasi, J. Duhaime, and P.-A. Turcotte (Eds.). Altamira Press, Walnut Creek CA, 247–266.

Riches, A., 2016. *Ecce Homo: On the Divine Unity of Christ.* Eerdmans, Grand Rapids MI.

Root, B. W., 2014. *First Century Galilee: A Fresh Examination of the Sources.* Mohr Siebeck, Tübingen, Germany.

Rosen-Zvi, I., and A. Ophir, 2015. Paul and the invention of the Gentiles. *Jewish Quarterly Review* **105**:1–41.

Rousseau, P., 2002. *The Early Christian Centuries*. Longman, London UK.

Rowe, C. K., 2007. *World Upside Down: Reading Acts in the Graeco-Roman Age.* Oxford Univ. Press, New York.

Rubin, T. A., 1990. *Antisemitism: A Disease of the Mind.* Continuum, New York.

294

Ruether, R. R., 1974. *Faith and Fratricide: The Theological Roots of Anti-Semitism.* Seabury Press, New York.

Ruether, R. R., 1979. The *Faith and Fratricide* discussion: old problems and new dimensions. In *Antisemitism and the Foundations of Christianity*, A. T. Davies (Ed.). Paulist Press, New York, 230–256.

Ruether, R. R., 1981. *To Change the World.* SCM Press, London UK.

Rutgers, L. V., 2009. *Making Myths: Jews in Early Christian Identity Formation.* Peeters Publ., Leuven, Belgium.

Ryan, M. D., 1990. Hitler's challenge to the churches: a theological and political analysis of 'Mein Kampf.' In *The German Church Struggle and the Holocaust*, F. H. Littell and H. G. Locke (Eds.). Mellen Research Univ. Press, San Francisco CA, 11–30.

Salzman, M. R., 2002. *The Making of a Christian Aristocracy: Social and Religious Change in the Western Roman Empire.* Harvard Univ. Press, Cambridge MA.

Sanders, E. P., 1985. *Jesus and Judaism.* Fortress Press, Philadelphia PA.

Sanders, E. P., 1986. Paul on the Law, his opponents, and the Jewish people in Philippians 3 and 2 Corinthians 11. In *Anti-Judaism in Early Christianity, Vol. 1, Paul and the Gospels*, P. Richardson and D. Granskou (Eds). Wilfred Laurier Univ. Press, Waterloo, Ontario, Canada, 75–90.

Sanders, E. P., 1992. The life of Jesus. In *Christianity and Rabbinic Judaism: A Parallel History of Their Origins and Development*, H. Shanks (Ed.). Biblical Archaeology Society, Washington DC, 41–83.

Sanders, E. P., 2002. Jesus, ancient Judaism, and modern Christianity, In *Jesus, Judaism, and Christian Anti-Judaism*, P. Fredriksen and A. Reinhartz (Eds.). Westminster/John Knox Press, Louisville KY, 31–55.

Sanders, J. T., 2000. *Charisma, Convents, Competitors: Societal and Sociological Factors in the Success of Early Christianity.* SCM Press, London UK.

Sanders, J. T., 2002. Establishing social distance between Christians and both Jews and Pagans. In *Handbook of Early Christianity: Social Science Approaches*, A. J. Blasi, J. Duhaime, and P.-A. Turcotte (Eds.). Altamira Press, Walnut Creek CA, 361–382.

Sandmel, D. F., 2009. Contesting texts, an afterword. In *Contesting Texts: Jews and Christians in Conversation About the Bible*, M. D. Knowles et al. (Eds.). Fortress Press, Minneapolis MN, 173–178.

Schaff, D. S., 1887. Introductory essay; St. Augustin as an exegete. NPNF Series 1, vol. 6, vii–xii,

Scheffler, E., 2011a. Luke's view on poverty in its ancient (Roman) economic context: a challenge for today. *Scriptura*, **106**:115–135.

Scheffler, E., 2011b. Reflecting on Paul's non-use of the Old Testament in the letter to the Romans. *Scriptura,* **108**:269–281.

Schelle, J., 1992. *Antidocetic Christology in the Gospel of John.* Fortress Press, Minneapolis MN.

Schiffman, L. H., 1981. At the crossroads: Tannaitic perspectives on the Jewish Christian schism. In *Jewish and Christian Self-Definition. Vol. 2: Aspects of Judaism in the Graeco-Roman Period,* E. P. Sanders, A. I. Baumgarten, and A. Mendelson (Eds.). Fortress Press, Philadelphia PA, 115–156.

Schiffman, L. H., 1985. *Who Was a Jew? Rabbinic and Halakhic Perspective on the Jewish-Christian Schism.* KTAV Publishing House, Hoboken NJ.

Schmithals, W., 1997. *The Theology of the First Christians.* Westminster/John Knox Press, Louisville KY.

Schneemelcher, W. (Ed.), 1991. *New Testament Apocrypha, Revised Edition, Vols. 1 and 2* (English Translation). James Clark and Co., Cambridge UK.

Schoenfeld, D., 1913. *Isaac on Jewish and Christian Altars: Polemic and Exegesis in Rashi and the Glossa Ordinaria.* Fordham Univ. Press, New York.

Schoeps, H. J., 1963. *The Jewish-Christian Argument: A History of Theologies in Conflict.* (Translated from the 1961 third German edition.) Holt, Rinehart and Winston, New York.

Scholer, D. M. (Ed.), 2008. *Social Distinctives of the Christians in the First Century: Pivotal Essays by E. E. Judge.* Hendrickson, Peabody MA.

Schott, J. M., 2008. *Christianity, Empire, and the Making of Religion in Late Antiquity.* Univ. of Pennsylvania Press, Philadelphia PA.

Schremer, A., 2009. The Christianization of the Roman empire and rabbinic literature. In *Jewish Identities in Antiquity: Studies in Memory of Menahem Stern,* L. I. Levine, and D. R. Schwartz (Eds.). Mohr Siebeck, Tübingen, Germany, 349–366.

Schremer, A., 2010. *Brothers Estranged: Heresy, Christianity, and Jewish Identity in Late Antiquity.* Oxford Univ. Press, New York.

Schröter, J., 2013. *From Jesus to the New Testament: Early Christian Theology and the Origin of the New Testament Canon.* Mohr Siebeck, Tübingen, Germany.

Schüssler-Fiorenza, E., 2000. Paul and the politics of interpretation. In *Paul and Politics: Ekklesia, Israel, Imperium, Interpretation,* R. A. Horsley (Ed.). Trinity Press, Harrisburg PA, 40–57.

Schwartz, S., 2010. *Were the Jews a Mediterranean Society? Reciprocity and Solidarity in Ancient Judaism.* Princeton Univ. Press, Princeton NJ.

Scroggs, R., 2011. *The People's Jesus: Trajectories in Early Christianity.* Fortress Press, Minneapolis MN.

Sechrest, L. L., 2009. *A Former Jew: Paul and the Dialectics of Race.* Continuum, London UK.

Seitz, C. R., 2006. The canonical approach and theological interpretation. In *Canonical and Biblical Interpretation*, C. G. Bartholomew, et al. (Eds.). Zondervan, Grand Rapids MI, 58–110.

Setzer, C., 2011. Jewish responses to believers in Jesus. In *The Jewish annotated New Testament*, A.-J. Levine and M. Z. Brettler (Eds.). Oxford Univ. Press, New York, 577–579.

Sevenster, J. N., 1975. *The Roots of Pagan Antisemitism in the Pagan World.* Brill, Leiden, Netherlands.

Shepardson, C., 2007. Defining the boundaries of orthodoxy: Eunomius in the anti-Jewish polemic of his Cappadocian opponents. *Church History, Studies in Christianity and Culture,* **76**(4):699–723.

Shutt, R. J. H., 1985. Letter of Aristeas (third century B.C. – first century A.D.): A new translation and introduction. In *The Old Testament Pseudepigrapha, Vol. 2,* J. H. Charlesworth (Ed.). Doubleday, New York, 7–34.

Simon, M., 1996. *Verus Israel: A Study of the Relations Between Christians and Jews in the Roman Empire (AD 135–425).* (Translated from the French by H. McKeating.) Littman Library of Jewish Civilization, London UK.

Smelik, W. F., 2012. Justinian's Novella 146 and contemporary Judaism. In *Greek Scripture and the Rabbis,* T. M. Law and A. Salvesen (Eds.). Peeters, Leuven, Belgium, 141–163.

Smith, D. E., and J. B. Tyson (Eds.), 2013. *Acts and Christian Beginnings: The Acts Seminar Report.* Polebridge Press, Salem OR.

Spicer, K. P., 2008. *Hitler's Priests: Catholic Clergy and National Socialism.* Northern Illinois Univ. Press, DeKalb IL.

Spiegel, J. S., 2015. Hell and the problem of eternal evil. *Toronto Journal of Theology,* **31**(2):239–248.

Spinks, D. C., 2005. *The Bible and the Crisis of Meaning: Debates on the Theological Interpretation of Scripture.* T and T Clark, London, UK.

Stanley, C. D., 2008. Paul's "use" of Scripture: why the audience matters. In *As It Is Written: Studying Paul's Use of Scripture*, S. E. Porter and C. D. Stanley (Eds.). Brill, Leiden, Netherlands, 125–155.

Stanton, G., 2002. *The Gospels and Jesus (Second Edition).* Oxford Univ. Press, New York.

Stark, R., 1996. *The Rise of Christianity: A Sociologist Reconsiders History.* Princeton Univ. Press, Princeton NJ.

Ste. Croix, de G. E. M., 1981. *The Class Struggle in the Ancient Greek World; From the Archaic Age to the Arab Conquests.* Cornell Univ. Press, Ithaca NY.

Ste. Croix, de G. E. M., 2006. *Christian Persecution, Martyrdom, and Ortho-doxy*. M. W. Whitby and J. Streeter (Eds.). Oxford Univ. Press, Oxford UK.

Stegemann, E. W., and W. Stegemann, 1999. *The Jesus Movement: A Social History of Its First Century*. Fortress Press, Minneapolis MN.

Stendahl, K., 1982. Ancient scripture in the modern world. In *Scriptures in the Jewish and Christian Traditions: Authority, Interpretation, Relevance*, F. E. Greenspahn (Ed.). Abingdon, Nashville TN, 203–214.

Stevenson, J. (Ed.), 1987. *A New Eusebius: Documents Illustrating the History of the Church to AD 337* (Revised by W. H. C. Frend). SPCK, London UK.

Stewart, R. B., 2011. Introduction: why New Testament textual criticism matters: a non-critic perspective. In *The Reliability of the New Testament*, R. B. Stewart (Ed.). Fortress Press, Minneapolis MN, 1–12.

Swidler, L., 1988. *Yeshua: A Model for Moderns*. Sheed and Ward, Kansas City MO.

Tabor, J. D., 2012. *Paul and Jesus: How the Apostle Transformed Christianity*. Simon and Schuster, New York.

Tanzer, S. J., 2009. The problematic portrayal of the "the Jews" and Judaism in the Gospel of John: Implications for Jewish-Christian relations. In *Contesting Texts: Jews and Christians in Conversation About the Bible*, M. D. Knowles et al. (Eds.). Fortress Press, Minneapolis MN 103–118.

Tàrrech, A. P., 1997. Holy spirit and evil spirits in the ministry of Jesus. In *The Holy Spirit and the Church in the Gospels*, C. P. Dragutinovic, et al. (Eds.). Mohr Siebeck, Tübingen Germany, 365–393.

Taussig, H., 2002. Jesus in the company of sages. In *Profiles of Jesus*, R. W. Hoover (Ed.). Polebridge Press, Santa Rosa CA, 169–194.

Taylor, J., 2013. Parting in Palestine. In *Partings: How Judaism and Christianity Became Two*, H. Shanks (Ed.). Biblical Archaeological Society, Washington DC, 87–104.

Taylor, M. S., 1995. *Anti-Judaism and Early Christian Identity*. Brill, Leiden, Netherlands.

Telford, W. R., 1999. *The Theology of the Gospel of Mark*. Cambridge Univ. Press, Cambridge UK.

Teppler, Y. Y., 2007. *Birkat Ha Minim: Jews and Christians in Conflict in the Ancient World*. (translated by S. Weingarten.) Mohr Siebeck, Tübingen, Germany.

The Fathers of the Church: A New Translation (Patristic Series). Catholic Univ. of America Press, Washington DC.

Thiessen, G., 1999. *A Theory of Primitive Christianity*. SCM Press, London UK.

298

Thiessen, G. and A. Merz, 1998. *The Historical Jesus: A Comprehensive Guide*. Fortress Press, Minneapolis MN.

Tovey, D. M. H., 2009. On not unbinding the Lazarus story: the nexus of history and theology in John 11:1–44. In *John, Jesus, and History, Vol. 2*, P. N. Anderson, et al. (Eds.). Society of Biblical Literature, Atlanta GA, 213–223.

Townsend, P., 2008. Who were the first Christians? Jews, Gentiles and the *Christianoi*. In *Heresy and Identity in Late Antiquity*. E. Iricinschi and H. M. Zellentin (Eds.). Mohr Siebeck, Tübingen Germany, 212–230.

Treier, D. J., 2008. *Introducing Theological Interpretation of Scripture: Recovering a Christian Practice*. Baker Academic, Grand Rapids, MI.

Trigg, J. W., 1983. *Origen: The Bible and Philosophy in the Third Century Church*. John Knox, Atlanta GA

Trobisch, D., 2010. The authorized version of his birth and death. In *Sources of the Jesus Tradition: Separating History from Myth*, R. J. Hoffman (Ed.). Prometheus Books, Amherst NY, 131–139.

Tyson, J. B., 2013. Acts, myth and history. In *Acts and Christian Beginnings: The Acts Seminar Report*, D. E. Smith and J. B. Tyson (Eds.). Polebridge Press, Salem OR, 15–18.

Vaage, L. E., 2006a. Ancient religious rivalries and the struggle for success: Christians, Jews, and others in the early Roman Empire. In *Religious Rivalries in the Early Roman Empire and the Rise of Christianity*, L. E. Vaage (Ed.). Wilfrid Laurier Univ. Press, Canada, 3–19.

Vaage, L. E., 2006b. Why Christianity succeeded in the Roman Empire. In *Religious Rivalries in the Early Roman Empire and the Rise of Christianity*, L. E. Vaage (Ed.). Wilfrid Laurier Univ. Press, Canada, 253–278.

Van Wahlde, U. C., 1993. The Gospel of John and presentation of Jews and Judaism. In *Within Context: Essays on Jews and Judaism in the New Testament*, D. P. Efroymson, E. J. Fisher, and L. Klenicki (Eds.). Liturgical Press, Collegeville MN, 67–84.

Varner, W., 2004. *Ancient Jewish-Christian Dialogues*. Edwin Meller Press, Lewiston NY.

Varner, W., 2013. On the trail of Trypho: two fragmentary Jewish-Christian dialogues from the ancient Church. In *Christian Origins and Hellenistic Judaism: Social and Literary Contexts for the New Testament*, S. E. Porter and A. W. Pitts (Eds.). Brill, Leiden, Netherlands, 553–565.

Vermes, G., 1973. *Jesus the Jew*. Fontana-Collins, London UK.

Vermes, G., 1993. *The Religion of Jesus the Jew*. Fortress Press, Minneapolis MN.

Vermes, G., 2003. *The Authentic Gospel of Jesus*. Allen Lane, London UK.

Vermes, G., 2005. *The Passion*. Penguin Books, London UK.

Vermes, G., 2008. *The Resurrection*. Penguin Books, London UK.

Vermes, G., 2010. *Jesus in the Jewish World*, SCM Press, London UK.

Vermes, G., 2012. *Christian Beginnings: From Nazareth to Nicaea*. Yale Univ. Press, New Haven CT.

Vermes, G., 2013. The Jewish Jesus movement. In *Partings: How Judaism and Christianity Became Two*, H. Shanks (Ed.). Biblical Archaeological Society, Washington DC, 1–25.

Walls, J. L., 2015. *Heaven, Hell, and Purgatory: Rethinking the Things That Matter Most*. Brazos Press (Baker), Grand Rapids, MI.

Watson, F., 2001. The quest for the real Jesus. In *The Cambridge Companion to Jesus*, M. Bockmuehl (Ed.). Cambridge Univ. Press, Cambridge UK, 156–169.

White, L. M., 2010. *Scripting Jesus: the Gospels in Rewrite*. HarperOne, New York.

Wilde, R., 1949. *The Treatment of Jews in Greek Christian Writings of the First Three Centuries*. Catholic University of America Patristic Studies, Vol. 81, Washington DC.

Wiles, M., and M. Santer (Eds.), 1975. *Documents in Early Christian Thought*. Cambridge Univ. Press, Cambridge UK.

Wilken, R. L., 1971. *Judaism and the Early Christian Mind: A Study of Cyril of Alexandria's Exegesis and Theology*. Yale Univ. Press, New Haven CT.

Williams, A. L., 1935. *Adversus Judaeos: A Bird's Eye View of Christian Apologiae Until the Renaissance*. Cambridge Univ. Press, Cambridge UK.

Williams, M. H., 2013. Jews and Christians at Rome: an early parting of the ways. In *Partings: How Judaism and Christianity Became Two*, H. Shanks (Ed.). Biblical Archaeological Society, Washington DC, 151–178.

Williamson, C. M., and R. J. Allen, 1989. *Interpreting Difficult Texts: Anti-Judaism and Christian Preaching*. SCM Press, London UK.

Wilson, B., 2008. *How Jesus Became Christian*. St. Martin's Press, New York.

Wilson, S. G., 1995. *Related Strangers: Jews and Christians 70–170 C.E.* Fortress, Minneapolis MN.

Wilson, S. G., 2006. Rivalry and defection. In *Religious Rivalries in the Early Roman Empire and the Rise of Christianity*, L. E. Vaage (Ed.). Wilfrid Laurier Univ. Press, Waterloo, Ontario, Canada, 51–71.

Worthen, J. F., 2009. *The Internal Foe: Judaism and Anti-Judaism in the Shaping of Christian Theology*. Cambridge Scholars Publishing, Newcastle upon Tyne UK.

Wright, R. B.., 1985. Psalms of Solomon: a new translation and introduction. In *The Old Testament Pseudepigrapha*, J. H. Charlesworth (Ed.). Doubleday, New York, 667–668.

Young, F. M., 1997. *Biblical Exegesis and the Formation of Christian Culture*. Cambridge Univ. Press, Cambridge UK.

Young, F. M., 2006. Prelude: Jesus Christ, foundation of Christianity. In *The Cambridge History of Christianity, Vol. 1, Origin to Constantine*, M. M. Mitchell, and F. M. Young (Eds.). Cambridge Univ. Press, Cambridge UK, 1–34.

Zindler, F. R., 2010. Prolegomenon to a science of Christian origins. In *Sources of the Jesus Tradition: Separating History from Myth*, R. J. Hoffman (Ed.). Prometheus Books, Amherst NY, 140–156.